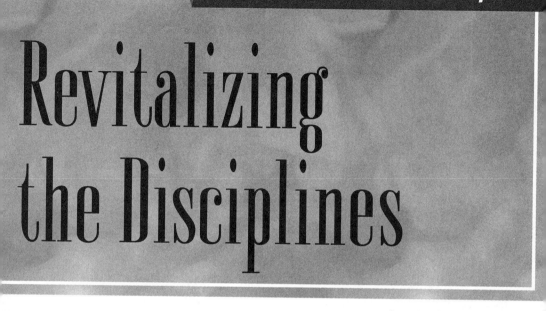

the best of ASCD's *Curriculum Update*

Revitalizing the Disciplines

Edited by **John O'Neil** and **Scott Willis**

ASCD

Association for Supervision and Curriculum Development ✦ Alexandria, Virginia

Association for Supervision and Curriculum Development
1250 N. Pitt Street • Alexandria, Virginia 22314-1453 USA
Telephone: 1-800-933-2723 or 703-549-9110 • Fax: 703-299-8631
Web site: http://www.ascd.org • E-mail: member@ascd.org

On July 14, 1998, ASCD will move to new headquarters: 1703 N. Beauregard St.,
Alexandria, VA 22311-1714. Telephone: 703-578-9600

Gene R. Carter, *Executive Director*
Michelle Terry, *Assistant Executive Director,*
 Program Development
Nancy Modrak, *Director, Publishing*
John O'Neil, *Acquisitions Editor*
Mark Goldberg, *Development Editor*
Julie Houtz, *Managing Editor of Books*
Charles D. Halverson, *Project Assistant*

Gary Bloom, *Director, Editorial, Design, and*
 Production Services
Eva Barsin, *Graphic Designer*
Tracey A. Smith, *Production Manager*
Dina Murray, *Production Coordinator*
John Franklin, *Production Coordinator*
Hilary Cumberton, M.L. Coughlin Editorial
 Services, *Indexer*
BMWW, *Typesetter*

Printed in the United States of America.   s6/98

ASCD Stock No. 198051   ASCD member price: $16.95   nonmember price: $20.95

Also available as part of a 2-volume set (ISBN 0-87120-312-X). Stock no. 198198.
ASCD members: $26.95   nonmembers: $32.95

Library of Congress Cataloging-in-Publication Data

Revitalizing the disciplines : the best of ASCD's Curriculum update / edited by
  John O'Neil and Scott Willis.
     p.   cm.
   ISBN 0-87120-309-X (pbk.)
     1. Curriculum planning—United States.   2. Education—United States—
Curricula.   3. Curriculum change—United States.   I. O'Neil, John.   II. Willis,
Scott.   III. Association for Supervision and Curriculum Development.   IV.
Curriculum update (Alexandria, Va.)
   LB2806.15.R48   1998
   375'.001—dc21   98-15117
                                                                CIP

03 02 01 00 99 98   10 9 8 7 6 5 4 3 2 1

REVITALIZING THE DISCIPLINES
THE BEST OF ASCD'S CURRICULUM UPDATE

PREFACE

The curriculum—the body of knowledge and skills that students are taught in school—is never static. But since the 1980s, a number of major trends have impelled educators to make especially significant changes to the K–12 curriculum in the various subject areas.

One of these trends is the call to provide students with learning experiences that are "authentic"—that closely resemble tasks that adults perform in real life. Another major trend is the standards movement, which seeks to define and apply clear standards for both content and performance in the disciplines. A third (and related) trend is the new sense of obligation to help *all* students achieve at a high level, rather than settling for the traditional bell curve.

These three trends, among others, have made an impact on what students are being taught in schools today. Curriculum developers have been hard pressed to keep up with the rapid changes in philosophy and goals. In this time of ferment, educators need good sources of information on how the curriculum in the various subject areas is evolving. This book is a collection of articles that were written to meet that need.

All of the articles in this book were originally published in *Curriculum Update*, a quarterly newsletter of the Association for Supervision and Curriculum Development (ASCD). *Curriculum Update* is sent to ASCD's entire membership, which includes principals, teachers, curriculum specialists, superintendents, and teacher educators, among others. Therefore, these articles were written to appeal to a broad audience of educators. These articles may be most useful, however, to those who are taking on the challenge of curriculum renewal, whether they are doing so at the classroom, school, district, or state level. These articles provide background information and plenty of practical ideas for pursuing the elusive goal of a "state-of-the-art" curriculum.

We have arranged the content of this book by subject areas—language arts, mathematics, social studies, and so on—as a convenience to the reader. (We realize this decision may seem to be at odds with another major trend in K–12 education—the movement toward interdisciplinary studies.) We would also like to acknowledge that, given our space limitations, we have been able to include only a subset of the disciplines that are typically taught in K–12 schools.

As editors of *Curriculum Update,* we have tracked many education trends and tried to assess their effects on the curriculum. The articles we have selected for this book represent, in our judgment, the most thought-provoking information about changes in the subject areas that we have been able to provide our readers. We hope you will find them interesting, informative, and useful.

JOHN O'NEIL
SCOTT WILLIS

Section 1

LANGUAGE ARTS

TEACHING YOUNG WRITERS

FEEDBACK AND COACHING HELP STUDENTS HONE SKILLS

SCOTT WILLIS

"The best stories are not written but rewritten." This simple premise is the key to a highly interactive approach to teaching writing that has been gradually spreading through K–12 classrooms, as more and more teachers ask students to revise their writing in response to feedback and coaching.

Teachers of writing are using other progressive approaches as well. They are encouraging peer review of students' writing; allowing students to write for authentic audiences; and teaching mechanics in the context of students' own writing. Other trends include writing across the curriculum, using computers, and focusing clearly on the assessment of writing.

Thanks to these new approaches, experts claim, today's students are willing and able to put pen to paper—or fingertips to keyboard—and translate their thoughts into writing that is clear and compelling.

WRITING AS A PROCESS

Today's teachers are building on 20 years' experience with teaching writing as a process, experts say. Before the "process writing" movement began in the late 1970s, many teachers simply assigned writing topics, then corrected and graded students' papers—which were typically first drafts.

The articles in this chapter were originally published in the Spring 1997 issue of ASCD's *Curriculum Update* newsletter.

In process approaches to writing, by contrast, teachers help students do what adept writers do: brainstorm ideas, organize their thoughts, write a first draft, solicit feedback, revise their work several times, then edit and proofread the final product. (Despite these stages, the writing process is recursive rather than linear, experts emphasize.)

From the start, the process writing movement put the focus on instruction, says Sarah Freedman of the University of California–Berkeley, former director of the National Center for the Study of Writing and Literacy. Beyond simply grading students' work, teachers began to coach students during the various phases of writing—as they pondered content or struggled with revision, for example. This shift in emphasis made "a big contribution," Freedman says. "It introduced pedagogy."

Even today, too many teachers of writing merely "assign and evaluate," says Jeffrey Wilhelm of the University of Maine, a classroom veteran who still teaches middle school students. Teachers need to provide lots of instructional support *while* students are writing, he says. "That's when students care about what they're doing."

Students lack a repertoire of writing skills, Wilhelm says. Most students don't know how to write a thesis statement or marshal supporting evidence. Nor do students know how to generate ideas, write a good "lead," or organize their writing to emphasize important points. To learn skills such as these, students must revise their writing based on feedback, experts agree.

Teachers need to instill in students the idea that "words are fluid; they can be worked with," says Virginia DeBolt, who teaches English at Murchison Middle School in Austin, Texas. Students don't take to revision naturally, she has found: "Students think you write something the first time and it's finished." Therefore, the teacher must show students *how* they can change a piece of writing to make it more powerful and effective.

Today's teachers are expecting students to revise their writing, says Jane Hansen, director of the Writing Lab at the University of New Hampshire. Teachers are encouraging students to clarify their main points, reorder paragraphs, and make judicious cuts. Students can also strengthen their writing in revision by providing specifics and details, Hansen says. "They tend to write in generalities."

Teachers of young students may have more modest expectations for revision. Janet Matsuoka, who teaches 3rd and 4th graders at Joaquin Miller Elementary School in Oakland, Calif., asks students to make limited revisions on the same piece of paper—to correct spelling errors or add details. Matsuoka tries to coach students while their work is in progress. That's the best time to give a lesson, she says, because "you're dealing with the writing right there, so students have ears to hear."

For Lynne Yermanock Strieb, who teaches 1st and 2nd graders at Greenfield Elementary School in Philadelphia, Pa., the goal is to get her pupils writing—with only "a light touch on revision and editing." Strieb sometimes prompts pupils to fix fundamental flaws, such as a tangled sequence of events. With young children's writing, if revision is overemphasized, "it becomes the teacher's work," she cautions.

On one occasion, Strieb recalls, a pupil wrote about a visit to Disney World but never mentioned it by name. Similarly, another pupil wrote about building a hamster run ("We made it out of sticks and glue . . .") but never specified what "it" was. In conferences with these pupils, Strieb suggested that they repair these omissions "so readers will understand."

A GOOD IDEA GONE WRONG?

Students should always consider revising their work, but teachers shouldn't make revision mandatory, Hansen says. Writers use different processes for different pieces of writing, she notes. A writer might revise a piece six times or publish a first draft, depending on the purpose of the piece. "Don't set up a rigid system," she says. "Writing is not a formulaic thing. You don't write by steps any more than you paint by numbers."

Too often, however, the writing process *has* been turned into a formula, some experts lament. "The writing process has often been overcodified in textbooks and workshops, presented as a rigid sequence rather than a flexible method with recursive components," says Charles Suhor, deputy executive director of the National Council of Teachers of English (NCTE).

Betty Jane Wagner, director of the Chicago Area Writing Project, is also concerned about "trivialization" of the writing process. Student writers are inhibited, she believes, when teachers adhere slavishly to a formula that dictates that "every piece must go through three to five stages."

The writing process is "hard even to talk about," says Joan Cone, who teaches English at El Cerrito High School in El Cerrito, Calif. Simply by labeling stages, a teacher implies a linear, step-by-step approach, she points out—whereas writing is actually very recursive.

"Writing is a complex process; if you narrow it, you lose kids," says Richard Sterling, executive director of the National Writing Project (see box). Teachers need to realize that there is no one right way to write, he says. Take making an outline. Some students find this step helpful; others hate it and do it in a perfunctory way; still other students make the outline *after* they have finished writing the piece. Rather than turning writing into "a lockstep experience," teachers should think in terms of multiple approaches.

"Teachers have discovered the power of allowing a certain leeway to students in approaching writing assignments," Sterling says. Some students prefer to write a piece from beginning to end, while others like to start *in medias res*, for example. "There isn't a wrong way to do this," he

---

The National Writing Project

The National Writing Project (NWP) is a teacher-centered staff development program that seeks to improve the teaching and learning of writing. The Project, which began in 1973, is based at the University of California–Berkeley and has 161 sites in the United States and 5 sites in Canada and Europe.

Each year at all NWP sites, successful teachers of writing from all levels of instruction are invited to participate in intensive five-week Summer Institutes. Afterward, these teachers join with other NWP teacher-consultants to plan and conduct yearlong staff development workshops in schools.

For more information, contact the National Writing Project, University of California, 5511 Tolman Hall, #1670, Berkeley, CA 94720-1670 USA. Phone: 510-642-0963. Fax: 510-642-4545. E-mail: nwp@garnet.berkeley.edu. Or visit the NWP Web site at http://www-gse.berkeley.edu/Research/NWP/nwp.html.

emphasizes. Students need to "try everything till they find a way that works for them."

Another criticism of process writing as it has played out in classrooms is that teachers have put too much emphasis on process and not enough on the product. Process writing for some teachers resulted in "no final product," says Cone, who believes that teachers must hold students accountable for final drafts. "We can't stay in the process mode forever."

PEER REVIEWERS

Obviously, for students to learn how to revise their writing, they must receive feedback on their work. Many teachers, besides providing feedback themselves, are encouraging peer review, experts say.

"Writers in classrooms need sounding boards," Hansen says. Teachers should set up interactive classrooms, she advises, where students are free—and eager—to consult one another. This sort of writers' workshop atmosphere is becoming much more common, she believes. "A writing classroom that's quiet is suspicious."

Students should develop the ability to help a peer rethink his or her material, says Kathryn Ransom, vice president of the International Reading Association. (Students listen to their peers more than they listen to teachers, she believes.) Ransom advises teachers to narrow the focus of feedback, asking peer reviewers to "focus on a very specific thing." Are there illustrations to support the thesis? Is there a clear statement of purpose? An attention-getting "lead"?

Wagner agrees that teachers should ask students to provide specific feedback. She suggests asking peer reviewers to "underline the word picture that jumps off the page" or "put a question mark in the margin where you need more information." Students should also evaluate their *own* papers, she says. They should note "This is my best imagery" or "This is where I was most persuasive," for example.

TEACHING SKILLS IN CONTEXT

As students learn about smooth transitions and rhetorical rhythm, they must also learn skills such as spelling, punctuation, and usage. How best to teach these skills is "one of the areas where there's disagreement" in the field, Ransom says. Some experts advocate teaching these skills primarily in the context of students' writing, while others favor a more systematic, sequenced approach.

"I want to take the middle road," Ransom says. "There is a place for brief, targeted, specific instruction," she believes, "but it should immediately be applied in real writing situations"—not in isolated practice exercises. "Rather than 77 practice sentences on quotation marks, let's generate a piece of writing with conversation in it," she recommends.

Skills instruction should be embedded in students' writing, Wagner agrees. "Drills in isolation don't carry over." Many teachers present short grammar or vocabulary lessons at the beginning of each class, she notes. Typically, teachers focus on a common error, such as sentence fragments or faulty pronoun case ("Jimmy and me went . . ."). With this approach, "the lesson is feeding back into the writing, which is where it matters."

DeBolt, however, finds she must teach spelling as a "separate entity," because teaching it in context means "you're limited to the student's small vocabulary." She has had more success teaching grammar in context, she says, because grammar "applies to all sentences."

Pamela Morgan, a teacher-consultant with the Maryland Writing Project, used to teach from a grammar book, but she found that very little of her lessons transferred to students' writing. Now she tailors her instruction so that students can apply new skills immediately in their writing. Morgan gives students mini-lessons in skills "that their writing says they need," rather than letting the curriculum dictate her focus. "Once I have samples of their writing, I know what skills I need to work on," she says.

For Morgan's 5th graders, these skills include subject-verb agreement, writing complete sentences, constructing paragraphs, and the proper use of commas ("Students go from one extreme to the other," she notes, "from using no commas to putting them everywhere").

Joan Cone also lets student papers guide her teaching. "I'll teach a lesson on things in their writing that went wrong," she says—such as how to spell *separate,* use quotation marks, or use the subjunctive mood. "All kids benefit from that corrective stuff."

Cone also takes a proactive approach by assigning the use of sophisticated punctuation. She might say to students, "In this essay, use three semicolons, two colons, and one piece of dialogue." Or she might ask students to include sentences of one, four, and seven words. "This practice serves them," she says, noting that she sees these skills applied in students' work later on.

AN AUTHENTIC AUDIENCE

One good way to motivate students to refine their writing, experts say, is to have them write for real purposes and authentic audiences. "It's really key to have a real audience," Wilhelm says. "That solves a lot of problems with motivation." When students write for a real audience, they keenly want their writing to be good, he says, and they develop their own critical standards.

For example, some of Wilhelm's students wrote a manual on "what you need to know to live in Italy for a year," aimed at a real audience of foreign exchange students and business transfers. This "real-world work" spurred the students to conduct surveys and interviews and do "a lot of research, writing, and revising," Wilhelm says. The students were far more motivated than they would have been by "a bunch of empty exercises."

Students concentrate more closely on their writing when they have "someone to do it for," says Rosa Sailes, a teacher-on-loan working with several Chicago high schools to improve writing instruction. When the audience goes beyond the teacher, students take more pride in their work and try to make their writing "as perfect as they can." Even in e-mail chatting, Sailes has found, students are very conscious of grammar and spelling—and very critical of mistakes.

After Morgan arranged for graduate students to correspond with her 7th and 8th graders, she found that students who used to resist revising their papers began to feel a need to produce perfect copy. These students were "concerned about the impression they were making on the other person." Morgan has also found that this new conscientiousness transfers to other work: Refining their writing becomes a habit for students.

Another way to provide a real purpose for student writing is to publish it. Publishing students' work "gives the writing value; it shows you feel it's worth doing," DeBolt says. Whether publishing a piece means reading it to the class from the "author's chair," including it in a portfolio or anthology, or actually printing it in a booklet or literary magazine, students find the experience motivating, she says. (DeBolt is looking into publishing on the Internet.)

Teachers should publish students' writing all the time, Cone says. "We should plaster our classrooms with kids' writing." When students know their work will be published, they often come up at the end of class and ask, "Can I take it home and write it again?" she reports. "And every time we publish, students are inspired by other kids' work."

GREATER EXPECTATIONS

Helping students find the writing strategies that work for them definitely pays off, says Elizabeth Close, who teaches language arts at Farnsworth Middle School in Guilderland, N.Y. Teachers in her district began teaching writing as a process in the late 1970s, Close notes. "We were early in."

Since that time, expectations for students' writing have changed dramatically. In the early 1970s, teachers were looking for students to produce "one good paragraph with a topic sentence," Close says. Today, by contrast, teachers expect students to be able to write at least three pages with "developed ideas" and vivid description that "draws pictures."

Students are rising to the challenge. Compared to their peers of yesteryear, "they are able to express themselves so much better," Close says. Students are more willing to write, and they can produce writing that is carefully crafted. Their work may not be as "error free" as the stilted one-paragraph compositions of the past, Close concedes, but both the quantity and overall quality of their writing are in another league altogether. "It's a totally different story."

Assessing Student Writing

Kathy Checkley

For most of her 25 years in teaching, Lois Johnson, like many of her colleagues, judged the quality of her students' writing by how well they had mastered the mechanics of writing. "We looked for correct sentence structure, periods in all the right places," says Johnson. Other aspects of writing weren't acknowledged, she notes, and the letter grade emblazoned on students' papers was the only feedback they received. "We didn't explain [to students] why they received the grades they did," Johnson says. The result of such an approach to assessment was anxiety. "Students were so scared of making a mistake while they were doing the writing, they couldn't get through the assignment."

Johnson, a 4th grade teacher at Cedar Grove Elementary School in Panama City, Fla., now assesses student writing very differently. She uses a rubric—a scoring guide of performance criteria—to help her evaluate and "appreciate" aspects of writing that go beyond grammar conventions, such as voice, organization, ideas and content, word choice, and sentence fluency. Now instead of a single grade, students receive a range of scores that indicate how well they've incorporated these traits of effective writing into their work.

The result of this approach to assessment, says Johnson, is enthusiasm. She enjoys teaching writing "more than ever before" and says she's seen "a love of literature bloom" in her students, many of whom now aspire to be writers themselves.

Finding a Common Language

Johnson's success with rubrics comes as no surprise to Vicki Spandel, senior research associate at the Northwest Regional Educational Laboratory in Portland, Oreg. Spandel helped develop the assessment tool that Johnson now uses (see box) when she teamed up with teachers in the

Six Key Qualities

The six-trait analytical writing assessment model focuses on the six key qualities of writing mentioned most often by teachers who evaluate student writing. The six traits are:

✦ **Ideas and Content.** Is the message clear? Does the paper hold the reader's attention? Are the ideas fresh and original?

✦ **Organization.** Does the paper have an inviting introduction? Are supporting details placed in a logical order? Can the reader move easily through the text?

✦ **Voice.** Does the writer speak directly to the reader? Is the writer sensitive to the needs of an audience? Can the reader sense the person behind the words?

✦ **Word Choice.** Are the words chosen specific and accurate? Do lively verbs energize the writing? Is the text free of jargon and clichés?

✦ **Fluency.** Does the writing have a cadence and easy flow? Do the sentences have a structure that invites expressive oral reading? Do sentences vary in length as well as structure?

✦ **Conventions.** Does the writer demonstrate a good grasp of standard writing conventions, such as grammar, punctuation, and paragraphing? Is punctuation accurate? Is spelling generally correct?

Adapted from the scoring guide (rubric) developed by the Northwest Regional Educational Laboratory in Portland, Oreg., in collaboration with teachers in the Beaverton (Oreg.) School District.

Beaverton (Oreg.) School District to find a better way to assess student writing at the district level and in the classroom.

Spandel and the teachers ranked stacks of student papers and described their reasoning for each of the rankings. "What emerged were six common threads, six umbrella terms that people mentioned when they evaluated student writing," Spandel explains. The six traits that are now on the rubric weren't invented, she says. "We just chose language to describe what works. The scoring guide is an outline that gives teachers a language they can use when they talk about writing."

Establishing a common language (scoring guide) is essential if students are to develop an understanding of what is meant by "quality writing," says Barbara Clausen, executive director of curriculum and assessment for the Bethel (Wash.) School District. Students have to know what constitutes good writing if their own writing is to grow, she says.

That's one reason why those who teach writing in the Bethel School District receive formal training in how to use the six-trait model. The scoring guide is used for the districtwide assessment of student writing, and teachers are encouraged to use the model in their classrooms. That way, says Clausen, teachers know "what makes a three a three" when scoring the thousands of papers from the 3rd, 6th, 9th, and 11th grade students who participate in the districtwide assessment. Such consistency is important because the district wants to track students' long-term performance in writing, she explains, and because teachers want students to know what characteristics are evident in high-quality writing.

"It's important to share the criteria and samples of good writing with students because then they have a vision of success . . . they need a target to aim at," agrees Spandel. Students need to see examples of good and poor writing and have opportunities to assess that writing. Through such exercises, she contends, students learn to be objective, to develop "a detachment that will allow them to be honest when they assess their own work."

LINKING ASSESSMENT TO STANDARDS

The move to an analytical assessment approach has the cautious approval of the National Council of Teachers of English (NCTE), which released its own standards for assessment (co-written with the International Reading Association) in 1994. The approval is cautious, says Miles Myers, NCTE's executive director, because "trait-feature models" can be used as inappropriately as traditional assessment models.

"Such rubrics are helpful as diagnostic tools for students," says Myers, but the trait-feature system can also lead to people teaching the traits in isolation from the other features. Teachers can show students "exemplars of performance," such as some excellent uses of language conventions, for example, "but these should be contained within an actual essay or story," he maintains. "While we often need to go back and focus on individual parts, it's most useful to see how all those parts work together." In some uses of the trait-feature system, says Myers, "students never see the total performance."

And the analytical assessment approach, alone, cannot provide educators with all the data they need to accurately gauge student understanding and achievement, adds Johnny Toliver, acting vice president for academic affairs at Delaware State University, and cochair of the task force that developed the assessment standards.

"When we initially talked about standards, the plan was to eliminate standardized testing," Toliver explains. But task force members agreed that an assessment is valid if teachers "are able to determine what modifications need to be made to the curriculum to improve student learning." Standardized testing, says Toliver, "can show what students can do on demand." So, if a number of students perform poorly on multiple-choice questions dealing with grammar or usage, that information "can help teachers determine if those are weak areas they need to address with their students." Writing samples may not provide such aggregate data, he contends.

Toliver concedes, however, that because too much emphasis was once placed on the results of standardized testing, "the English curriculum was driven by national standardized tests . . . that were not the best assessment of a student's ability to write." Had the IRA and the NCTE not pressed for change, he says, too many people would still see such standardized tests as the only measure of the success of a curriculum, and standardized tests themselves might not have been revised to "assess student writing in a way the profession accepts." Tests such as the SAT have been revised, however, and now, says Toliver, it's more important to see "how assessment standards are reflected in the classroom."

ACCENTUATE THE POSITIVE

Myers hopes that standards-based assessment practices help offset the perception that those who teach writing "list only what's wrong with

Portfolios and Assessment

Giving students opportunities to reflect on their work is one of the practices supported by the standards for the assessment of reading and writing developed by the National Council of Teachers of English (NCTE) and the International Reading Association (IRA). "Portfolio assessment," writes the IRA/NCTE Joint Task Force on Assessment, "can be reflective, involving students in their own learning and assisting teachers in refocusing instruction."

Portfolios also give teachers examples of how students perform over time and in a variety of situations, adds Ruth Culham, senior research associate at the Northwest Regional Educational Laboratory in Portland, Oreg.

Still, schools that decide to adopt portfolio assessment "have to be careful not to make the portfolios mere scrapbooks," Culham cautions. Educators must determine, before adopting portfolios, what it is they want the portfolios to show. In general, she says, schools have four types of portfolios to choose from:

✦ *Sampling of Works.* This type of portfolio is often used in primary grades to compare early writing samples with later writing samples, explains Culham. These portfolios are often sent on to the student's next teacher.

✦ *Selected Works.* In these portfolios, students collect samples of their writing in response to a teacher prompt. "This is the self-reflection port-folio," says Culham. In responding to questions such as, "What is your best work?" students become more critical and objective. Teachers find that "kids have a lot to say about their work when given an opportunity," she says.

✦ *Longitudinal.* These portfolios are oriented toward district goals for student achievement and "must include September and June data" to provide an accurate assessment, Culham notes.

✦ *Passport.* Students use these portfolios to collect samples of work that will allow them "to go someplace new," says Culham. Such "passport folios," as she calls them, can be used for college entrance or to move students from one grade in high school to another.

a student's work." Papers swimming in red ink have no place in today's classroom, he maintains. "We're trying to restore some balance in the discussion by asking that teachers concentrate on what students can do while also asking them to stretch in a particular area."

For example, says Myers, when students graduate from using simple sentence structures, they often have trouble with restrictive and nonrestrictive clauses. He advises teachers to applaud students for making an effort to write more complicated sentences. "What a teacher needs to say to the student is, 'Hey, it's great that you're writing more complex sentences. Now let's focus on how to put together these complicated ideas.'" Teachers should acknowledge that students' skills are expanding and give them the guidance to do those new tasks successfully, Myers contends.

Ellen Tatalias agrees, and that's why an analytical model of assessment appeals to her. Tatalias, who teaches senior-level writing courses at Northwestern LeHigh High School in New Tripoli, Pa., says rubrics provide precise information and help put student writers "on a level playing field" with those who are evaluating their work. "Giving kids more information is going to guide them. The greater the clarity you can bring to an assessment, the easier it will be for students to improve," she says.

Tatalias adds that any assessment should "recognize the many dimensions of the writer." Writing, she maintains, "has to be understood with the ear, and that wasn't possible with the traditional means of assessment." An analytical model of assessment, says Tatalias, helps teachers "hear" rhythm and sentence fluency and consider such traits as voice and audience awareness—"the things that bring vitality and life to a piece of writing"—when reviewing student writing.

But, Tatalias notes, one of the most positive results of using an analytical assessment model is that more students are included in the community of writers. "When we used a holistic model, it was not surprising that when we did our schoolwide testing, our best writing samples came from students who were in the upper academic achievement levels," Tatalias explains. In using rubrics, she says, "we were looking at different aspects of writing, and many of our best pieces came from those students we may have ignored before" because they had not mastered the conventions of writing. The new assessment approach has been "very affirming" for those students, Tatalias observes. "This is a much more humane way to evaluate writing, a much more humane way of looking at students' writing and recognizing their potential for growth."

Editor's Note: Copies of Standards for the Assessment of Reading and Writing *are available from NCTE for $6.95. NCTE has also developed other publications to help educators translate the standards into practice. Call 1-800-369-6283 for order information.*

WRITING AND TECHNOLOGY

LARRY MANN

Technology's potential for engaging more students in the writing process is encouraging. Three case studies illustrate how teachers are using computers to help students become better and more willing writers.

Rebecca Feaster, a kindergarten teacher in Memphis, Tenn., has one computer in her classroom at Oak Forest Elementary. But with that one computer, "we've started doing really wonderful things," she says. By the end of the year, and with the help of technology, every child in her class "publishes" at least one 8-page book. Some children publish several.

To help her kindergartners get started with writing, Feaster begins with drawing. Her students might draw snowflakes, for example, and then at the computer, they dictate words to her that describe their snowflakes. Feaster prints these words, extra large, on a laser printer, and then children paste their words on their pictures. Pleased with the authentic look of their "real book words," they begin to develop a love of language.

Using a computer helps students become more fluent writers, Feaster finds. "When children write by hand, they only want to write something short," she observes, "since they know they'll have to go back and do the whole thing over with corrections. Because of their poor handwriting, children are easily frustrated. But with the computer, children are not discouraged. Corrections and revisions are easy. The process is failure-proof because anything can be fixed. They feel like they can be more expressive." And students' own illustrated books are a big hit in the classroom library.

As her students begin thematic books, Feaster provides sentence frames, such as, "The hot chocolate is _____." Conferring with one another, her kindergartners choose words they like, and either dictate their words to her, or type them at the computer themselves. These sentence frames become the first lines of "chapters" for their books.

At the computer, Feaster guides her students using *KidWorks II*, software with a typing program as well as a drawing program. An exciting feature of this software is that it can read back what children have written, or children can record their own voices reading their own words.

For spelling, Feaster uses a phonics approach, coaching her young writers to discern the beginning, end, and then middle sounds of words. Short vowel sounds, which make up about 80 percent of vowels, receive special emphasis in her classroom instruction. Her term for standardized spelling is "book spelling." Instead of saying, "Let's spell it correctly," which she sees as threatening, Feaster assures her kindergartners there's nothing wrong with their own spellings on first drafts. But on revisions and final drafts, she requires them to find "book spelling" for their words by checking classroom lists or by finding their words in books. Because dictionaries present special challenges for kindergartners, she lets them use spell-checking programs when writing at the computer.

Feaster notes that before her classroom had a computer, her students never wrote in-depth stories. She believes this experience with computers has greatly expanded her kindergartners' reading comprehension and thinking processes.

PROJECT-BASED LEARNING

Patti Scanlon, a colleague of Rebecca Feaster's at Oak Forest Elementary, uses project-based learning in the school's computer lab. Scanlon refers to the lab as a whole language computer lab because in addition to

21 computers, it has lots of books, and is a place for peer tutoring and conferencing. "This is good for kids," Scanlon explains, "because they do more critical thinking and work at a higher level than in a computer lab without books or lots of talking."

One project that originates in the lab is the school newspaper. Meeting twice a week, a student group with reporters from each grade produces a weekly 6-page paper. For planning their stories, Scanlon's young writers use a software product called *Inspiration*, a program that helps writers outline their stories. She also involves students in creating rubrics for evaluating their own work.

Another group that Scanlon teaches is known as the *Webweavers*. Twenty-five K–6 students have created a home page on the Internet for Oak Forest Elementary (http://conect.memphis-schools.k12.tn.us/ OakForest/.) Links at this Web site include pages for each of the participating students.

BECOMING BETTER WRITERS

At Penn High School in Mishawaka, Ind., Mary Nicolini is director of the Writing Center. Although the center has more than 80 computers, she'll be the first to insist that "you can't just put kids in front of a computer and expect improvement." Before embracing technology as a tool, teachers must have a philosophy of the teaching of writing, she says.

"When I first became director of this center," Nicolini remembers, "I was accosted by all kinds of software grammar programs with bells and whistles. I didn't want a grammar program; that's not how students become better writers."

"Writing is a social act," explains Nicolini. "Talking is a big part of the writing process. That alone is a big hurdle for teachers to realize. Talking about your writing is almost as important as doing it."

In Nicolini's writing center, where talking is encouraged, she expedites writing processes with three software programs that help students generate ideas:

• *Inspiration*, a graphic organizer that helps students create visual representations of their ideas. "Many, many students are visual learners," claims Nicolini.

- *Aspects*, a groupware program networked within the writing center. With this real-time chat program, students quickly discover the need for clarity and precision of thought.
- *Daedalus*, a HyperCard program with prompts that guide writers through a series of questions that require critical thinking. After this point, writers move to the drafting stage.

What differences has Nicolini observed among her student writers? "I've noticed an attitude change. I don't have empirical data for this, but I see that students are less intimidated by writing. And they're much more inclined to revise on computers than on paper, so there is an increase in fluency."

WRITING ACROSS THE CURRICULUM

KAREN RASMUSSEN

When Gene Sweeney became principal of Penn High School in Mishawaka, Ind., he intended to make writing the center of the curriculum. Three years later he jokes, "I lied. What we actually want to do is make *thinking* the center of the curriculum."

Sweeney, who began his career as an English teacher, believes that writing enables students to deepen their understanding of all subjects, not just language arts. Writing helps students clarify their thoughts and "put inert knowledge into action," he claims. Writing across the curriculum also permits students to exhibit their grasp of all subjects, he says, and allows teachers to see students using higher levels of thinking.

"Writing makes thinking visible. Clear writing reflects clear thinking," says Mary Nicolini, director of the Penn High School Writing Center. Writing allows students to analyze and synthesize materials and articulate what they know, experts agree.

For Nicolini, "writing across the curriculum" is writing that's done in a content area other than language arts to communicate an understanding of content. "If you think in all subject areas, you should be able to write in them," she says. Writing should be employed as a process of discovery, not as an exercise in which students regurgitate what they've been told, she adds.

The nucleus of the writing emphasis at Penn High School is the Writing Center. It's a place where teachers and students learn how writing contributes to the understanding of every subject.

AN INTEGRAL PART OF TEACHING

Nicolini's job is to help teachers make writing an integral part of teaching. "When a teacher comes to the Center, we essentially work as a team and the Writing Center becomes a big workshop," Nicolini explains. Teachers identify the main learning objectives of a unit, lesson, or activity, "and we'll work backward from that."

For example, a science teacher recently brought his earth science class to the Writing Center for a unit on rocks. Students classified different types of rocks, made graphic representations of their findings, and then wrote descriptions of each type of rock. "The unit was successful," says Nicolini, "because it required students to sort through and select information" rather than merely to memorize classifications.

The shift in emphasis from rote memorization to using writing to demonstrate understanding of concepts has also garnered support from math educators and researchers. The recent Third International Mathematics and Science Study (TIMSS) found that U.S. math teachers typically stress how to solve problems, in contrast to educators in other countries who help students understand mathematical concepts. The National Council of Teachers of Mathematics (NCTM) Standards have called for educators to make the math classroom a place for discourse.

For Anne Doran, a 4th grade teacher at Holden Elementary School in Birmingham, Mich., TIMSS and the NCTM *Assessment Standards* prompted her to review and revise her teaching methods. "The TIMSS study stated that [U.S.] children do more problems than children in other countries, but understand them less," relates Doran. "I'm more interested in spending time on one problem rather than assigning lots of them."

She maintains that "using writing to teach math has a dual purpose: it allows students to express their understanding of math concepts and allows me to assess their understanding." Ultimately, Doran believes, concentrating on concepts is beneficial for her students. Once they grasp what they are doing, "they can relax and enjoy math. They leave the class saying, 'Gosh, this is fun!'"

NEW ASSESSMENTS

Although many teachers have discovered that writing enhances understanding, they have learned that writing across the curriculum requires them to revise their lesson plans and try new assessment methods.

Doran has discovered that students' journal entries, written in response to a specific question on a concept, help her gauge student understanding. She looks for content over language arts skills, she explains. "I don't emphasize spelling and grammar in math writing assignments. However, if I say at the beginning that they must express their answers in a sentence, they will get points taken off it they don't," Doran says.

In general, Doran finds that assessment is the most challenging aspect of introducing writing into math lessons. When grading math problems, there is a clear right or wrong answer, but with writing, "it's harder to quantify subjective terms," Doran states. "You must develop more creative assessment tools and many times you have to develop a rubric for each assignment," she explains.

Harvey Hurst, a government teacher and head of the Humanities Division of Penn High School, says that introducing writing across the curriculum has required him to reevaluate how he grades assignments. "I'd never heard of a rubric until a few years ago. It has been a learning experience for me to figure out how much emphasis to place on the mechanics of writing versus the content," he says. Ultimately, teachers "find that rubrics provide focus and help them identify what they are looking for."

According to Hurst, who gives students a writing prompt at least twice a week, the biggest hurdle for most teachers is that teaching and assessing writing are time-consuming. Although block scheduling has allowed teachers in his school some flexibility with their lessons, some teachers "worry that writing assignments will take a long time to grade," he says.

Still, Hurst believes that the effort is well spent. As a result of increased writing assignments, "students are more aware of the subject they are being taught" and have learned to be critical thinkers, he contends.

For his part, Hurst, a teacher for 35 years, has discovered that writing across the curriculum has revitalized his teaching. Before the emphasis on writing, he relates, "I was getting lazy, but writing has given me a new outlook on teaching. It has recharged my battery."

WHOLE LANGUAGE

WHAT IS WHOLE LANGUAGE?

SCOTT WILLIS

Educators, parents, and policymakers often misunderstand whole language, its advocates claim. Even some whole language teachers long for a concise definition they can share with parents. A dictionary definition cannot capture the complexity of whole language, however. Whole language is both a theory about how children learn language and a set of principles to guide classroom practice, experts say.

What are the basic tenets of whole language? According to whole language theory, teachers should:

• *focus on meaning, not the component parts of language.* Children learn language from whole to part. Therefore, instruction in reading and writing should begin by presenting whole texts—engaging poems and stories—rather than zeroing in on the "bits and pieces" that make up language (words, syllables, and sounds in isolation). By keeping language "whole," teachers focus on its purpose—to communicate meaning—rather than reducing language to a set of abstractions that children can't relate to.

• *teach skills in context, not in isolation.* Children learn the subskills of language—such as letter-sound relationships, spelling, punctuation, and grammar—most readily when these skills are taught in the context of reading and writing activities. Teachers should coach children in skills as the need for the skills arises, rather than marching children in lockstep through a sequenced skills curriculum.

The articles in this chapter were originally published in the Fall 1995 issue of ASCD's *Curriculum Update* newsletter.

- *expose children to lots of good literature.* High-quality children's literature is the heart and soul of a whole language program. By acquainting children with stories and nonfiction works that capture their interest, teachers motivate children to become adept readers and writers—and plant the seeds of a lifelong love for books. Shared literature also provides a meaningful context for teaching skills.

- *get children writing, early and often.* Teachers should encourage young children to write as soon as they can hold a pencil, rather than waiting until they have learned to read. Reading and writing develop best in tandem. When children write, they master phonics relationships because they must constantly match letters with sounds to write what they want to say. Lots of early writing experience also helps children become comfortable with putting their thoughts on paper and leads them to think of themselves as writers.

- *accept "invented spelling."* Whole language teachers do not expect perfect spelling from the beginning. Instead, they encourage children to make their best efforts. Children's crude approximations—usually called "invented spelling"—reveal to what degree the young writers have cracked the phonetic code. Over time, children's spelling becomes more conventional, and teachers gradually insist on more correct spelling.

- *allow pupils to make choices.* Teachers should let children choose at least some of the books they read and topics they write on. When children have some control over their learning, they are more motivated and retain what they learn longer.

The basic premise of whole language is "teaching language in the context of *using* language," says Ken Goodman of the University of Arizona. Whole language teachers involve children in using language purposefully to meet their own needs, he says. They support children's language development, rather than seeking to control it.

"Whole language is an attempt to build curriculum based on what we know about natural language learning," says Jerome Harste of Indiana University–Bloomington. It avoids using a skill-sequence approach that seems logical to adults. Breaking language into small parts to be learned in sequence "seems logical only until you watch how little kids are handling language," he says. Language development is actually more wholistic.

WHAT IT'S NOT

Whole language is defined as much by what it is *not* as by what it is, some experts say. Whole language teachers generally avoid these practices:

• *breaking language into its component parts.* This overly analytical approach subverts the whole-to-part nature of language learning.

• *teaching skills in isolation or in a strict sequence.* Children learn skills best when a need to know them arises in the course of reading and writing.

• *relying on basal readers with controlled vocabulary.* Whole language teachers are skeptical of basal readers that follow a part-to-whole model, which runs counter to whole language theory. Basal readers present subskills in sequence, control vocabulary, and simplify sentence structure. Because they are so contrived, basal readers often serve up stilted passages that children find insipid compared to "real" literature.

• *using worksheets and drill.* Whole language teachers avoid activities where children practice skills in isolation. They consider drill activities too abstract to make sense to some children, and demotivating to all children because the drills are divorced from meaning. Unlike literature, such activities provide no purpose for learning skills and inspire no love of reading.

• *testing subskills.* Many whole language teachers are dubious of tests that focus on children's mastery of subskills, rather than on their ability to read for meaning and to write well. Most prefer more wholistic assessments, such as miscue analysis and portfolios.

FINDING THE SUREST WAY TO LITERACY

SCOTT WILLIS

Can children become literate by reading and writing? This apparent paradox is at the heart of the debate over "whole language"—a debate that, after 15 years, shows signs of heating up rather than abating.

Since the 1980s, whole language has strongly influenced the way children in North America are taught to read and write. In the 1960s and

'70s, basal-reader programs drilled children in phonics skills. Instruction emphasized the *parts* of language—letter sounds, consonant blends, long and short vowels—rather than using language to communicate. Children read bland stories with strictly controlled vocabulary, then filled out an unending stream of worksheets.

Whole language discredited this part-to-whole approach and ruined the reputations of Dick and Jane. In whole language, *meaning* is paramount. Rather than learning phonics skills out of context, children are taught about the parts of language while they pursue "authentic" reading and writing. High-quality children's literature and children's own writing are central—and provide the context for skills instruction.

Whole language practices are more effective, proponents argue, because they match children's natural language development. Children learn spoken language through being immersed in a world of talk—without carefully sequenced instruction. To learn to read and write, children need conditions similar to those that helped them learn to speak: a literate environment, lots of modeling, and a teacher who supports their development.

The whole language philosophy has swept the primary grades, experts say. Although most teachers still use a basal reader (many are required to), most have also incorporated elements of whole language into their instruction.

But as whole language comes of age, it is also coming under siege. Critics are citing California's low 1994 NAEP scores as proof that whole language is a failure. Of the 50 states, California has been considered in the vanguard in moving to whole language. Yet of the 39 states ranked by "the nation's report card," California tied for last place (with Louisiana) in average reading proficiency. Of all the jurisdictions reported, only Guam scored lower.

California's low scores have prompted a reappraisal of whole language. This article explores the arguments on both sides of the debate.

TEACHING PHONICS "IN CONTEXT"

Whole language has won nearly universal praise for its use of children's literature and its emphasis on writing. It has drawn fire, however, for its approach to teaching skills such as spelling, punctuation, grammar—and especially phonics.

These skills should be taught in the context of authentic reading and writing activities, whole language advocates believe. Phonics should *not* be learned and practiced in isolation. Basal readers, worksheets, flashcards, and "the letter of the week" should all be rejected because they make phonics overly abstract and boring.

"Everyone—even the most hardcore whole language advocates—acknowledges that kids need to learn letter-sound relationships," says Gay Fawcett, director of curriculum and instruction for the Summit County (Ohio) Education Service Center. But whole language teachers do not teach phonics skills in a carefully sequenced hierarchy. Instead, they allow the teaching of skills to "emerge naturally" from activities the class is engaged in.

When teaching reading, a whole language teacher begins by presenting a piece of literature, then encouraging pupils to look at textual features, explains Dorothy Strickland, professor of reading at Rutgers University. After pupils have become acquainted with a text, they examine all the conventions of print, such as periods and question marks. Then they take a closer look at phrases and words, noticing features such as initial consonants. When this process is repeated "on a daily basis, with a variety of texts," children begin to form generalizations about written language and internalize the rules. Whole language "gives kids opportunities to figure it out for themselves," Strickland says—a technique that yields more powerful learning.

Constance Weaver, professor of English at Western Michigan University, recommends two strategies for teaching phonics in context. The first is shared reading from a big book. Teachers should choose literature "where the sound elements are interesting," she suggests, such as poems with ear-catching alliteration and rhyme. Scrutiny of the texts can "help kids grasp the principle of how two or three letters together make a sound," for example. The second strategy is shared writing, where teachers and students compose together, discussing how words should be spelled and why. Teachers must plan such activities carefully, Weaver adds, to guide children to important understandings.

"Whole language is the best phonics program there is," asserts Jerome Harste, professor of language education at Indiana University-

Bloomington. Rather than learning phonics rules by rote and applying them on worksheets, children in a whole language classroom *think* much more about the phonetic system as they write, he says.

Rather than just telling about letter-sound relationships, whole language teachers help children *discover* phonics principles, says Regie Routman, a language arts resource teacher in Shaker Heights, Ohio, and author of *Transitions: From Literature to Literacy*. Pupils constantly test their own hypotheses. They look at patterns in words, hypothesize rules, and make word lists that help confirm or disprove their thinking.

For example, a class might make a list of rhyming words they've encountered—*play, day, say, way*—then discuss the pattern pupils see. (The teacher wouldn't just state, "One-syllable words with a 'long *a*' sound often end in *ay*," Routman says.) The class might also discuss other ways to spell the "long *a*" sound, such as *eigh* or *ai*. "With the teacher's guidance, students discover the rules and patterns over time through lots of talk, experimentation, and observation, rather than through the teacher's telling them," Routman says.

Whole language teachers "highlight and demonstrate" phonics principles, says Heidi Mills of the University of South Carolina, coauthor of *Looking Closely: Exploring the Role of Phonics in One Whole Language Classroom*. On a daily basis, whole language teachers demonstrate in context "how letters and sounds work." Rather than trying to teach skills in isolation, teachers "capitalize on children's insights and ideas," which are sparked by reading and writing activities.

Whole language teachers need a record-keeping system to monitor the progress of individual children, Mills says. Teachers should observe each child weekly and maintain portfolios and individual files. (Many teachers keep records of children's miscues—mistakes made when reading aloud—to document learning.) "Teachers who adopt a 'kidwatching' stance know so much more about their children" than teachers who march through a skills curriculum, she says.

Whole language teachers make sure pupils "interact with print in a meaningful way," says Tim O'Keefe, a whole language teacher in Columbia, S.C., and coauthor of *Looking Closely*. For example, O'Keefe asked his pupils to write their names in a "sign-in journal" every morning. The children became intrigued by commonalities in their names, such as the first letters of *Chiquita* and *Charles*. O'Keefe used their interest to encourage them to reflect systematically on patterns in written language.

Individual children's insights should be shared with the class, O'Keefe says. If a child notices the *ch* blend at both ends of the word *church*, for example, that discovery is made public so other pupils can learn from it. O'Keefe also works with children one-on-one. "Writer's workshop"— when pupils are writing stories or nonfiction—is "the perfect time to work with kids individually" to help them develop the skills they need to work on, he says.

Teaching phonics and other skills in context works well, O'Keefe testifies. "I've seen it happen with my own eyes."

THE CASE AGAINST

Many detractors of whole language, however, believe that teaching phonics "in context" is not feasible—that the approach is haphazard and leaves too much to chance. Much more effective, these experts say, is systematic, direct instruction in phonics.

To become readers, children must learn the connections between letters of the alphabet and the sounds they represent, says Jeanne Chall, professor emerita of Harvard's Graduate School of Education and author of *Learning to Read: The Great Debate*. Teachers must make sure their pupils understand the phonetic system. A teacher with a class of 30 pupils "can't do that in the context of the literature," Chall asserts. Such phonics instruction is merely "incidental"—and inadequate.

"Sometimes you have to take things out of context" to teach them effectively, Chall maintains. "God doesn't say everything has to be in context."

Teaching phonics in context is not an adequate strategy for managing a whole class, agrees Marilyn Jager Adams, professor of cognitive and linguistic sciences at Brown University and author of *Beginning to Read: Thinking and Learning about Print*. In teaching Joey about the *e* on the end of *made*, for example, "you lose the bulk of the audience," she says. "The rest of the kids are counting the holes in the ceiling tiles." And when instruction is strictly context-bound, pupils may not grasp general points the teachers makes.

Steven Stahl, professor of reading at the University of Georgia, likes many aspects of whole language but is concerned that it "leaves out" direct teaching of skills. Most children need at least some direct phonics instruction to learn to read, he says.

Stahl expresses skepticism that a whole language teacher can teach skills when the need for them arises in context, seizing the teachable moment. "What if that moment arises when the teacher is [working] with another kid?" he wonders. "The teacher can't be everywhere." Although teaching skills in context is "a great romantic notion," teachers shouldn't just "trust to serendipity," he says.

Stahl dismisses the argument that teaching phonics out of context is developmentally inappropriate or boring. "Teaching phonics can be deadly dull, but it can also be interesting," he says. Rather than using worksheets, teachers should introduce the letter *a*, for example, then have students read a story with lots of *a*'s in it, he recommends. "Good phonics instruction feeds into kids' reading of connected text," he says. "Kids can take a detour to learn something about words without losing sight of the overall goal" of reading for meaning.

Children need "very focused skill development early on," says Bill Honig of San Francisco State University, author of the forthcoming book *How Should We Teach Our Children to Read?* In his former position as California's superintendent of schools, Honig was closely identified with the state's language-arts framework, which promoted a "literature-driven" approach. Honig now believes the effect of that framework was "disastrous for huge numbers of kids in California."

Although the framework said phonics is important, that endorsement was "just one line—a throwaway," Honig says. "We took for granted that teaching of phonics would happen." Instead, teachers neglected or ignored phonics as they placed more emphasis on literature, he laments.

The belief that it's bad to break words into their constituent parts is wrong, Honig says bluntly. "You *have to* look at parts to learn to read." Children need to be able to decode words automatically so they can use their mental energy to concentrate on meaning, he says. Therefore, in 1st grade, children need intensive instruction in letter-sound relationships, sight words (high-frequency words that must be recognized at a glance), and word attack ("sounding out") skills.

Phonics instruction needs to be focused, sequenced, and comprehensive, Honig contends. "You need an organized system" to teach skills and then have children practice them—like piano scales, he says. "And you need materials designed and appropriate for that [purpose]." The old, rote approach to teaching phonics didn't work, Honig concedes. But the new approach helps children understand how the phonetic system works, he says. "Today, phonics is a thinking skills program."

"Whole language has gone way too far in underemphasizing word attack and phonetic skills," says Bob Slavin, codirector of the Center for Research on the Education of Students Placed at Risk, at Johns Hopkins University. In whole language classrooms, "you see very little phonics, or [see it taught] only incidentally," he alleges. "Many children need a more systematic presentation of word attack skills." Two of his own children would have "crashed and burned" as readers without a systematic presentation of phonics, Slavin says.

THE DOWNSIDE OF PHONICS

Advocates of whole language counter that direct, systematic teaching of phonics is actually detrimental to beginning readers.

The part-to-whole nature of isolated phonics instruction makes learning to read more difficult, argues Ken Goodman of the University of Arizona, a pioneer of the whole language movement. "In our zeal to make it easy, we've made it hard. How? Primarily by breaking whole (natural) language up into bite-size but abstract little pieces. It seemed so logical to think that little children could best learn simple little things," he writes in *What's Whole in Whole Language?* That approach is incompatible, however, with the way children actually learn language, he says.

Goodman also lambastes basal readers for creating "inauthentic and meaningless texts" by controlling vocabulary. The prose that results is "incomprehensible nonsense," he charges. Children learn much better from "real" literature that has "predictable patterns," such as *The House That Jack Built* or *I Know an Old Lady Who Swallowed a Fly*, he says. (Stahl, however, vigorously disputes this characterization of basals, which he claims haven't used controlled vocabulary in 15 years. "Dick and Jane are in the history collection," he says.)

Some children who are taught through an intensive, analytical phonics approach learn to decode but dislike reading, warns Dale Hayes, professor of reading and special education at Brandon University in Brandon, Manitoba. When phonics is overemphasized, some children interpret reading as a decoding act, with comprehension "trailing behind."

Many children remember skills better if the skills are presented within a high-interest story, says Marie Carbo, executive director of the National Reading Styles Institute. It's difficult for children to remain interested in phonics if they don't see the connection to reading literature. "We forget the zombies we had in many classrooms during the skills era," when teachers rarely read aloud, she says. "We forget how much some children hated reading." During the heyday of that approach, resource teacher Routman adds, children who had trouble learning sounds and their corresponding letters were placed in "low" reading groups and were never exposed to good literature.

Direct teaching of phonics is a class-centered approach, whereas whole language is child-centered, says Gary Manning, professor of education at the University of Alabama at Birmingham. "I would teach certain phonics skills to individuals or small groups," he says. "It doesn't make sense to teach them to the whole class, because it's too early for some children, too late for others." Phonics and grammar make more sense when the learner sees a purpose for them and needs to use them, he contends. "I'm a constructivist: I believe learning develops inside-out; it's not a pouring in" of information.

"If you believe that what's taught is directly learned, then you set up a very sequenced direct-instruction program," says Yetta Goodman of the University of Arizona, a leading whole language theorist. But if you believe in constructivism—that children *respond* to what is taught—then you create a rich literate environment where the teacher knows when to push and when to stay on the sidelines. "If given rich experiences, kids will find ways to come to literacy," she contends.

"If a systematic, sequenced approach works, why did we have kids who didn't learn in the 1960s and '70s, when over 95 percent of kids were in a basal program?" Goodman asks. She adds that two of her grandchildren who have been taught through a rigid phonics-and-workbooks approach are struggling readers and don't like to read.

Advocates of whole language vehemently deny that their approach is haphazard. A good whole language classroom has a great deal of structure, Strickland says. "It's not a laissez-faire classroom by any means." She dismisses as "baloney" the charge that whole language only relies on the teachable moment. On the contrary, whole language teachers plan activities carefully and monitor their pupils closely to ensure they are developing skills, she says.

POORLY IMPLEMENTED?

But critics of whole language also charge that, whatever the ideal, teachers by and large have fallen short in putting whole language in practice. Many teachers have held whole language and teaching phonics to be mutually exclusive—and have abandoned the latter, critics complain.

"Many of our teachers have felt, 'Oh, dear—we're not supposed to teach phonics,'" although they were never told that by the district, says Ann McCallum, language arts coordinator in Fairfax County, Va., where the program incorporates elements of whole language. (McCallum is featured in the ASCD videotape program *Making Meaning: Integrated Language Arts*.)

Some teachers misunderstand whole language as "just celebrating where the kid is," McCallum says. Because of the de-emphasis on basals and workbooks, some teachers see whole language as "kids rolling around on the floor with books," she says. "You just give them books and it will all work out nicely. That just doesn't work."

Whole language is not well understood among teachers, says Dick Allington, chair of the department of reading at SUNY–Albany. Many teachers have the mistaken notion that they should not address the skills and strategies of reading, he asserts. In essence, these teachers have returned to the discovery learning mode, he says: "Leave kids alone and immerse them in a rich environment, and they'll learn by themselves."

Others believe such claims are overstated. In their "zealousness" to become whole language teachers, some teachers may have gone too far in downplaying skills, resource teacher Routman says. "A small minority of teachers thought phonics would come automatically for all children." But most teachers are now taking "a balanced position," she believes.

WHAT RESEARCH REVEALS

Does research help resolve how best to teach reading and writing?

Studies that compare whole language to more phonics-intensive approaches show no clear advantage on either side, according to some experts. In a meta-analysis of comparative studies, Stahl found no difference between whole language and traditional instruction in their effects on student achievement. Some studies favored one approach or the other, but these effects "washed out" in the big picture. No studies that looked at children from low-SES homes favored whole language, he points out.

Jeffrey Fouts of Seattle Pacific University, coauthor of *Research on Educational Innovations*, confirms that comparative studies show "no appreciable difference in results" between whole language and direct instruction in phonics. But he cautions that this area is "very difficult" to research. Defining which classrooms are using which approach is problematic: "Very few teachers are [doing] either all whole language or all direct instruction," he notes. Isolating variables to show cause and effect is fraught with difficulties.

Adams, in reviewing comparative studies, concluded that "intensive, explicit phonic instruction is a valuable component of beginning reading programs." Most comparative studies "indicate that approaches including systematic phonic instruction result in comprehension skills that are at least comparable to, and word recognition and spelling skills that are significantly better than, those that do not," she writes in *Beginning to Read.*

Complicating the research issue is the debate over what counts as research. Phonics supporters endorse *quantitative* research, which uses empirical measures (such as standardized tests) to look at large groups of children. Whole language advocates, on the other hand, prefer *qualitative* research, which describes what takes place in classrooms.

In their analyses of the research, Chall and Adams have ignored studies that didn't fit their paradigm of experimental research, says Manning. They define reading (in behaviorist terms) as "getting the words right," whereas whole language defines reading as "getting the meaning." Experimental research doesn't reveal how children develop as readers and writers, Manning says. Because that is precisely what whole language advocates want to discover, they pursue qualitative research.

Yetta Goodman prefers this latter brand of research, which she calls "interpretive." Researchers who pursue it are "drowned in data," she says. Some sit in classrooms "day in, day out," tape recording. One researcher studying literacy during play among preschoolers spent three days a week for a year observing children, she notes. These researchers also interpret what they see and hear, "carefully analyzing and coming to conclusions."

"I don't want to count research that isn't real," Goodman says. "Real language takes place in homes and schools, not clinics."

"We're only beginning to get a sense of how to do research on whole language," says Terry Salinger, director of research for the International Reading Association. The best research on whole language, she believes, is ethnographic—looking at the development of individuals or small groups of children over time in a whole language environment. Such research is "very illuminating," she believes. From it, "we can generalize aspects of development and instruction."

The weaker research on whole language relies on standardized tests, Salinger says. Most standardized tests assess what's taught in more traditional programs, which focus on subskill instruction. "In many ways, [phonics-based programs] prepare kids for standardized tests," she says. But standardized tests don't yield "a sense of how kids are orchestrating these skills into coherent literate behavior." Nor do they capture children's attitudes about reading and writing, she adds.

Although Stahl concedes that standardized tests are flawed measures of reading ability, he notes that they correlate with other measures, such as teacher judgments. "If kids don't do well on standardized reading achievement tests, they're probably not doing well on other measures either." Whole language adherents ignore this fact, he says.

All the research—including standardized tests, interviews, and observations—points to the same conclusion, Chall says. Studies "come down very clearly" that systematic phonics is better. "We've been giving tests so long, and they all correlate," she says. "If you complain, it's because you don't like the results."

Some whole language practitioners, however, are not troubled by standardized tests. Whole language instruction does not put children at a disadvantage on standardized tests, says Routman—unless the tests include sections on phonics in isolation. These should be replaced with sections that test reading comprehension. "There's nowhere in life where you have to do phonics in isolation," she points out.

"Generally, my kids have done fine on standardized tests," says Linda Erdmann, a whole language teacher from Harwich, Mass. But she is frustrated by the tests because her pupils can do "so much more" than the tests reveal. For example, they can discuss authors and identify writing styles, and they are highly motivated to read. "They devour books," she reports.

"There's research that both sides can point to," says Fawcett. If our primary concern is that children be able to sound out words, then whole language is not working as well as direct-phonics programs, she says. If our top priority is for children to "love and comprehend reading," then whole language works better. This philosophical difference means the research question "will continue as a stalemate," she believes.

PATCHING WHOLE LANGUAGE

Is the answer to blend both approaches? Some experts advocate bolstering whole language programs with direct instruction in skills. Many teachers, they say, use an eclectic approach of this sort. "Practitioners are putting stuff together to create something that works," says Michael McKenna, professor of reading at Georgia Southern University. He notes that many self-described whole language teachers use basals. "Attacking multiple fronts is probably the way to get the job done."

Educators can "take the best of both worlds," says Margaret Pleta, principal of Covert Avenue School in Elmont, N.Y. Pleta's district is locked into a basal and workbook approach, but she has provided teachers with staff development training in whole language practices. She also encourages teachers to supplement the basal with literature and to provide a print-rich environment. "It can coexist," she reports.

If done well, an eclectic approach is "probably very sensible," says Salinger. She sees that approach as "a kind of adaptation" of whole language.

The idea of "patching" whole language with systematic phonics instruction does not sit well, however, with advocates of whole language. The patching idea reflects a mistaken understanding of whole language, says Ken Goodman. "One cannot reconcile direct instruction with natural learning. Meaningful, predictable, authentic texts are incompatible with carefully controlled vocabulary and decontextualized phonics instruction," he has written in ASCD's *Educational Leadership.*

"You can't have it all ways," says Harste. Curriculum must be anchored on educators' notion of the learning process. Educators can't see the learning process as rote *and* as needing to be functional. "Eclecticism is curable by taking a theoretical stand," he says tartly.

"We keep trying to find consensus," says Yetta Goodman. "We need to agree that we have serious disagreements, and we need to find a way to talk," she insists. "We've been working toward consensus too long."

BEYOND THE BACKLASH

Whole language will withstand the current backlash against it, most experts believe. But it may be transformed by the backlash.

"Extreme" whole language will not survive, predicts Michael Pressley, professor of educational psychology at SUNY–Albany. "Something more in the middle has a better chance" to prevail, he believes, because a balanced approach is "best supported by data and top-drawer curriculum materials—and terrific teachers are doing it."

"The term *whole language* may disappear, but what it represents won't," says Manning. Whole language has had a big impact, even in traditional classrooms, in spurring more literature-based teaching, more reading aloud, and more writing. "It won't go away."

Some worry, however, that the pendulum may swing alarmingly far in the other direction. McKenna fears a return to the phonics-first programs of the past. "Hold your breath—it looks like we may be going back to the '60s," he says. "It didn't work then, and it won't work now."

"I'm worried about the big picture," says Routman. Whole language teachers need to make clear that they're teaching skills along with great literature, she says. "Unless parents realize this, we're in trouble."

Many advocates believe whole language is taking the rap for systemic problems in education. In California, where whole language has been blamed for low NAEP scores, the average class size in 1st grade is very high, children are linguistically diverse, and schools have curtailed inservice training in the last 10 years, Harste says. "Why can't we hypothesize that some of those things are the cause" of the low scores?

But Harste does not fear that the influence of whole language will be erased. "Despite the hopes of adversaries, there's no going back," he says. "The field of education has been forever changed—and it won't change back."

WHAT DISADVANTAGED CHILDREN NEED

SCOTT WILLIS

Each year, unnumbered children who have not had rich early literacy experiences enter kindergarten and 1st grade. No parent has read them bedtime stories every night or taught them their ABCs, for example. (These children are often, but not always, from low-SES homes.) Compared to peers who have been raised on a steady diet of Dr. Seuss or Winnie the Pooh, these children are clearly at a disadvantage. What should schools do to ensure that these disadvantaged students succeed in learning to read and write?

Opinion is sharply divided on this question. Advocates of whole language emphasize that these children need experiences with whole texts. Other experts recommend that these children receive lots of direct skills instruction.

The latter prescription for these children "blows my mind," says Yetta Goodman. "If other kids become literate by being in a rich literate environment, why would you prescribe narrow, boring experiences" focused on phonics for these kids? she asks. "Why give them the most sterile experiences?" Ken Goodman warns that the belief that these children must learn skills before they can read anything that makes sense "digs them into a rut."

When children come to school without having had wholistic experiences with written language, "that's all the more reason why they need them," says Manning. Why do schools have so much failure with disadvantaged children? he asks. "Because we're using a part-to-whole paradigm with them," he says. These children lack early literacy experiences, so they aren't ready to make part-to-whole relationships. By teaching them phonics in isolation, "we're dooming them to failure."

Disadvantaged children "need to hear the rhythm of the language," says Fredi Norris, a whole language teacher from Rockville Centre, N.Y. They also need opportunities to learn story structure (beginning, middle, and end) and to "get caught up in the power of a good story." Some of these children "don't even know nursery rhymes," she says. "They *need* that stuff."

"Why would these kids need to know 'short *a*' more than other kids?" Norris asks. A focus on such skills "would turn them off," she believes.

Children who come from a print-rich home environment "can tolerate having language abstracted," as happens in a phonics-first approach, says Harste. But disadvantaged children "should not be looking at print in the abstract." This approach hasn't worked in the past, he says. These children need a meaningful context for learning skills.

Stahl sees the situation differently. Whole language—which puts children in a literate environment and allows them to explore—provides a continuation of the home environment for advantaged children. "These kids are getting more of what they've gotten already," he says. But children who haven't been read to, who don't have background experience with print, "don't know how to negotiate that environment," he asserts. These children need someone to teach them more explicitly about print. Otherwise, "they don't pick up on it."

Whole language proponents think children develop skills "from enjoying reading interesting stories," says Chall. This approach fails particularly with high-risk children, whose parents don't teach them at home. "Children who have weaknesses need a lot of extra help, not incidental instruction." Research shows that direct instruction is particularly helpful for average and below-average achievers, she says. "Systematic, structured teaching helps low-income children."

Chall points to California, which has a high population of poor and minority children. "When you do away with direct teaching, those children fall down." Alluding to California's recent low NAEP scores, she says, "We're finding over and over again that this is true."

While she agrees that disadvantaged children need to explore text and book language, Adams says it's "inarguable" based on research that explicit guidance in the sound-spelling relationship "makes a huge difference" for them.

All children are at risk without direct phonics instruction—even children who have had every middle-class advantage, says Slavin. "A lot of kids just don't click" without it. Middle-class children get "rescued"—their parents teach them or hire tutors—but children from poor families often lack this safety net, he says.

PROVIDING BOTH

The best approach lies somewhere between both extremes, Salinger believes. Disadvantaged children may well need more systematic skills instruction, but they also need exposure to literature, which they have lacked. "If everything they've heard is oral—TV and radio—book language will seem bizarre to them," she notes. Whole language will give them a "level of comfort" with the sound of literature. "That's essential."

Disadvantaged children need both instruction in phonics and exposure to literature, says Routman. "And a good whole language program will give them both."

"There's no doubt that these children need language development," says Carbo. Whole language gives them this "in much greater doses" than a phonics-centered approach. Disadvantaged children make the best progress when they receive "a tremendous amount" of modeling—when they listen to book recordings or hear the teacher read aloud frequently, she says. This prescription fits the whole language paradigm better. "Both sides have some of the answer—but whole language has more of the answer," she believes.

To help disadvantaged children, "the best bet is to invest in kindergarten," Adams says. All young children benefit if engaged in activities (such as games and rhymes) that direct their attention to the sounds of language. By finding ways to engage kindergartners with print, stories, and the sounds and structure of language, teachers can make sure young children have "phonemic awareness"—an understanding of the logic of written language.

A lack of phonemic awareness appears to be the major cause of reading difficulties, says Reid Lyon, a neuropsychologist with the National Institute of Child Health and Human Development. Some children lack the intuitive understanding that words are made up of individual sounds. (The word *cat,* for example, comprises the sounds c-a-t, but "the ear doesn't recover that," Lyon says. "It hears one big pulse of sound.") This understanding lays the groundwork for later learning. Teaching phonics to children who don't have phonemic awareness is "a big waste of time," Adams says. "The very kids who need it most are just not responding."

INVENTED SPELLING

SCOTT WILLIS

One aspect of whole language that has caused confusion is its acceptance of "invented spelling"—the spellings young children devise as they learn to write. Invented spellings often lack vowels or median consonants: *frd* for *friend* or *vkashn* for *vacation.* These spellings represent children's early attempts to match letters to the sounds they hear in words.

Whole language teachers allow young children to use invented spelling because, they believe, an emphasis on correct spelling would be developmentally inappropriate and would dampen children's enthusiasm for writing. It would also force young writers to restrict their vocabulary severely. Some parents, however, have been alarmed to find their children's schoolwork full of what they consider misspellings left uncorrected by the teacher.

Whole language teachers have pupils composing much earlier, says Strickland, so of course spelling will be rudimentary. "As adults, we have to live with *tf* for *tough*—it's okay at this stage." If teachers insist on "perfection right from the beginning," then children just copy, she says—they don't compose at all. Compared to their peers in traditional classes, children in whole language classes are better (or equally good) spellers and better composers, she asserts.

Children's invented spellings are "the best indication" that they are developing an understanding of the phonetic system, says Ken Goodman. Correcting children's spelling is a natural thing for teachers to want to do, but it "shuts down" the process of children's searching for the letters they need to represent the sounds. "It distracts children—it says to them, 'Don't trust your ear.'" Children's spelling gradually becomes more conventional, he points out. They discover standard spelling through reading.

The fear that children will never learn correct spellings is unfounded, experts say. "If kids are reading and writing a lot, if they're exposed to print, their spelling will move toward the conventional," says Weaver. Similarly, the fear that children will need to *unlearn* their invented spellings is unsupported by research. In fact, children often spell the same word different ways within the same piece, she notes.

At what point should teachers insist on correct spelling? "People I respect differ a lot on this," Weaver says. "So much depends on the individual child." Some are ready in kindergarten; some are hardly ready by the 4th grade. Children who don't have a good visual memory will make slower progress, she says.

Invented spelling may help teach letter sounds, says Chall, but "parents are worried sick over children's spellings." Sooner or later, somebody has to show pupils conventional spellings and hold pupils to them, she says. And 3rd grade is "a really late time to do that."

Although it sometimes upsets parents, invented spelling is a wonderful way to develop phonemic awareness—linking letters with sounds, Adams says. As children practice, they "pull in" more and more phonemes, final consonants, and vowels. "They gradually pick up the complexities." Nevertheless, conventional spelling does need to be taught, Adams believes. Children pick up standard spellings quickly if they've done independent writing, which gives them "the mental Velcro to absorb those spellings," she says.

HIGH EXPECTATIONS

Teachers need to be clear about their expectations for spelling, McCallum says. They should tell children, "Book spelling is your ultimate goal—and we'll get there as fast as we can." Teachers should expect conventional spelling by the time children are out of the primary grades, she advises.

To set high expectations, Routman suggests 1st grade teachers create a "Word Wall" listing high-frequency words that must be spelled correctly. For example, teachers should expect *went* to be correctly spelled because children use that word so often in their writing.

Teachers shouldn't discourage children by marking up their papers with red ink or forcing them to spell words correctly, Manning says. But teachers *should* recopy children's writing if it's to be shared, he says, so children see only models of standard spelling.

Teaching spelling in isolation—through lists of spelling words—often doesn't transfer to children's writing, Manning says. In whole language classrooms, children's spelling abilities are far superior, and they can spell far more words than if they had been taught by the list method, he says.

As teachers meet with children to discuss their rough drafts, they can give specific spelling information to children, such as explaining the "silent *e*," says Mills. Some of the best spelling instruction comes during editing, she says. In classrooms where correct spelling is emphasized from the start, children are "panicked" when asked to compose. They say, "I can't write."

Traditional programs have emphasized spelling and grammar skills, says Harste, rather than getting one's ideas down on paper. "In the past, we prepared secretaries. Whole language prepares writers."

REWRITING THE BOOK ON LITERATURE

CHANGES SOUGHT IN HOW LITERATURE IS TAUGHT, WHAT STUDENTS READ

JOHN O'NEIL

Move over, Dick and Jane. Silas Marner: you, too, can take a walk.

Slowly but inexorably, the literature found in school curriculums—and the instructional strategies used to teach it—are beginning to change. Although changes in classroom practice are often slow in coming, experts in the field see some significant shifts in thinking regarding the role of literature in the curriculum K–12.

What's considered "in" are efforts to make literature more engaging and relevant to students and to take advantage of the power of literature to enhance reading and writing skills or to help integrate the curriculum. On the way "out" are chopped-up, bowdlerized literary selections in the primary grades, classroom approaches that depend on the teacher to explain the "meaning" of literary works to rows of passive students, and reading lists that consist almost exclusively of works by "DWEMs" (dead white European males). This article describes some selected trends and issues influencing the teaching of literature in elementary and secondary schools.

REAL LITERATURE

Perhaps the predominant change in what literature is taught in elementary schools is a new interest in using more "real" literature in the

This article was originally published in the June 1994 issue of ASCD's *Curriculum Update* newsletter.

curriculum. Dick and Jane, it seems, are on the way out, and classrooms are filling up with dog-eared versions of children's classics and fiction and nonfiction on every conceivable topic. The catch phrase for the new interest in using literature in elementary classrooms is "literature-based" programs. "The literature-based trend is very strong," says Carl Smith, professor of education at Indiana University and director of the ERIC Clearinghouse on Reading, English, and Communication.

In general, literature-based programs differ from traditional approaches by surrounding students with rich, authentic, whole pieces of literature from the earliest grades; by teaching reading skills in the context of real literature; and by using literature throughout the curriculum.

What would a visitor see in a classroom using a literature-based approach? For one thing, the classroom itself would be rich with print, says Rudine Sims Bishop, professor of education at the Ohio State University. In most of these classrooms, trade books are in abundant supply, either in the school library or in classroom libraries. The textbooks tend to be used as a resource; they do not serve as the sole source for the entire language arts curriculum. "It's a literate environment," says Bishop. Students "are surrounded by all kinds of books."

The books, moreover, would be diverse—in topics, culture of the characters and the authors, and difficulty. Students and teachers would be talking to each other about their reading. Pupils would be "using books for information" to help them in subjects other than reading or language arts. "I would see literature used throughout the curriculum," says Bishop.

Experts in the field say that literature-based programs draw support from the increasingly popular "whole language" approach to developing student literacy. "The whole language philosophy includes a literature base for language arts instruction," says Smith. "Probably the beginning point of whole language" is "getting kids out of the basal [readers] and into real books."

Some experts see whole language and literature-based approaches as a correction in course for an elementary-level curriculum that has over-emphasized the teaching of discrete reading skills at the expense of treating students to high-quality literature. What's now needed, many say, are approaches that bring about balance in the use of literature to teach reading skills.

In traditional language arts programs in the early primary grades, experts say, literature has often taken a back seat to the teaching of phonics and other decoding skills. "It's partly how one views how people learn to read," explains Bishop. Traditional methods have emphasized the teaching of various subskills (e.g., sound-letter relationships, vocabulary words) plus comprehension skills (e.g., learning to identify the main idea or the sequence of events), she says. Although these skills are important, the teaching of these skills too frequently became ends in themselves. Basals included stories designed to teach children phonics, adds Charles Suhor, deputy executive director of the National Council of Teachers of English (NCTE). The problem was, the books ended up reading "as if they were written to illustrate phonics," rather than to tell an interesting story. As a result of the emphasis on skills, worksheets and drill sheets built around discrete subskills abounded. Teachers sometimes drilled students endlessly on the skills, leaving little time for students to put their skills into practice by looking at or reading a good book (or having one read to them).

Traditional reading theory held that students learned to read through repeated exposure to new words, notes Jim Hoffman, professor of language and literacy studies at the University of Texas. So basal readers began to include stories constructed to provide this repeated exposure— repeating the same word up to 40 times in a selection, says Hoffman. The result? The stories that children read too often followed the "Dick and Jane" pattern of sanitized and tightly controlled vocabulary that proved bland and monotonous to read.

In whole-language and literature-based programs, the teaching of skills is supposed to be placed squarely in the context of reading good literature. The theory is that "the teacher will [incorporate the skills] organically, as the occasion arises in the conduct of reading" together, says Smith. For example, in a classroom following the literature-based philosophy, the teacher might read a story aloud to the whole class, says Smith. Students might pair up and read to each other. Afterward, the teacher might teach vocabulary words found in the story. "The literature becomes the focal point from which other things arise."

A major feature of the changes sought in the use of literature in the early elementary grades is that programs must be balanced and flexible, drawing on the best of skills-based and literature-based strategies, experts say. A working paper drafted by the California Department of Education notes: "Over the years, in the quest to teach early reading successfully, educators have used a variety of approaches, ranging from methods that emphasize literature and the processes of reading and writing (to the exclusion of phonics and other skill-based strategies) to the traditional code-oriented approaches that emphasize skills at the expense of literature and reading and writing. Neither of these extremist approaches has been effective for all students." The preferred approach in California and elsewhere is a literature-based program that includes phonics and other decoding strategies.

NEW BOOKS SOUGHT

A major factor influencing the use of literature in the elementary grades is the role that basal readers, trade books, and other reading materials play in the curriculum. Most experts contacted for this article favored changes in the content of basal readers (as well as less dependence on the textbook in general) and greater use of a wide range of trade books.

Some experts point to promising signs that basal readers are changing to reflect new views on the teaching of reading and the renewed interest in good literature. More frequently, the textbooks contain whole stories, rather than edited, "dumbed down" versions; and decontextualized drills on skills are less commonly a feature. Some of the newer elementary readers "look more and more like literature anthologies than they do 'Dick and Jane,'" says Smith. In some cases, "they look like trade books mashed together."

Both Texas and California, which together represent a significant share of the market for basal readers, have issued new guidelines for publishers stressing integrated, literature-based programs.

California took the plunge first, issuing a new curriculum framework (which textbook publishers are supposed to address) for language arts in 1988. The framework called for literature-based, integrated programs that taught explicit skills in the context of literature. Publishers did not fully follow the guidelines, however, says Glen Thomas, director of curriculum frameworks and instructional resources for the California Department of Education. The programs submitted "were not integrated; they were not balanced," he says. For example, "none of them taught spelling in the context of reading and writing."

Since then, however, Thomas feels that the changes advocated by the framework have gained broader appeal in the field. The calls to boost the use of real literature and to integrate literature across the curriculum "are more pronounced now," he thinks. "We're still probably out in front of the market, but less so than in years past." The state plans to adopt new textbooks and instructional resources for grades K–2 this year, he adds, and he believes the new materials will better reflect the new emphases.

Texas may already be a step ahead of California. Guidelines for textbook publishers issued by Texas in 1990 said that in addition to incorporating traditional reading skills, language arts textbooks must provide "a pluralistic anthology of quality children's literature"; contain unabridged literature; and integrate reading with writing, speaking, and listening activities.

A study by researchers at the University of Texas on 1st grade basal readers adopted under the new guidelines (and placed in classrooms this school year) suggests the new books *do* differ from older books in some important ways. Adaptations of the literature in the new basals are minimal, and the vocabulary control and repetition that characterized the old basals have been significantly reduced, the study says. In addition, the teaching of skills in the new books has not been diminished, but the presentation of those skills has changed. The skills have been placed in the context of the literature, rather than standing in isolation, and are usually taught *after* students read the selection.

Because the basal readers sold in Texas will be marketed nationally, the changes are likely to have a significant impact on the use of literature in the early grades, says Hoffman, one of the study authors (and also, it should be noted, an author of one of the basal readers). In the past, publishers have usually been reluctant to make major changes until they felt sufficient demand in the field for a new approach. The fact that the publishers *did* respond to the new guidelines suggests that they believe many educators are ready for a more balanced approach to reading and literature. Still, Hoffman admits that neither anti-basal whole language advocates nor strong proponents of the traditional skills-based approach are likely to fully embrace the compromise. "The extremes in both directions will not be satisfied," he says. Moreover, the implementation of the new basals will have to be carefully watched to see how they influence classroom practice. "It's a big leap in the way we approach reading instruction," says Hoffman. "A lot of people are sitting back with their fingers crossed" on this new type of program.

INTEGRATED CURRICULUM

One of the successful aspects of California's approach has been the effort to use literature throughout the curriculum, says Thomas. Many teachers are interested in ways to use literature in different subject areas, and the Department of Education has issued a popular series of books of recommended readings in different subjects.

For California teacher Pam Cook, literature provides the vehicle for integrating the curriculum. Cook, who teaches 5th and 6th grades at Redwood Heights Elementary School in Oakland, uses literature to help teach concepts in subjects such as science and social studies. She "pulls" literature selections from the lists of recommended readings included in California's frameworks for language arts, history, and social science, she says.

As part of a science unit on wolves, for example, Cook has her students read Jack London's *White Fang* and a book about dogsledding. In social studies, students read historical fiction to gain a more in-depth understanding of early colonial history and ancient civilizations. One book students "really like" is *The Sign of the Beaver* by Elizabeth Speare, which deals with the relationship between Native Americans and white settlers, Cook notes.

Educators in other states share similar aims. "I see literature as being the driver of cross-disciplinary themes," says Carol Santa, coordinator of language arts and social studies for School District No. 5 in Kalispell, Mont. The district has tried to move to an integrated curriculum model heavily grounded in literature, especially trade books. The district has procured classroom sets of trade books that support certain themes, Santa says, and teachers are using the old textbooks only as a resource. "We haven't bought any new ones," she says.

Five elementary schools in the district are using literature as a "launching point" to integrate the curriculum, Santa says. For example, students in 5th grade embarked on a unit on human rights. In so doing, they read the Bill of Rights, a biography of Sojourner Truth, and nonfiction pieces about the Black codes, women's rights, and so on. A 3rd grade class studied insects and spiders, and students read fiction and nonfiction stories on those topics. The teacher also wove in skill-building on such things as how to keep an observation journal and how to take effective notes, says Santa. "They're using the trade books to show children how to learn," she says.

The move to a literature-based, integrated approach was fueled by two desires: to have students read "real" books and "to simplify teachers' lives," says Santa. Integrating the curriculum, she explains, means teachers can focus on core concepts and themes and not have to jump from one subject to another so abruptly. On standard achievement test results, she adds, students continue "to perform very well."

WHAT ARE THEY READING?

A continuing trend at all levels of education—elementary, middle, and secondary—is a move to broaden the scope of the literature curriculum, experts say. Teachers of literature from the earliest grades to the highest, for example, report trying to assign readings by more diverse authors; moreover, many language arts textbooks and libraries are becoming more multicultural. In addition, many teachers now encourage students to read broadly, sampling works from contemporary authors as well as reading the classics that make up the so-called "canon" of the great works of literature.

Of course, the effort to supplement (or supplant, as some fear) some of the works considered "classic" is hotly debated in the field. Some experts believe that truly worthy "classic" literature is still widely taught; others think that some notable authors and works are slipping out of the curriculum in favor of marginal works designed to appeal to student interests.

Although few national data exist, some experts feel that the literature read by students in elementary and middle schools these days is more likely to include selections that address children's "issues," as well as works by and about African Americans, Asian Americans, Hispanics, Native Americans, and so on.

At the secondary level, more national data show what literature students are reading; but experts continue to differ over the extent to which the literature curriculum is changing.

"Research indicates that the canon is alive and well" in schools, says Suhor of the National Council of Teachers of English. "Works for whole-class study have changed very little" over the past few decades (although Suhor adds that supplementary reading materials have changed).

A study of book-length works taught in grades 7–12, conducted by Arthur Applebee at the National Research Center on Literature Teaching and Learning, suggests that the prominence of time-tested authors and classic works has changed little over the past 30 years. Several plays by Shakespeare (*Romeo and Juliet, Macbeth, Julius Caesar,* and *Hamlet*), Twain's *Huckleberry Finn,* Hawthorne's *The Scarlet Letter,* Steinbeck's *The Pearl* and *Of Mice and Men,* and Lee's *To Kill a Mockingbird,* for example, continued to be taught in more than 50 percent of schools when the survey was conducted in 1988.

So has the canon opened up to include more contemporary works and books by authors from diverse cultures? "In widespread practice, it clearly has not," says Applebee. Still, Applebee says that interest among teachers in diversifying their reading lists has grown since his study was published, and that this interest is beginning to push publishers to adjust selections in their literature anthologies.

Sandra Stotsky, research associate at the Harvard Graduate School of Education, believes that many teachers already have substituted more contemporary and diverse offerings for older selections. The "top 10" literary selections and authors may be time-tested classics and recognized literary titans, but that doesn't mean that all students read them, Stotsky says. Moreover, if one looks at entire reading lists for individual teachers, one would likely find a smattering of acknowledged classics mixed with more recent fare.

DIVERSITY A PRIORITY

Stephen Tchudi, professor of rhetoric and composition at the University of Nevada, Reno, says that teachers have good reasons for broadening the literature curriculum. One is that the traditional curriculum practically ignores literature written by non-whites. "It's no joke to say that the canon was determined by dead white guys," he says.

Making the literature curriculum more multicultural "is one of the big trends," says Bishop of Ohio State University. "There are more books [by diverse authors], and publishers are re-issuing books that had gone out of print" to meet demand. Diversity in the reading that students are asked to do for class assignments is essential, because "when kids don't see themselves reflected in the books that are sanctioned by the adults around them, they get messages that they don't really count," says Bishop. Further, a diverse reading list helps pupils empathize with characters in different circumstances from their own. Literature "gets inside the life of those characters and helps you see through different eyes," says Bishop. As a consequence of this reasoning, more teachers are trying to ensure that students sample broadly from works by and about different cultures.

The effort to make the literature curriculum more multicultural is not without its critics, however. Several commentators have remarked recently that books and stories that marginalize non-whites are being displaced by works in which most whites are villains. Stotsky cites such works as Toni Morrison's *The Bluest Eye* and Lawrence Yep's *Dragonwings* as stories in which no white characters are portrayed in a positive fashion. The purpose of including more diverse works no longer seems to be to help students respect and better understand one another, she says.

Albert Shanker, president of the American Federation of Teachers, took a similar position recently when he cautioned that some multiculturalists appear bent on getting "rid of one set of stereotypes only to replace them with another. . . . This is a change, but it is not an improvement, and there is a good chance that it will intensify the hostility that already exists among some groups."

ARE THE CLASSICS RELEVANT?

Another reason for broadening the literature is to allow students to read more selections targeted for their age group, their interests, and their abilities. Some of the literature considered "classic" is too difficult for students to read, enjoy, and learn from, Tchudi says. "People have recognized that forcing students to read books beyond their level just kills their interest in literature," says Tchudi. Even Shakespeare, he points out, wrote for adult audiences—is it obligatory that *all* kids should read his works before graduating? Expanding reading lists to include more works written for young adults, moreover, will not result in a loss of academic rigor, he believes. "To me, relevance does not mean pandering to kids' tastes or abandoning standards." The role of the teacher in selecting literature, he says, is to find the "intersection" between students' needs and the demands of the discipline. "The canon has had a long time to prove itself in schools . . . and is anyone really satisfied with the results of that?" he asks.

Suhor also questions the idea that "classics" should fill the literature curriculum in secondary schools. "Who's to say that one must have had the classics by the time one has finished the 12th grade?" he says. Pupils could read some works in college or as adults. Moreover, "some classics are more readable than others." It's important to recognize that "you can study any good literature rigorously," says Suhor, whether it's Chaucer's *Canterbury Tales* or Robert Cormier's *The Chocolate War.*

Other experts worry that the trend toward including more literature deemed relevant to students' tastes carries with it negative consequences, however. "It's certainly positive" to choose different kinds of works related to students' interests, says Stotsky. But it can be carried to extremes. She argues that the literature curriculum may have been diluted as it was broadened, partly because of the perception that the classics lack relevance to today's students. But often it's the language—not the themes of enduring human concerns—that causes students to feel that older literature isn't relevant. What's more, Stotsky says, when older works are supplanted in elementary and middle schools, students are less likely to be able to handle the language in secondary school English classes.

"Teachers have to have some sense of balance," says Stotsky. "We've gone too far in catering to what we perceive as student interests. Relevance can be carried only so far." If teachers overemphasize motivational works, "we do have the danger of a dumbed-down curriculum for everybody."

Others say that though teachers should definitely put great literature on their reading lists, they shouldn't be troubled if students only gradually come to appreciate it. Many readers go through stages, avidly consuming "all the horse books, or all the Stephen King novels," says Alleen Pace Nilson, professor of English at Arizona State University. They "just need a little nudging" by the teacher to broaden their appetite. Good teachers "aren't just giving students what they already know and like," says Suhor. They're going to "take students to the next steps" by assigning increasingly challenging works.

Several teachers contacted for this article confirmed that they teach a broad range of literature, and that students have some degree of choice in selecting at least part of the literature they read in school.

For example, Linda Rief, who teaches 7th and 8th grades at Oyster River Middle School in Durham, N.H., says that her main goal in teaching literature is to ensure that students "love reading and find authors whose books they will search out and read." About 80 percent of the reading students do is of their choice, Rief says, and *everyone* reads on Friday, herself included. Her classroom has bookshelves crammed with 500–700 selections. In class, she teaches widely recognized staples, such as *Romeo and Juliet* or *Huckleberry Finn*, as well as time-tested student favorites, such as S.E. Hinton's *The Outsiders*, hoping to expose students to all kinds of literature.

Gail Siegel, who teaches 7th and 8th grades at Ross School in Ross, Calif., says she hopes students "will leave here with an appreciation for a wide variety of literature." Siegel uses a bit of everything in her classroom—poetry, nonfiction, short stories, novels, even newspapers. And she admits that students often need some nudging to read widely from works considered "classics," as well as books that are just plain entertainment. Few students will read *A Midsummer Night's Dream* or *Lord of the Flies* on their own, she notes. "Kids tend to want to read *The Pelican Brief*" or whatever is the hot book of the moment, she says. "We spend a lot of time arguing over what's literature and what's airplane reading."

CONNECTING WITH TEXT

One of the reasons for making a broader range of literature available to students, of course, is to increase the chance that they'll "engage" or "connect" with that literature. For the same reason, many educators are trying to change the way they *teach* literature—whether the work in question is Charles Dickens' *Great Expectations* or Paul Zindel's *The Pigman.*

"Kids today insist on relevancy," says R. Stephen Green, assistant to the superintendent of the Lawrence Township, Ind., public schools and a former English teacher. "The instructor needs to create an environment where what's being taught connects to their world." But this doesn't meaning dumping the classics: it means exploring the underlying themes of the human condition and using lots of different classroom approaches to get students involved. Further, Green says teachers have to use strategies that allow students to "engage" in the analysis of text from a variety of entry points, by attending to students' different learning styles.

For example, Green observed a class in the midst of studying *King Lear.* As one of the activities, the teacher had students create reversible hats that exemplified two sides to a character, such as King Lear, Cordelia, or the Fool. The lesson helped students understand that duality of characters in the play and brought out that we all "change hats" throughout our lives. "Bringing the literature to life, making it relevant . . . is where the best teaching and learning is," says Green. "Students are searching for that kind of involvement."

The philosophy about teaching literature that has recently swept the field—in theory, if not yet in classroom practice—is known as "reader response" theory, experts report. At this stage, reader response theory has influenced higher education more than K–12, Applebee believes. "What's changing [in K–12 education] is that we're seeing a growing concern for literature as a source of independent student response."

Basically, reader response theory differs most radically from previous theories about teaching literature in the degree of emphasis placed on the reader's response to and interpretation of the text. "Teaching begins with the sense that students are making with the text," says Applebee. In reader response theory, the text's meaning is considered to reside in the "transaction" between the reader and the text, not in the text alone.

This is a departure from the old school of literary criticism, wherein all meaning was presumed to reside in the text, and the teacher's role was to lead students to predetermined conclusions. This often led to a "guessing game," with students trying to figure out what the teacher wanted them to discover in the work at hand.

When approaching a text, teachers under the traditional model usually "started with theme, plot, character, and symbols," downplaying what the reader felt about the selection, says Suhor. In practice, reader response theory considers very carefully how students respond intellectually and emotionally to the text.

In presenting a piece of literature, instead of telling students, "This is a wonderful work," a teacher should elicit students' own genuine responses, no matter how odd their perspectives on the work, says Joan Cutuly, a 20-year teaching veteran from Las Vegas, Nev. Let students attack the work if they choose, Cutuly says; the important thing is to let them know their feelings about it *count*. "Start with their outlandish criticisms," she advises, "then pick up the pieces and put them together." Students who like the work will typically speak up in its defense, she says.

By validating students' responses, teachers can spark a lively discussion from which a careful literary analysis will flow. "We've all got a group of experiences, and reactions to what we read," Cutuly says. If students' feelings about a work are made the first focus of discussion, then "everybody has somewhere to start," she says. Rather than beginning with a discussion of symbolism or metaphor, for example, teachers should allow an exploration of these aspects to develop from students' own observations about the work. "Allow kids to raise questions," Cutuly says—such as, Why did Eudora Welty give her character such an odd name as "Phoenix"? "You've got to create a *need* to understand metaphor," rather than just handing students an explanation of how an author uses metaphor, Cutuly emphasizes.

Class discussions play a key role in trying to elicit student response— and in trying to help them better understand the literature and their reaction to it. "The study of literature is about reading books and discussing them," says Carol Jago, who teaches 10th grade English and creative writing at Santa Monica High School in Santa Monica, Calif. In Jago's view, an effective literature teacher doesn't "lord over" students by emphasizing her knowledge of the text. Instead, she acts as a catalyst for the discussion, helping students brainstorm questions, participating in the discussion, but not "pontificating." The model she uses is more like an "adult book club," she says—a discussion among peers, not "the professor lecturing [the students] and asking tricky questions."

Is Every 'Response' Valid?

Although practices informed by reader response theory have captured the professional journals and conferences, some experts are concerned that *too* much emphasis on student response can backfire. Some advocates of reader response appear to posit that "everything is relative—that your idea and my idea are equally good," says Smith. In such a scenario, even what the author said about a text is considered of no more merit than what any one reader might suppose. "That really worries me," Smith adds. Others are concerned that a spirit of "anything goes" would reign if teachers attended to reader response theory, and that students wouldn't learn mature, formal responses to literature.

"That's a common misconception about reader response [theory] in general," says Applebee. "Student-centered approaches don't mean that anything goes." Neither should the notion of getting students to discuss how they *feel* about a text mean that the analysis should stop there. The "How do you feel?" question is "an opening gambit," says John Clifford, professor of English at the University of North Carolina–Wilmington. "It's valid as step one in a process of trying to get the students to connect the reality of *Hamlet* with the reality of their own lives." But any good teacher would take the discussion far beyond that.

"It sounds like a Pollyanna theory, but it isn't," Patricia Phelan, a language arts resource teacher at Crawford High School in San Diego, says about reader response theory. Students simply will not understand or care about the literary work "until they make *some* connection" with it, she says. So teachers *must* use various hooks to get students connecting and responding to the text. But the emphasis on getting students to respond to the literature doesn't mean that any response is as good as another. Students are "continuously urged to return to the text to find validation" for their views. It takes a skillful teacher to mediate the dialogue, she adds. "When teachers let kids just talk, without direction to the talk, there isn't much learning."

What would a class on a piece of literature look like, if the teacher took reader response theory seriously? There are lots of possible approaches, but Phelan suggests one example. She'd probably start by using cooperative learning, because that would probably "get a wider response . . . and allow everybody to be heard." Students would then be asked to respond to the literature in different ways. Some might present their views in posters or a dramatization. Allowing students to respond using such techniques "seems to help the kids understand," Phelan says. The students would also do plenty of writing, but the writing would be for a variety of purposes. "There would be a great deal more writing of different types." This might include writing short responses to prompts, creating "dialog journals," and writing more formal pieces.

CHANGE IN DISCUSSION

As with many proposed reform initiatives, the wholesale changes being advocated for the teaching of literature must now make the tough transition from theory to practice. Currently, the kinds of practices advocated as the leading edge—reader response theory, literature-based programs, and so on—are not widely practiced. Applebee says the past few years have been marked by a "change in the discussion that's just making its way into the classroom."

A series of studies completed at the National Research Center for Literature Teaching and Learning suggest that, in many ways, the teaching of literature has changed little through the years. Part of the reason, Applebee writes in a recent book published by the NCTE, is that new theories about literature have largely ignored pedagogical issues. So teachers have taken an eclectic path: organizing the curriculum around traditional genres, chronologies, or themes; using reader response techniques to foster student involvement; and relying on traditional techniques for studying individual texts.

"What is lacking is a well-articulated overall theory of the teaching and learning of literature, one that will give a degree of order and coherence to the daily decisions that teachers make about what and how to teach," Applebee writes. The extent to which the field generates such a framework is likely to play a significant role in whether changes in the teaching of literature will continue to be episodic, or whether they will become widely practiced.

Section 2

MATHEMATICS

REAL-LIFE APPLICATIONS

◆

BRINGING MATHEMATICS TO LIFE

SCOTT WILLIS

If, as a student, you ever wondered why you were being taught something in a math class, consider these lessons Joy Donlin uses to teach her 6th grade students about fractions:

• When teaching equivalent fractions, Donlin gives her students a real recipe and a set of measuring cups and spoons. "You hate to wash dishes," she tells them, "so use the fewest utensils possible to measure out the ingredients." ("That's really what you do when you're cooking," she notes.) Students discover they can use the $\frac{1}{4}$-cup measure six times to measure out $1\frac{1}{2}$ cups, for example.

• To help her students learn to add and subtract fractions, Donlin uses the stock market pages of the newspaper. Students observe that a stock has moved from $61\frac{7}{8}$ to $61\frac{3}{4}$, for example. Because they are "just learning" which fraction is greater, the newspaper's indication that the stock is "down one-eighth" helps them understand.

• To convey the relative size of fractions, Donlin also makes use of a set of wrenches. "The $\frac{5}{16}''$ wrench is too small," she tells her students, "and the $\frac{1}{2}''$ wrench is too big. Which one should I try?"

Mathematics "makes sense" to students when lessons draw real-world connections, says Donlin, who teaches at Bates Middle School in Annapolis, Md. She wants her students to "experience" math, not just memorize it, and she wants them to know where they will use the math skills they're learning.

The articles in this chapter were originally published in the Summer 1996 issue of ASCD's *Curriculum Update* newsletter.

In her efforts to bring math to life, Donlin is not alone. Inspired by the curriculum and teaching standards developed by the National Council of Teachers of Mathematics (NCTM), teachers across North America are striving to make math relevant to students' daily lives, not just something found between the covers of a textbook. The NCTM standards call on K–12 math teachers to emphasize problem solving, mathematical reasoning, and real-world applications, and many teachers are enthusiastically following suit.

MAKING USE OF MANIPULATIVES

One way teachers are grounding mathematics instruction in the real world is by using manipulatives—tangible objects that students can use to explore number concepts. Manipulatives help students bridge the gap between the concrete and symbolic realms.

During a lesson in geometry, Diane DeRoy asked her 2nd graders if increasing a circle's diameter would increase its circumference—a suggestion her pupils soundly rejected. So she took an apple off her desk and showed them just what she was asking. "The kids all changed their minds," says DeRoy, who teaches at Mitchell Elementary School in Woodbury, Conn. DeRoy also uses commercially produced manipulatives, such as pattern blocks, base-10 blocks, and Unifix cubes.

Traditionally, math students were taught a procedure to follow—to multiply, divide, or find a square root, for example—but they "really didn't know *why*," DeRoy says. When students work with manipulatives, however, they can actually see why a procedure works.

Manipulatives can also clarify concepts for older students. In algebra, the concept of a "variable" is abstract, but many 14- and 15-year-olds are still "really concrete" in their thinking, says David Bahr, who teaches math at Concordia Lutheran High School in Fort Wayne, Ind. Bahr uses "algebra tiles" to help his students grasp this and other concepts.

Algebra tiles come in a variety of shapes, Bahr explains, and each shape stands for something different. A triangle might stand for x, a square for y, a circle for x^2, and so on. Students can solve equations, multiply, and factor with the tiles, and they note patterns in the tiles as they do so.

One algebra rule, for example, is that $3x$ can be added only to another x, Bahr notes. In the past, teachers would teach this rule by saying something about not adding "apples and oranges"—but students would still add $3x$ to $4y$ and get $7xy$. With the algebra tiles, however, students can plainly see that different variables stand for different things, and hence can't be added, Bahr says.

PROVIDING APPLICATION PROBLEMS

Beyond using manipulatives, teachers are bringing math to life by presenting students with "application problems"—math problems set in real-life contexts.

To teach addition to her pupils at North Fayette Elementary School in Fayetteville, Ga., Judy Chambers uses a set of menus from local restaurants. Chambers asks her pupils to add the cost of a hamburger, fries, and a piece of pie, for example. She also asks pupils to "spend" a set amount of money by selecting items from a gift catalog. Children learn better when math problems deal with "things they recognize," she believes.

Beth Walima, who teaches a multiage class at Rockport Elementary School in Rockport, Mass., derives math problems from events in the world, such as the heavy snowfalls last winter, and from themes her pupils study. Last year, when her class went "maple syruping," pupils calculated the number of taps, which is based on the number and size of the maple trees. When math is learned in such real-world contexts, "it's fun," Walima says.

"Listening to kids [yields] opportunities to weave math into their lives," adds Fred Hiltner, who teaches at Capital Elementary School in Juneau, Alaska. Hiltner derived a three-day math activity from an argument between two of his pupils over whose sled was faster. At his request, pupils brought in seven different types of sleds: rectangular and saucer-shaped, flat-bottomed and grooved, and so on. Pupils voted for the sled they thought was fastest; then the class held a tournament. Afterward, they analyzed the outcomes of the races and explored why some sleds were faster. This kind of authentic activity helps children understand that "math is connected to life; it's not just working with numbers," Hiltner says.

Teachers can also find real math problems "embedded" in literature, says Jacque Smith, who teaches 3rd grade at the Malcolm Price Laboratory School in Cedar Falls, Iowa. After reading about the Native Americans' transition from using dogs to using horses as their pack animals, for example, her class solved math problems dealing with the weight of tepee poles and supplies, and the fact that horses can carry four times as much weight as dogs can.

When problems are situational, students "get into pretty involved math," Smith says. "I'm just amazed at what the kids can do. Five years ago, I would have said, 'There's no way they could solve some of these problems,'" she admits. "It's really refreshing for me as a teacher."

Math problems can be derived from many everyday sources, teachers say. "The newspaper is a wonderful source of problems," says Annette Raphel, who teaches math at Milton Academy in Milton, Mass. After reading a news story about a man who used his *VISA* card to buy a painting for $2.5 million—thereby earning countless frequent-flyer miles—Raphel's 4th graders planned trips that would consume those miles. Another article about a man who saved a million pennies led her students to explore such questions as, "How many is a million? How much would a million pennies weigh? How high would they stack? How many truckloads would they fill?"

Raphel has also challenged her students to determine how much Planter's should charge for a can of mixed nuts—a "ratio and proportion problem" that also required students to convert grams to ounces. A local gourmet shop provided the price of each nut per pound. Students worked with the data, then wrote letters to Planter's telling them how much to charge and why. "There was an element of fun to that," she says.

In another lesson, Raphel taught her 7th graders the history of the cost of a first-class U.S. postage stamp and asked them to predict the cost in the year 2010. Students arrived at their predictions in various ways: by using graphing, ratios, and percentages, among other approaches. There was "no right answer," Raphel points out, but students had to defend their solutions.

Geometry also lends itself to application problems. Chris Lyndrup asks his geometry students to design a container to hold three tennis balls. The container can be any shape, but the fit must be as perfect as possible,

Using Math to Design and Build a City

Students in David Bahr's Discrete Mathematics course apply what they learn in a unique way—they design a city.

In a full-semester project, Bahr's students (mostly seniors) must design a city with an efficient road network. They must also create an election process to ensure that the city council fairly represents all resident populations. In addition, students must contact construction companies and make a plan for building their cities, to apply what they've learned about "critical path analysis."

To prepare for this challenge, students first learn about "routing graphs," which are used to plan routes for garbage trucks and mail carriers so they don't waste gas or steps. Contractors also use routing graphs to lay out roads in new communities. Bahr takes maps of students' neighborhoods and asks students to route a mail carrier through them.

Bahr's students also study election theory, including alternatives to the popular vote, such as ranking methods where voters might select both a first- and last-place candidate. (One candidate could get the most first-place votes yet still lose because she also got many last-place votes, Bahr explains.) Once they've studied the theory, students scrutinize the school's election processes for student government and write position papers on what method would be most fair.

Students put all this new learning to use in the "Design and Build a City" project. They work on the project for five or six days in class, Bahr says, collaborating in groups of four or five. They must write an 8- to 10-page rationale for their design decisions, including all relevant mathematics. They must also make 15-minute oral presentations to "sell" their cities. In completing their projects, many students integrate other subjects, such as economics and recycling.

The project allows students to be creative in applying the math they've learned, Bahr says. Some students have sited their cities on islands, on Mars, even under the ocean. "One student actually got quotes from a construction company on building under water," Bahr recalls.

with no "slippage." This task, which requires students to apply area and volume formulas and to construct models, "ties together all they've learned," says Lyndrup, who teaches at Byron Center High School in Byron Center, Mich. "It's also a nice break away from the book."

Students in Lyndrup's course on Functions, Statistics, and Trigonometry have used the piano to study functions. A piano has 88 keys and strings, Lyndrup explains, each with its own vibrating frequency. A local music store provided the class with a list of all the frequencies, and students derived an equation to express the relation between key position and frequency. Then students read about a Bösendorfer piano in Germany with nine extra keys at the bottom of the keyboard. "The kids had to use their formula to determine the frequencies of the added keys," Lyndrup says.

Technology can also help provide application problems. According to Sandra Dawson, who teaches math at Glenbrook South High School in Glenview, Ill., technology allows math students to use real-life data collected through experiments. For example, students can use a light sensor to measure the intensity of a light source from various distances, graph the data points, then use their calculators to find the relevant equation. "With technology and experiments, you can make mathematics a laboratory science," Dawson says. Working with real data makes math both more real and more exciting for students, she finds.

To introduce new functions to his students at Benjamin Banneker Academic High School in Washington, D.C., Jeffrey Choppin has used a "calculator-based laboratory." This hand-held machine, which includes a motion sensor and other measurement devices, allows students to conduct experiments dealing with motion, temperature, and light. Different experiments—dropping a basketball or swinging a bucket, for example—produce different functions, Choppin explains. When students use the calculator-based laboratory, quadratic equations and sine or cosine waves are "not this completely abstract model," he says. Students see more of a connection between what they're learning and the world around them.

Putting Reasoning First

Time on application problems is well spent, Choppin believes, because these problems "force students out of the cookbook, follow-the-procedure method." When students try to solve application problems, they must think about what they're doing, he says. "They're not just putting pencil to the page without understanding."

Teaching for understanding, rather than promoting the rote use of algorithms, is a central tenet of the NCTM Standards. In accordance with the Standards, many math teachers are teaching computation not as an end in itself but as a means to a more important goal: the development of mathematical thinking skills.

"We're trying to make sure that kids get the chance to think and reason," says Gail Burrill, a high school math teacher from Hales Corners, Wisc., who is NCTM's president. In the past, Burrill admits, "I spent my class having kids imitate *my* way of thinking through a problem." Now, however, "I start with what kids are already thinking," she says. "Kids have innovative, powerful ways of thinking," which may be very different from the teacher's but equally valid.

Math teachers should listen to students and build on the knowledge they already have, rather than "starting from scratch," Burrill advises. Students get more involved and excited when they can contribute their ideas, she says. This approach creates "a very different role for the teacher," she notes. Teachers must elicit students' thoughts and be alert to misconceptions. They also must find ways to "nudge" students into more correct thinking.

Shifting the focus of instruction from computation to reasoning requires "a whole philosophical switch," says Smith. Now, students learn basic skills in the context of problem solving, not as a prerequisite. "They don't have to know a hundred tiny little pieces beforehand," she says. As a result, students are more willing to pit their wits against math problems.

Students used to lack "the disposition for problem solving," Smith recalls. "Elementary kids couldn't get the idea; they would focus on the numbers," she says. Rather than thinking about the meaning of the problem or their goal, pupils were just "looking for a quick trick," such as, "subtract the smaller number from the larger." Now, however, "I'm really excited by what I see—by how well they think," Smith says.

Perhaps most important, many students who struggle with computation are no longer tracked into classes where they do nothing but practice basic skills. Now these students are exposed to higher-level math concepts, so they do not fall hopelessly behind their peers.

"Students can do more advanced concepts even if they don't have all the basic skills," Donlin asserts—especially when they can use a calculator as support. Donlin is adamant about "presenting lower-ability students with the same invigorating, rigorous instruction that the high-ability students get." Less-able students are "not energized by doing 50 long-division problems," she notes drily.

"I used to be guilty" of bogging down some students in practicing basic math skills, Raphel admits. Those students "never got enchanted or seduced by math; they never got to the good stuff."

Students can have "a conceptual foundation" even if their computation skills are rocky, Burrill agrees. What's more, "computation skills grow as students see them used" in real-life contexts, she says. "In the past, we've taught these abstractly through algorithms, with few application problems."

Students who are weak at arithmetic can do complex problems, affirms Sandy Jernberg, who teaches 3rd and 4th graders at the Pillsbury Math, Science and Technology School in Minneapolis, Minn. "I had trouble having faith in that, until I saw it," she says. "It blew me away."

However, teachers don't want to neglect computation, either. "You need a good balance" between computation and problem-solving skills, says Dan Hupp, who teaches 7th and 8th grade math at Great Salt Bay Community School in Damariscotta, Maine. "The stronger the foundation" in computation skills, "the farther you can spring from that," he says. Some math programs don't give students the "necessary component skills" to be successful at creative problem solving, he warns.

Rather than doing "drill and kill," teachers should weave computation into engaging problems, Hupp advises. He worries that some young teachers misread the NCTM Standards and place too little emphasis on computation.

VALUING STUDENTS' OWN STRATEGIES

Students often devise their own approaches to computation, teachers note. To foster thinking, rather than memorization, teachers are letting students devise their own math strategies, rather than just teaching them the "preferred" algorithms. "If we just channel them into *our* way of solving a problem, we're doing them a disservice," Walima believes.

To add 29 and 36, for example, the traditional algorithm would require students to "carry the one." However, if students have done hands-on work with grouping, they could also "make 29 into 30 and add on 3 tens and 5 more," says Walima.

When pupils are invited to share their problem-solving strategies, teachers gain insight into each child's thinking, Hiltner says. Moreover, this approach better accommodates a range of developmental levels and learning styles. Imposing algorithms may even harm children by undermining their confidence in their own ability, Hiltner believes. "It makes them dependent on someone else's strategy," he says. "It's really evident when a child is ready to look at a standard algorithm," which is just another strategy, he points out.

Of course, helping students use *efficient* strategies is also a goal, teachers say. When Walima has her students share their various approaches to solving a problem with the class, she might point out "how much quicker" a particular method was. Similarly, Smith sometimes asks her students to "find the shortest route" to the solution.

STIMULATING DISCOURSE

Communicating about math goes hand in hand with the new emphasis on developing students' reasoning abilities, teachers say. "You don't know what you know till you put it in language," Raphel asserts.

Classroom discourse about math helps students clarify their thinking and helps teachers observe students' thought processes. In the past, students who talked in class were reprimanded, Lyndrup says. Now, teachers encourage student discussion.

When students talk about math, they internalize concepts and build long-term knowledge, DeRoy says. Students can't get by with "just parroting" the teacher or textbook when they must explain their thinking in detail. Talking also reveals students' misconceptions, she notes.

Discourse about math is vital to understanding, Smith believes. She often starts a lesson by posing a problem and letting her pupils "pull together their various thoughts." When they do, pupils usually see "big discrepancies." After debating the relative merits of their points of view, the class finally reaches consensus, with Smith's guidance. She also fosters discussion by having pupils in small groups verbalize how they would solve a problem, then share their ideas with the whole class.

Like Smith, Jernberg lets her pupils disagree with one another—respectfully. (She teaches them the appropriate language and tone to use, and emphasizes that "every idea counts.") At first it's "hard to get kids to sit and listen to each other," she says, "until they start to see the value in sharing their opinions."

Teachers are also encouraging their students to *write* about math. Donlin's students write an answer to a math question every day. When teaching her class how to add fractions with unlike denominators, for example, Donlin asked them to write answers to the question, "Why doesn't $\frac{1}{2} + \frac{1}{3} = \frac{2}{5}$?" Students gave different answers, depending on their level of understanding, she says. Some students wrote that the addends had to have a common denominator; others, that the sum had to be bigger than $\frac{2}{5}$, and so on.

Writing is "a wonderful way to find out how a child is thinking," Walima agrees. But the ability to express one's thinking in words does not come automatically to children, she cautions. Many young children will say, "I just knew it," when asked by the teacher, "How did you know?" With enough modeling from the teacher, however, "they can eventually explain or draw pictures."

Modeling is essential, says Jernberg, whose students explain their reasoning in math journals. "Even at 3rd and 4th grade, it's kind of pushing it to get them to explain" their thinking in writing, she says. "They're really awful at first." The teacher must model the process continually until students catch on.

Raphel's students also keep math journals. From reading her students' journals, Raphel will see, for example, "six different ways of solving a particular problem," which she can then share with the class. And students will write things they wouldn't say out loud—that they feel frustrated, for instance, or are not "called on" often enough. Thanks to the journals, "no child is invisible," Raphel says.

Some teachers are finding ways to incorporate discourse about math into student assessment—by using portfolios, for example. Choppin counts portfolios as 10–15 percent of his students' grades.

Assessing students through writing is very different from using "in-class, high-time-pressure tests," which used to be the only way students were assessed, Choppin says. "Writing is the best way to find out what students know," he believes. "Can they explain accurately and concisely? Or is there a lot of gray area?"

Choppin also gives occasional "group quizzes," during which students may talk and interact. When given this freedom, students are "energized," he says. Choppin concedes that, with group quizzes, "sometimes the strong [students] may carry the weak," but every assessment technique has potential problems. And the benefits of group quizzes "far outweigh" the drawbacks, he maintains.

SEEING MATH EVERYWHERE

Bringing math to life requires imagination and a willingness to experiment, teachers say. Because math is inherent in so many things we encounter in our everyday lives, teachers can make use of almost anything that comes to hand.

"I want my students to see math everywhere, to be excited about it, and to know they can do it," Jernberg says. "The math is more relevant when students see it in their lives." Not surprisingly, the results of making real-world connections are gratifying: "The kids beg for math time, and they groan when it's time to quit," she reports.

MATH FOR THE ANXIOUS

KATHY CHECKLEY

The same teaching strategies and curriculums that help students connect math to the real world can also profoundly affect how students perform within the world of the math classroom, say experts. When students are encouraged to work in cooperative groups, when they're given opportunities to communicate their understandings—both verbally and in writing—and when a variety of assessment tools are used, students once apprehensive about math find they can, indeed, "do" math.

"Math anxiety is eased in situations where the goal is cooperation instead of competition," says Christian Hirsch, co-director of the Core-Plus Mathematics Project.

"In traditional classrooms, math is presented in a very logic-based manner, which appeals to relatively few students," adds Jeffrey Choppin, math teacher at Benjamin Banneker Academic High School in Washington, D.C. "New teaching methods appeal to a broader range of learning styles and, thus, broaden the number of students who know they can learn mathematical principles."

The increased confidence of those who once shied away from math—primarily women and minorities—is becoming evident on college campuses. Carolyn Tucker is chair of the Mathematics Department at Westminster College of Salt Lake City. The college's math curriculum, she observes, has been influenced by NCTM-inspired reform efforts—and the changes are beneficial to both men and women. "In a traditional curriculum," Tucker notes, "individual achievement is rewarded." Because women are less competitive then men, she says, and because women tend to work better in group settings, they benefit from the cooperative learning and hands-on approaches featured in the new [K–12] curriculums.

Research supports the optimism shared by experts. According to *The Learning Curve*, a report released by the National Science Foundation (NSF), members of all racial and ethnic groups are now "satisfactorily completing courses in science and mathematics," and achievement scores in these fields are on the rise for students of all races.

Educators must expose the myths about math, says Andrew Page, a math instructor for the Chatham County Board of Education in Savannah, Ga. "Americans believe that there are people who are just 'born' with mathematical ability," Page explains. "Students need to learn that there isn't a certain 'math' gene."

Larry Suter, deputy director of the division of research and evaluation at NSF, agrees. An image he'd like to "destroy" is that "people are born with natural scientific or mathematical ability." Suter says the evidence included in reports such as *The Learning Curve* proves "that any-body can learn this stuff."

Still, cautions Ann Pollina, dean of faculty at the all-girls Westover School in Middlebury, Conn., while "mathematics education is changing in positive ways for women and the disenfranchised," educators must not be lulled into relaxing the focus on equity. Pollina, who is also the head of the mathematics department at Westover, says student-centered, problem-based curriculums do, indeed, engage more women and minorities, but "simultananeously involving technology in the curriculum" gives her pause. Technology is a male-dominated field, she explains, and it's also expensive. "So you're already stacking the deck a bit for those more comfortable with technology and with the more affluent school systems that can afford to provide students with that technology."

Moreover, Pollina says, educators also need to be concerned with "how few people are taking math" in general. Not enough girls *or* boys are taking math, Pollina contends.

Tucker agrees. "All professions need to be infused with math knowledge," she says. "We need a more mathematically literate society, and we need to convey the message that math is a fun subject, not one to be avoided."

THE TEACHERS' PICKS

KATHY CHECKLEY

These "model" curriculums were recommended by many of the teachers we talked with for this article.

In his first six years as an elementary school teacher, Matt Ludwig taught mathematics by following a format teachers have used for years: Introduce the mathematical concept in a lecture, supply students with a new formula, show them how to use it, and then ask students to solve pages of problems using the formula.

In the last two years, however, Ludwig has dramatically changed his approach. This 6th grade teacher at Kate Mitchell Elementary School in Ames, Iowa, no longer supplies students with a prescribed strategy. Instead, he expects his students to discover the mathematical principles embedded in the real-world problems they are asked to solve.

"It's very conceptual," Ludwig says of the curriculum that enables him to take such an approach. "With Mathematics in Context, students solve problems by using their prior knowledge and through experimenting with new ideas. The teacher's role is to continually ask questions so as to guide and build students' understandings."

Mathematics in Context (MiC) is a four-year curriculum for the middle grades, initially developed by the Freudenthal Institute in The Netherlands. The National Center for Research in Mathematical Sciences Education at the University of Wisconsin adopted the curriculum and "Americanized" it, says Margaret Meyer, staff development coordinator for MiC. "We retained the math concepts and content" of the Dutch curriculum, she explains, "but we made it more colloquial, using contexts [U.S.] students would be familiar with."

This emphasis on real-world contexts distinguishes MiC from traditional curriculums, says Meyer. "One problem, for example, asks students to examine a parking lot that has a certain number of spaces filled. Students are then shown another parking lot with a different number of spaces filled and are asked, 'Which parking lot is fuller?'" Through this exercise, Meyer explains, students see that they can't directly compare the two parking lots if the two lots don't contain the same number of parking spaces. "The notion of relative comparison becomes clear," says Meyer. By immersing students in such contexts, students "reinvent" math and are "led to discovering the rules and principles of mathematics."

What's also unique about MiC, she adds, is that students are able to build their understandings of mathematical concepts over time. Take percentages, for example. "Typically, teachers cover percentages in one year's curriculum in the middle school," Meyer explains. "Percentages then become an all-consuming part of the curriculum. Teachers know students need to 'get it' and students know they need to 'get it' because it's not part

Teacher Tested, Teacher Approved

When the University of Chicago School Math Project (UCSMP) began creating curriculum materials more than 10 years ago, they had one ultimate goal: to transform K–12 math classrooms across the United States. Now, according to Carol Siegle, the assistant to the director of the UCSMP, there are more than three million users of the materials nationwide. And, says Siegle, while UCSMP never wanted to create a national curriculum, the project was the first to suggest many of the strategies now supported by the NCTM standards, including using a student-centered approach.

Why is the UCSMP so popular with teachers? Siegle thinks it's primarily because "teachers find the materials interesting to teach and students find them interesting to use." Siegle also speculates that teachers appreciate the ongoing staff development support offered to them and the willingness by UCSMP to consider teachers' suggestions when revising and updating curriculum materials.

Of the myriad math curriculums that seem to have replicated aspects of the UCSMP model, Siegle says graciously, "Our goal is to make change. We're happy when other projects have joined us in change."

For more information about UCSMP's elementary and secondary curriculum materials, call (312) 702-9770. E-mail address: ucsmp@cicero.uchicago.edu

Other "Teacher Approved" Curriculums

✦ **Investigations in Number, Data, and Space** is a K–5 curriculum offered by the Technical Education Research Center (TERC), designed to offer students meaningful mathematical problems, emphasize depth in mathematical thinking, and expand the number of mathematically literate students. *For information, call TERC Communications at (617) 547-0430. E-mail address: Communications@TERC.edu.*

✦ **Mathcounts** features 7th and 8th grade curriculum materials, created every year by the National Society of Professional Engineers and the NCTM. Through the activities included in the Mathcounts kit, students also prepare for a series of local, state, and national mathematics competitions. *To obtain a free Mathcounts kit, call Camy Rowan at (703) 684-2828.*

of the next year's curriculum." In contrast, percentages are introduced in the MiC curriculum in the 5th grade, but students will work with percentages throughout middle school, "which allows for a deeper, fuller understanding of the concept," says Meyer.

The MiC curriculum also allows students to draw connections between concepts that before were taught in isolation, Ludwig adds. When learning about those percentages, for example, students are introduced to decimals and fractions as well. In other curriculums, he says, "we would just target percentages and never talk about fractions and decimals."

Giving students opportunities to see connections is an important feature of the MiC curriculum, says Meyer. The curriculum has 40 units— 10 per grade level—and each year, students focus on four mathematical concepts: number, algebra, geometry, and probability and statistics. And, Meyer points out, because the problems are contextual, the curriculum is also interdisciplinary. In one unit, students compare how beans grow in different mediums. When students measure the sprouts each day and create their own data, she explains, they "see the connection between math, growth, and biology."

MAKING MATH APPEALING

Ensuring equity is at the heart of curriculums that feature problems set in contexts students recognize, says Christian Hirsch, professor of mathematics and mathematics education at Western Michigan University. Hirsch is co-director of the Core-Plus Mathematics Project (CPMP), which is field-testing a single-core, three-year high school curriculum that, like MiC, helps students develop their understanding of key mathematical concepts through the problem-solving process.

"One of the guiding philosophies of Core-Plus is to accommodate diversity," says Hirsch. "Therefore, the contexts in which problems are set are as widespread as possible to appeal to students from many different cultures."

In the first two years of the program, for instance, students will study the patterns of change in the most commonly spoken languages; determine how unemployment may or may not be related to crime; and even explore how to design pop-up cards and books.

The Core-Plus curriculum abounds with challenging and thoughtful questions, questions that "demand thoughtful and insightful answers," says Tommy Eads, math teacher and technology coordinator at North Lamar High School in Paris, Texas.

Eads is among a cadre of teachers field-testing the Core-Plus curriculum. A veteran teacher of 28 years, he says one of the biggest challenges in implementing Core-Plus is changing teaching styles and adjusting to a student-centered learning environment. "Teachers have to learn to formulate the right questions rather than supply the right answer," he explains.

The power of this approach was driven home to Eads when he was helping his 2nd grade son with math. "He had trouble using the prescribed algorithm for subtracting, so I told him to do it in a way that made sense to him." From that experience, Eads gained a better understanding of what he now expects of his students. "The problem with the way math was traditionally taught is that students were not allowed to think through the method, to work out the problem in their own ways."

"Teachers' attitudes about students have to change," agrees Ginny Hanley, a math teacher at Brookwood High School in Snoellville, Ga. "Teachers have to let students take ownership and learn the math in their own ways."

Hanley has been teaching the Core-Plus curriculum for two years and appreciates the genuine curiosity that the problem-based curriculum inspires in students. Students in her Core-Plus classes are inquisitive, Hanley observes, and, because students discover the answers for themselves, they're also confident in their ability to solve *any* problem. "I never hear, 'I can't do this,'" she maintains. Her students, Hanley adds, also seem to have a true understanding of "the importance of math in the real world."

Real world companies, like Campbell Soups, also see the importance of developing students' problem-solving abilities. Eads invited the company to review the Core-Plus curriculum because North Lamar High School "is really trying to make a connection with industry." Campbell Soups will consider hiring many North Lamar graduates, Eads says, and those students "will need to know a considerable amount of mathematics to be successful in a company like Campbell Soups—they want students to know statistics and to be able to write well. They also want students to feel confident about public speaking and to be able to work cooperatively." Core-Plus, says Eads, gives students opportunities to enhance their skills in all of these areas.

In fact, Eads adds, the only concern Campbell Soups raised about the Core-Plus curriculum is its emphasis on using calculators in the classroom (the curriculum assumes that all students will have access to a graphing calculator), fearing that some students wouldn't fully develop their computational skills as a result.

Some students just don't have strong computational skills, but they still understand the mathematics—and that's the point of calculators, says Arthur Coxford in defense of the curriculum he helped create. Coxford is a co-director of the CPMP and a professor of mathematics at the University of Michigan. "A lot of things we ask students to do in the curriculum are facilitated by their having access to a calculator," Coxford explains. Core-Plus has a strand on statistics, for example, which was not usually covered in more traditional curriculums, he says, because it took too much time to draw graphs by hand. Drawing graphs, he continues, "is not an inspiring task, nor does it really require students to develop what we think are the more important skills—that of being able to analyze the graphs once they see them." Using calculators, Coxford maintains, "allows students to concentrate on what's really important."

SUCCESS FOR ALL STUDENTS

Both the Mathematics in Context and Core-Plus curriculums propose, through their designs, that all students can learn mathematics. As a result, students whose teachers use these curriculums are not ability-grouped, and non-college-bound students are given the same mathematical experiences as those who are headed for universities. "We identified a common core of broad mathematics that all students benefit from," says Hirsch. College-bound students benefit because "the college prep program of the past was very narrow and served a very small number of people"—namely those who sought math degrees. The Core-Plus curriculum, explains Hirsch, introduces students to the kinds of mathematics needed to go into careers in business and the social sciences.

Non-college-bound students perhaps stand to gain the most from curriculums like Core-Plus. The general-education math curriculum, says Coxford, was very limited in scope, focusing primarily on arithmetic. Machines will handle that function, he asserts, "so these general-math students will be shortchanged when they compete for jobs that will require further use of mathematics."

Curriculums like MiC and Core-Plus also build in teachers a new respect for the intellect of students. "We learned that middle school students are capable of doing significant math," says Meyer. "In truth, the students take the curriculum far beyond what we intended."

Adds Ludwig, "I have different expectations for my students. I expect them to verbalize and write about their understandings. No longer do they get by with simply knowing the procedure. I expect students to share their thinking."

Hanley expects her students to "walk out of here with a greater math appreciation or math sense." And, it's likely that they will, she says, because most of the students in her Core-Plus classes want to take a fourth-year math course, "even if they don't have to."

For more information on the Core-Plus Curriculum Project, contact Christian Hirsch at (616) 387-4526. E-mail address: christian.hirsch@wmich.edu. Or, call Arthur Coxford at (313) 764-1817, e-mail address: acoxford@umich.edu. For information on Mathematics in Context, contact Margaret Meyer at (608) 263-1798. E-mail address: mrmeyer@macc.wisc.edu

THE IMPACT OF THE NCTM STANDARDS

STANDARDS 'REVOLUTION' TAKES HOLD

SCOTT WILLIS

In the field of mathematics education, the *Curriculum and Evaluation Standards for School Mathematics* issued by the National Council of Teachers of Mathematics (NCTM) are nothing less than a call to revolution—a call that is being heard and heeded, experts agree.

The *Standards* document proposes dramatic changes on many fronts. It specifies that the mathematics curriculum should emphasize problem solving, communicating about mathematics, and making connections between math topics. It advises that students have hands-on experiences; use manipulatives, calculators, and computers; and work in cooperative groups. It also broadens the traditional scope of mathematics topics studied to include more statistics and probability.

Since their release in March 1989, talk about the standards has never died down. Journal articles discuss them; workshops address them; policymakers tout them as a model for other subject areas. And there has been action. Across the country, mathematics curriculums and assessments are being remodeled to reflect the recommendations in the standards. But whether the standards will actually produce sweeping changes in the way mathematics is taught and learned in U.S. classrooms remains to be seen, experts concede. This article examines how far the standards

This article was originally published in the January 1992 issue of ASCD's *Curriculum Update* newsletter.

revolution has proceeded and to what extent it has crossed the classroom threshold.

SHIFT IN EMPHASIS

The NCTM standards are revolutionary because they are "moving us beyond the kind of mathematics that is ingrained in our system," says Iris Carl, NCTM's president. The standards are shifting the emphasis in math instruction from the memorization of formulas and algorithms to the use of mathematical reasoning to solve real-world problems, she says.

The *Standards* document urges that teachers make clear the connections between mathematical symbols on the page and the world children live in. The emphasis on applying mathematical knowledge to authentic problems "eliminates kids' asking, 'What are we studying this stuff for?'" Carl says.

"Children come to school loving math," says Shirley Frye, a former president of NCTM. But mathematics has too often meant little more than memorization, and that "has really turned them off." The *Standards* recommendations are aimed, in part, at building on students' natural interest in the subject. Applications activities are motivating, Frye asserts; when students grapple with real-world problems, they are willing to persevere until they find a solution.

Also revolutionary is the degree of consensus that the standards represent. Never before in the history of the United States has there been consensus on what students should know at different levels of schooling, says John Dossey, a professor of mathematics at Illinois State University and a past president of NCTM. That the standards have captured such a consensus makes them unique, he believes.

Yet, despite their revolutionary nature, the standards are not so foreign that a teacher willing to be a risk taker wouldn't try to implement them, says Carl. Frye agrees. The standards offer "credible recommendations that could indeed be implemented in 'my' classroom," she says.

But will the promise of revitalizing mathematics education that the standards hold be realized in thousands of classrooms across the United States? The *Standards* document represents primarily a consensus of leaders in the field, not of the grass roots, experts admit. And the revolution the document calls for requires the support of teachers, whose efforts are most critical to the standards' implementation. The extent to which teachers are joining the ranks is not yet clear, experts say.

CHANGING CURRICULUM

One strong indication that the standards are likely to have an impact on classroom instruction is the number of states that are rewriting their math curriculums. According to a survey by the Council of Chief State School Officers (CCSSO), 34 states have revised, or are in the process of revising, their curriculum frameworks based on the NCTM standards.

California, for example, is developing a new math framework that will be "entirely consistent with the NCTM standards," says Joan Akers, a mathematics consultant with the state department of education. For the past two years, California elementary teachers have been trained in using "replacement units" that reflect the new thinking on how to teach topics such as fractions, she adds.

Ohio has developed a model mathematics curriculum based on the standards, says Frank Schiraldi, assistant director of curriculum, instruction, and professional development at the state department of education. Each Ohio school district must develop a math curriculum consistent with the model by the 1992–93 school year.

Administrators and teachers have welcomed the model curriculum, says Margaret Kasten, mathematics consultant to the Ohio department of education. "Most people see this as a great opportunity."

Ohio is pursuing a three-pronged staff development effort to support the new curriculum, Schiraldi says. The state department of education is collaborating with the Ohio Council of Teachers of Mathematics (OCTM) to create 10 six-person teams to promote change in designated regions; a systemic change grant from the National Science Foundation (NSF) is being used to change math and science education in the middle grades; and recently created regional teacher development centers are also offering support. "We are working diligently to see that all [these efforts] interface," Schiraldi says.

The Ohio department of education has worked closely with OCTM to promote the standards, Kasten says. Given its wide membership, the OCTM has "impact on virtually every school district" in the state.

CHANGING ASSESSMENT

Assessment of mathematics is also shifting in response to the standards, experts say. The National Assessment of Educational Progress (NAEP), for example, used the standards when developing its 1990 mathematics test, which included some open-ended items, says Rolf Blank, project director of the CCSSO's State Education Assessment Center. But there is "still debate as to what extent the NAEP tests follow the standards," he notes.

Other changes in assessment are less ambiguous. The standards are having "a pretty big effect at the state level," Blank believes. "Some 20 states are revising tests in science or math."

One of those states is Maryland, according to Jay McTighe of the Maryland School Performance Program. Maryland's new criterion-referenced math assessments are based on learning outcomes "highly influenced" by the NCTM standards, he says. The new tests, first used last May in grades 3, 5, and 8, use far fewer multiple-choice items, frame problems within a situational context, and require students to *apply* knowledge and skills.

Fifth grade students taking the test, for example, might be given raw data from a survey about pets and then asked to tabulate the data, create a graph to represent it, and answer questions about it, such as, "What fraction of the people surveyed owned either a dog or cat?"

Such tests go far beyond multiple-choice, allowing students to explain their reasoning and to draw graphs and diagrams. But such tests also must be scored by people, not computers—which is expensive, McTighe notes. (The scorers are Maryland teachers, retired teachers, and graduate students trained in applying scoring rubrics.)

The benefits are well worth the cost, McTighe believes. "The real strength of this [kind of assessment] is that it strongly supports the kind of teaching recommended by the standards," he asserts. "People say, 'This is a test worth teaching to.'"

Use of the new test is "forcing teachers to learn about the standards," says June Danaher, chief specialist in mathematics for the Maryland department of education. Progress toward implementing the standards will continue in Maryland, she believes: "It has to, because of our assessment program."

What the NCTM Standards Say

What's revolutionary about the NCTM standards? Primarily, experts say, the fact that they remove computation from its reigning role in the mathematics curriculum and make it serve a more important goal—the development of mathematical thinking.

Specifically, the standards call for K–12 mathematics teachers to emphasize problem solving, mathematical reasoning, real-world applications, communication about mathematics, integration of mathematical topics, collaboration among students, and the use of manipulatives and technology.

Highlights of the recommendations include the following:

✦ Students need to experience genuine problems regularly.

✦ Instruction should persistently emphasize "doing" rather than "knowing."

✦ Computational skills should not be a prerequisite for working with word problems; experience with problems helps *develop* the ability to compute.

✦ Calculators should be available to all students at all times, and every student should have access to a computer for individual and group work.

✦ For grades 9–12, *all* students should experience a core program, which should vary for college-bound students only in depth and breadth of treatment and the nature of applications.

Evaluation

The standards devoted to evaluation advise using multiple assessment techniques (including written, oral, and demonstration formats) and using calculators, computers, and manipulatives in assessment. Among the specific recommendations are the following:

✦ Assessment should yield information about students' ability to apply knowledge to solve problems, to use mathematical language to communicate ideas, and to reason and analyze.

✦ Assessment should provide evidence that students can formulate problems, apply a variety of strategies to solve problems, verify and interpret results, and generalize solutions.

Teaching Standards

The NCTM's *Professional Standards for Teaching Mathematics,* released in March 1991, is the companion document to the curriculum standards. The teaching standards emphasize that teachers are "the key" to changing mathematics teaching and learning, and that they "must have long-term support and adequate resources."

The teaching standards recommend, in part, a shift toward

✦ classrooms as mathematical communities.

✦ logical and mathematical evidence as verification, and away from the teacher as the sole authority for right answers.

✦ conjecturing, inventing, and problem solving, and away from merely emphasizing finding the correct answer.

Copies of the *Standards* documents are available from NCTM, for $25 each or $42.50 for both. Quantity discounts are available. Executive summaries and brochures are also available. To order, contact The National Council of Teachers of Mathematics, 1906 Association Dr., Reston, VA 22091; (800) 253-7566.

CHANGE IN THE CLASSROOM

While clear signs exist that curriculum and assessment are changing on a wide scale in response to the standards, the extent to which classroom instruction has been influenced is much less clear, experts agree.

The standards are having at least some influence in 30 percent of U.S. classrooms, Carl estimates. "What excites me is that we've got a tremendous number of primary teachers" working to put the standards into practice, she says. Unlike in the past, these teachers are laying the groundwork for study of geometry and algebra at higher grades, she adds.

Implementation in classrooms is "progressing well," Dossey believes. More progress has been made in the primary grades than in the middle grades, he says, because change was happening in the early grades even before the *Standards* document was released. At the secondary level—which has changed least—the use of technology, such as graphing calculators in algebra, has increased somewhat, he says.

One-third of secondary teachers want to implement the standards, one-third don't want to change, and one-third are "going with the flow," says Zalman Usiskin of the University of Chicago School Mathematics Project (UCSMP).

Other experts' opinions are more sanguine. "There's a great deal more implementation activity than people realize," Frye asserts. One sign, she says, is the extremely high level of awareness the standards enjoy among administrators. Superintendents, assistant superintendents, and directors of curriculum are all coming to NCTM-sponsored meetings with their copies of the *Standards,* she says. "They don't have to be sold on them." Administrators also realize that they must provide inservice training and long-term support to help teachers implement the standards, she adds.

School districts that do provide strong staff development are certainly likely to see greater implementation of the standards. The Orange County, Fla., school district, for example, has created a coaching model of staff development, with support from an Exxon Education Foundation grant. One teacher at each of 30 elementary schools has been trained as a math "specialist," says Linda Levine, the county's program specialist for elementary mathematics. Now in their third year, the specialists conduct workshops and invite other teachers to observe in their classrooms. "They're now mentoring a new set of specialists," Levine says.

The specialists have credibility with other teachers because they are classroom teachers themselves, she says, and also because they initially did *not* have a special strength in math. Levine calls the specialists "a real good seed—a small handful of teachers that may really make a difference in the long run."

Susan Joyner, a kindergarten teacher at Rock Springs Elementary School in Apopka, Fla., is one of the specialists. The change in her math instruction has been "like night and day," she says, as she has been freed from dependence on textbooks and worksheets. Now she uses lots of hands-on manipulatives and focuses on communicating about math— with "no drill and kill."

"From the time the day starts, it's math all day long," Joyner says. Her students encounter math in a wealth of contexts: when they determine how many students are absent; consider page numbers; create patterns going up and down steps or jumping rope; and when they explore how to share when there are too few of something to go around. This last problem requires them to grapple with the advanced topic of division.

"The children are always problem solving," Joyner says, emphasizing that she creates a risk-free environment. The math curriculum flows from the children's spontaneous interest in the things and events around them, she says. "You really take advantage of teachable moments."

Joyner likes the more active and flexible role that this kind of teaching requires of her, but she adds, "I'm not sure every teacher would be up for it."

Teachers at Cherry Run Elementary School in Burke, Va., clearly *are* up for it. "We make sure that everything we do is by the NCTM standards," says 6th grade teacher Sherry Gorrell. Teachers at the school use manipulatives and emphasize communicating about mathematics, as recommended by the standards.

In a lesson on prime, composite, and square numbers, for example, Gorrell asks her students to represent various numbers by arranging that number of blocks in as many different rectangular arrays as they can. Working in groups, the students do so, then cut copies of their arrays from graph paper. Gorrell posts the paper copies on the blackboard.

"What sorts of patterns do you see?" she asks. Students' observations—for example, that 12 can be represented by three different rectangular arrays—lead to a discussion of factors and multiples. When a student notes that certain numbers have only one rectangular array, Gorrell explains that these numbers are called "prime."

A discussion of exponents follows. When students become confused, Gorrell refers to the manipulatives to help them clarify their thinking. For example, she uses blocks to demonstrate how "3 squared" differs from "3 × 2."

Gorrell likes the results she gets from teaching in accordance with the standards. "I've taught a long time, and I've never seen as much interest, motivation, and understanding," she says.

Bette Singletary, who teaches 1st grade at Cherry Run, also makes extensive use of manipulatives. "We always work from the concrete to the abstract," she says.

In one lesson on estimation, measurement, and graphing, Singletary has her students work with apples, Unifix cubes, and string. After students estimate the circumference of their apples, they wrap string around them, cut the string, and then measure it against Unifix cubes. Then, using the data collected, the class works together to graph the results. Using the manipulatives "certainly does ensure better understanding," Singletary says.

SOME OBSTACLES

As implementation of the standards proceeds, several obstacles have emerged, experts concede. One major obstacle is assessment.

"We're still testing in a strange way," Carl says. Standardized tests emphasize "19th century arithmetic skills," even though math educators are united in the belief that students need to be able to do much more, especially problem solving. Similarly, the mathematics portion of the SAT still covers mostly algebra and geometry, even though math educators believe other topics, such as statistics and probability, are equally important.

Because many tests haven't changed, and because parents are concerned about test scores, teachers are reluctant to shift the focus of instruction from what has traditionally been taught. The assessment mismatch "brings to a screeching halt the good things that teachers are willing to try," Carl says.

A case in point is the effect of the Maryland Functional Mathematics Test, which all Maryland students must pass to graduate from high school. The test keeps 9th graders "under the gun" from the beginning of the school year until late October, says Joan Burks, math resource teacher at Watkins Mill High School in Gaithersburg, Md. Teachers feel "a great deal of pressure from central office that the results have to be improved," Burks says. "It has tremendous impact."

Until the test is over, some 9th grade classes do little but drill, Burks says. Once the test is past, however, students are free to do much more: work with spreadsheets on the computer, study probability and statistics, and grapple with real-world problems such as determining the relation between the dimensions of a board and how much weight it will bear, for example.

Dossey, however, charges that assessment is "a convenient excuse" for not making changes. If one test makes all the difference at a school, he says, that single focus is the problem—not an assessment mismatch.

"Large national testing publishers are eager to support [the NCTM recommendations] and will be coming out with tests that support the standards," he says. The real issue, he believes, is whether educators will adjust their local assessment programs.

Lack of time is another obstacle to putting the standards in practice, Frye says. "Teachers need time to plan in order to make significant changes," she asserts. She also cites the "practical reality factor" that is too often ignored in change efforts. When class sizes are large, for example, teachers can't be expected to do in-depth analyses of students' work. Some reform advocates seem to ignore the problems that teachers face every day, she says.

Finding the right teaching materials can also pose an obstacle. As a member of her county's textbook adoption committee, Joyner feels frustrated. "We're having such a hard time," she reports. "These publishing companies are using all the right words—'cooperative learning,' 'manipulatives'—but when you look into the heart of it, it's the same old thing: drill and kill."

Despite the inevitable obstacles, most experts are optimistic that the NCTM standards have indeed sparked a revolution in mathematics education. But they emphasize that it will be years before the new ways of teaching and assessing mathematics are firmly established. "This major change in mathematics will probably take us a decade," Frye says.

Carl concurs. "It's going to be the end of the decade before we can say even the people who are really trying are fully implementing the standards," she believes.

Most experts believe the momentum will continue to build. "I think it's going to keep going, mainly to the extent that it's aligned with the President's six goals," says David Haury, director of the ERIC Clearinghouse for Science, Mathematics, and Environmental Education at Ohio State University. Haury foresees "a pretty big push" to implement the NCTM standards in the 1990s, with the national drive for standards as the main impetus.

In Ohio, change is already happening rapidly, according to Kasten. "Within a few years, the vast majority of [Ohio] teachers will be implementing at least the spirit of the standards, if not every recommendation," she predicts.

Carl is confident that the standards will bring about fundamental, lasting change in mathematics instruction. "It's not a window of opportunity; it's a door," she asserts. "It's being realized, suddenly, that math is a gateway. If you don't understand math, your choices are limited."

Another reason the NCTM standards will propel change, she believes, is that they were developed by educators, not imposed upon them. "These are not federal standards, they're not from the National Science Foundation; this is the math community speaking," she says. The math community also appears to be listening—and acting.

Section 3

SOCIAL STUDIES

GEOGRAPHY'S RENAISSANCE

Restoring Earth to the K–12 Curriculum

Kathy Checkley

After decades of being almost invisible in the K–12 curriculum, geography is making a comeback in U.S. schools. This renaissance can be attributed, in large part, to the successful collaboration between geographers and educators who were galvanized into action after state and national test results revealed that an overwhelming number of students were geographically illiterate. Now geography education is becoming as vibrant and complex as the Earth it studies.

It's little wonder that our students lack geographic knowledge, experts say. Geography has never been a subject of strong focus in U.S. schools and teachers are not trained to teach the subject. "Since the 1930s, teachers who have been asked to teach geography in our schools are social studies teachers," says Robert Dulli, assistant vice president and director of the National Geographic Society's Geography Education Program. "So you have some teachers who are prepared to teach social studies, some who are really strong in history, and some who are really strong in economics." But most of these teachers, he notes, aren't strong in geography.

The scope of geography is also misunderstood, says Roger Downs, geographer in residence at National Geographic. "For many people, geography is place location. In other words, many think if you are a walking gazetteer or atlas and you can do well at Trivial Pursuit, you know geography." It's important, Downs continues, to know location, but it's not enough. "If you knew the dates on which major events have occurred for

The articles in this chapter were originally published in the Spring 1996 issue of ASCD's *Curriculum Update* newsletter.

Geography's Perspectives

Through geographic perspectives, societies and nature can be interpreted and explained. According to the standards, geography has two specific perspectives, spatial and ecological:

The Spatial Perspective

Geography is concerned with the spatial dimension, the space and place, of human experience. Understanding spatial patterns and processes—by asking "where is it?" and "why is it there?"—allows us to better appreciate how people live on Earth.

The Ecological Perspective

Human societies depend on diverse small and large ecosystems for food, water, and all other resources. Human actions modify physical environments and the viability of ecosystems at local to global scales. We need to understand that the survival of humans and other species requires a viable global ecosystem and depends on our understanding and respecting the complex web of relationships between living and nonliving things on Earth.

Adapted from *Geography for Life, 1994 National Geography Standards*, National Geographic Society.

the past three hundred years, that would not make you an American historian, but it is necessary that you know those dates in order to do history." Likewise for geography, he says. Memorizing location is necessary, "but it's not sufficient, and what has happened in the past is that many people have viewed it as necessary and sufficient."

Students' dismal test scores are one unfortunate consequence of inadequate teacher training and an ignorance of geography's breadth. But what really causes an uproar over geographic illiteracy is the realization by those in the political realm that schools are not preparing graduates to be effective citizens in society, says David Lanegran, professor and chair of the geography department at Macalester College. "When geography was dropped from the curriculum, students became disconnected. They didn't understand how their actions impacted others," Lanegran explains.

If taught well, geography can become "an important area of study in developing a responsible citizenship," adds Joseph Stoltman. Stoltman, a geography professor at Western Michigan University, says that the 12th grade students who were given the 1988 National Assessment of Education Progress (NAEP), did "pretty well" in locating countries, but were deficient in all other areas. "The principles of geography didn't come through," he says. "We wanted students to know where things are located and understand why. We wanted them to know the environmental costs of location, as well as the economic benefits."

ALLIES IN ACTION

That students scored well in any area of the 1988 NAEP was, according to Stoltman, a result of a burgeoning movement to restore geography to the classroom. "After a number of articles pointed out the inability of students to locate countries on the map, greater attention was paid to geographic illiteracy," he explains.

Much of the muscle behind the growing crusade was the National Geographic Society. In 1986, the Society launched the Geography Education Program and charged it with building a national alliance of geography educators, modeled after a successful state alliance in California.

"We had a discipline that's not in the school system," says Dulli. "We had a structure of geographers all across the country who have a very strong interest in geography education, so we asked them to join us."

Those who talk about the distance between academia and K–12 education "would be impressed with the outreach efforts made by professional geographic associations, educational geographic associations, and colleges and universities," adds Stoltman. "When you bring that kind of academic power to bear on what's happening in schools, you get more people to listen and participate. The focused effort encourages involvement."

And involvement of K–12 teachers was key to the success of the national alliance, Dulli adds. "Our goal was, and is, to get geography back in the school system—and what does that mean? It means working with teachers. If you're going to change education, you've got to go classroom by classroom."

Recognizing, of course, that they couldn't "bring every teacher to Washington," National Geographic, instead, decided to bring a core of teachers to their headquarters in Washington, D.C., train them, and then send them home to train other teachers.

Marianne Kenney was one of that first corps of teachers to accept the opportunity and responsibility to change how geography was taught in public schools. A veteran high school social studies teacher, Kenney attended a summer institute at National Geographic in 1986 and learned that she had only a very basic understanding of geography and, therefore, could only teach the basics. Through the summer institute and other workshops sponsored by the Society, Kenney learned that geography was more than the maps and regions to which she had once limited the discipline. Geography, she found, also "involves the movement of people and ideas across the landscape." Kenney also discovered how to use her local community as an extension of her geography lesson. "I could take kids to a shopping center and ask them to draw conclusions. What business would you put here to revitalize the economy?"

In 1993, Kenney joined the Colorado State Department of Education to help develop state geography content standards, based on the national geography standards she helped create. As Social Studies Specialist, its her job, Kenney says, "to help other teachers the way I was helped." Teachers who attend Kenney's workshops expect her to assist them in developing standards-based curriculum. And the best way to do that, Kenney says, is "to roll up your sleeves and develop standards-based curriculum. We give them two solid weeks in standards boot camp."

One activity, for example, is called "Picture the Standards." Teachers are divided into six groups and each group is given one of the standards. "They are then asked to draw a picture of the concept of their standard." Teachers choose the content and also develop assessment tools that link curriculum to the standards. The best of these units are entered into the state teacher resource bank and are made available to other educators in the state. "Our system is a good model for how other states can train teachers to implement the geography standards," says Kenney, who maintains that professional development is the key to improving geography education.

"If teachers don't buy into the standards, if they don't think aspects of geography are important, those aspects won't be taught."

CONNECTING WITH FAMILIES

Comprehensive teacher training certainly enhances how geography is taught in schools, but of equal importance to geography's renaissance, says Lanegran, is the focus on community and family participation. The improvement in geography education may "be a result of families getting involved, of the school board and local decision makers saying we need more geography in the curriculum," he says.

It's important that geography become more mainstream and that families get involved because "parents really are their children's best teachers," says Lori Morrow, Geography Frameworks Consultant for the School Effectiveness Unit at the Colorado Department of Education. "Getting geography in the home will result in that knowledge being transferred to the classroom."

Morrow trains teachers to work with families who participate in Colorado's Family Geography Challenge, a state-wide program that encourages families to focus on geography at home. And, just as state content standards guide classroom instruction, standards also guide the activities families do.

For example, says Morrow, "standard #3 says that students will understand how natural processes shape the Earth's surface patterns and systems." To complete the activity based on that standard, families create islands, complete with their various elevations and landforms, from butcher paper provided to them. Then, says Morrow, "we'll discuss how climate and vegetation patterns change as the elevation changes." It's a perfect activity for Coloradans, she continues, "because they're up and down the mountain so much."

Morrow expects that, this year, 45 families from urban, suburban, and rural sites will be registered to participate in the Family Geography Challenge.

TURNING THE TIDE

Communicating geography's import to families, establishing a 50-state geography alliance, tapping teachers' enthusiasm and drive, all these— paralleled with efforts to shine a national spotlight on the need for improved geographic education—had an impact. Results from the 1994 NAEP, which tested 4th, 8th, and 12 graders, showed that the majority of students in the United States had at least a basic understanding of geography.

To truly understand the significance of the 1994 NAEP results, however, it's important to note the differences between the 1988 and 1994 tests, says Stoltman. "When you look at raw scores, those for the 1994 NAEP were slightly better (than the 1988 NAEP) and probably not statistically significant. But when you look at the nature of the test, students did considerably better."

For example, in addition to broadening the survey to include 4th and 8th graders (the 1988 NAEP tested only 12th graders), the 1994 NAEP required that students answer both selected-response (multiple choice) and constructive-response questions; all questions on the 1988 NAEP were multiple choice. This change made the 1994 test more difficult, says Stoltman, because "students had to read the information, make conclusions, and generate new information."

The 1994 NAEP was also structured differently. "Geographers, citizens, and teachers worked together to develop a framework for assessments," Stoltman explains, so the test had a "much better philosophical underpinning" and better reflected how geography was being taught. "In the classroom, teachers were beginning to use authentic assessments. The constructive responses on the 1994 NAEP introduced a level of authentic assessment" and, therefore, provided a much more valid indication of students' geographic knowledge.

Although heartened by the 1994 NAEP results, Stoltman and others maintain that a "basic" understanding isn't enough. Geographers and educators concur that students must, at least, perform at the "proficient" level, if they are to "participate in the civic life of the community."

It's time to begin preparing for the 1999 NAEP, says Stoltman, which will no doubt be designed to reflect the national geography standards.

Teachers must become familiar with developing instructional approaches using the standards, Stoltman maintains. "The expectation is that, when students open the page of the test and look at the question, it will be very closely related to what they've studied. The context will differ, but they will have to be able to apply the process."

Lanegran agrees. "We need to take geography from the knowledge level to the application level," he says. Students must learn to use geography to solve problems, to "think with their eyes," and to "look at the landscape and understand it, understand why things occur in particular places." That, says Lanegran, is the geographic know-how all citizens should have.

WHAT IN THE WORLD IS GEOGRAPHY?

KATHY CHECKLEY

Picture this: You're gazing at a painting that allows you to peer into two back yards. Your vantage point is a window, perched above this setting. You notice that the yard on the left is very neat, with trimmed grass and a weeded garden. The yard on the right stands in stark contrast, with overgrown vegetation and a hammock that seems to invite relaxation.

As you contemplate why these yards are so very different—even though they share the same physical landscape and climate—you also ponder a geographic concept. Christopher Salter, chair of geography at the University of Missouri–Columbia, asks students to consider the yards in his lecture on cultural geography because it helps illustrate the meaning and significance of *place*. How these neighbors use the land in different ways reflects their sense of personal identity, explains Salter. "What's different are the cultural attitudes of the homeowners, who have very different mindsets about what their yards should be."

Understanding the physical and human characteristics of place is only one of the geographic concepts we need to grasp if we are to be "geographically informed." So say the creators of *Geography for Life*, the 1994 National Geography Standards, written in response to the alarming lack of geographic knowledge among students in the United States. As defined in the *Geography for Life Executive Summary*, geographically informed persons are those who understand that "geography is the study of people, places, and environments from a spatial perspective. Geographically informed persons understand and appreciate the interdependent worlds in which they live."

LINKING PEOPLE TO THE EARTH

Geography is about connections, about the relationship between human beings and their world. The Earth's physical features and systems influence how we live; likewise, decisions we make about how we live affect the Earth's surface.

Take the hydrologic cycle, for example. As water circulates through this system, it changes the Earth's surface in its wake. "Water shapes the planet," explains Kim Hulse, assistant director of the Geography Education Program at the National Geographic Society (NGS). "When water falls on the land, it erodes it. We have gullies because water carries the land away; we have canyons because rivers cut into the Earth."

When too much water falls on the Earth, however, those rivers can overflow, and people who live near these bodies of water may modify the landscape to control the resulting flooding.

Earth acts, humans react—that's geography, an interaction of physical processes and human responses to those processes. Geographers study this science from these two different points of view. Physical geographers, explains Salter, will talk, "almost incidentally" about the affect physical processes have on people, while cultural geographers are very interested in "how we perceive our environment and make decisions based upon those perceptions." For those decisions to be informed decisions, say experts, citizens must have a solid grounding in both physical and cultural geography, so they'll better understand the consequences of their actions.

Drop a stone in water and the water ripples. We must help students understand, says Hulse, why it's important not to just study the stone, but also to look at what happens over there with the ripples. "In an increasingly interdependent world, you can no longer live like you are the only person in the world," she explains. Students must understand that they are part of a system.

Students need to see that "the decisions we make do impact other parts of the world and that what happens in other countries impacts them," agrees Marianne Kenney, social studies specialist for the Colorado Department of Education. "Students need to see that we really are connected."

THE WORLD IN SPACE, THE WORLD IN PLACE

If geography requires us to understand connections, it asks us to do so by analyzing those connections in spatial terms.

"The driving force in geography is the idea of space—spatial relationships, spatial patterns, and spatial arrangements," says Roger Downs, geographer in residence at NGS. "Take the word *space* and think about its use as a modifier. Space is the dimension that makes geography work."

To think of the world in spatial terms, we must know and understand "how to use maps and other geographic tools to acquire, process, and report information from a spatial perspective; how to use mental maps to organize information about people, places, and environments in a spatial context; how to analyze the spatial organization of people, places and environments on Earth's surface," according to the national geography standards (which Downs helped write).

This knowledge, say experts, equips us to ask what David Lanegran calls the fundamental question of geography—where?

"Location is the key to all decisions," says Lanegran, professor and chair of the geography department at Macalester College, in St. Paul, Minn. "What makes geography geography is location." Knowing when something happens is important, he says, "but it's really important to know where something happens."

"Sometimes geography contributes significantly to the event," agrees Susan Gay, an instructor in the curriculum and instruction department at the University of Nebraska. And once we know where something happens, we can use geographic tools—maps, globes, aerial photographs, satellite images, and so on—to help analyze events from a spatial perspective. By studying data with such tools, we are then able to see the patterns that occur, says Gay, and make decisions based upon those patterns.

If Boris Yeltsin, for example, had studied a map that showed the distribution of Islamic people in relation to Slavic-Roman people, he may have avoided the chaos in Chechnya, explains Salter, adding that geographers could have predicted the Chechnian conflict based on the population patterns, and on another fundamental geographic concept—that people respond to place. "The Chechnians' sense of space," says Salter, "is leading them to this bloody battle. They've never felt a part of Russia and want to be free of the body politic of Russia."

Just as it can help us analyze current events, looking at data from a spatial perspective can also help us interpret the past. Thom Stroschein teaches social studies at Carrollton Elementary-Middle School in Baltimore. In planning an interdisciplinary unit on intolerance, Stroschein used geography to help students make sense of the political climate that contributed to the Holocaust.

"We went to the Holocaust Museum and examined the number of Jews given up by each country," explains Stroschein. The data will become more meaningful when students also consider location and then "formalize questions about the political systems of the countries involved. Why were some countries more willing to cooperate with Nazi Germany than other countries? Why were some countries neutral? How did natural, physical barriers impact political relationships?"

What they learn through this exercise, says Stroschein, will help students analyze other historical events from this spatial perspective. "When we look at the Khmer Rouge and Cambodia, for example, students will examine what kind of relationship existed between Cambodia and its neighbors." Students will consider location in analyzing why other countries did nothing to prevent the holocaust there.

Stroschein points out that learning about the politics of location has contemporary applications, as well. When a shooting occurred at his urban school, students were outraged at the media coverage that resulted, which they considered biased. Stroschein helped students analyze the event from a geographic perspective, asking them to think about how their local geography—the location of their school—influenced the coverage. What stereotypes, for example, are associated with urban schools, and how might those stereotypes have influenced media coverage? Geography, Stroschein suggests, gives students a way of analyzing such heated events objectively.

AN ANALYTICAL TOOL

Geography also provides citizens with a means to plan for the future and create policies that guide how to best use and manage Earth's precious resources.

In Colorado, water—how to get it and how to distribute it—should be considered when reviewing any land development proposal, says Lori Morrow, geography frameworks consultant for the state education department's school effectiveness unit. Morrow maintains that its critical to take geography into account when making important decisions about land usage in the arid West. "Understanding geography will enable us to create better plans for development," says Morrow. "The more geographically aware [we are], the better decision making at the polls."

"Citizens are basically the decision makers on the nature of the local landscape," agrees Salter. Citizens need to know what information to examine in determining "whether a community should allow a new landfill, a new road, a new development. Geography, Salter concludes, is the tool that helps citizens make those environmental decisions.

NEW TOOLS FOR GEOGRAPHY EDUCATION

KATHY CHECKLEY

Geography's renaissance comes at a time when educators are also learning how to use new technology to enhance education. As teachers determine how technology can stimulate students' geographic understanding, they're also deciding which of these tools can best assist them.

TOOLS FOR STUDENTS

There is no doubt that the way geography is being taught today has been influenced by technology, educators say. Internet connections and electronic mail have transformed many a geography classroom into interactive laboratories, with access to almost unlimited resources, people, and timely information.

"Technology brings the world into the classroom," says Bonnie Bracey, technology teacher in residence at the Arlington (Va.) Career Center. Bracey, the national "point person" for those who need technology information, says technology "helps students understand how ideas travel and teaches them to look at the world in an integrated way."

Carol Robitschek agrees. Robitschek, who teaches 5th graders at Surfside Elementary School in Satellite Beach, Fla., uses electronic mail to communicate with other schools across the United States and around the world. Through such exchanges, Robitschek's students are able to make cultural comparisons. Students in her class, for example, compare what they watch on television with what Canadian students watch. They then compare their viewing habits with students in other countries. "It allows my students to connect with people from far away places," Robitschek says. "In this way, students see the 'big picture' and understand that, while we're all the same, we're also very different and we need to respect those differences."

Online connections also allow students to experience the impact of Earth's natural forces in ways they weren't able to before. "When the earthquake in San Francisco hit," says Bracey, her students were online, "talking" with students who were living through the natural disaster. "Thanks to technology, the event wasn't remote, it was real."

Other technology, such as computer cartography or graphic software programs that enable students to draw maps, can help students master skills that once filled prospective geographers with dread. "I'm a clumsy person," says David Lanegran, geography professor at Macalester College who, therefore, agonized over cartography. "It was time-consuming and stressful because I knew I'd make mistakes." Students today who aren't skillful with their fingers may not suffer such anxiety, Lanegran says, "because they know if they make a mistake, they can start over."

TOOLS FOR TEACHERS

For all of technology's advantages, however, teachers run the risk of it being yet another distraction in the classroom, say experts.

"The Internet helps students understand how we are all linked, but students can get lost as they search for information," says Susan Gay of the University of Nebraska.

One way teachers can minimize online distractions, she says, is by creating "weblets"—databases of downloaded web pages that are modified so the browser can find information on a local hard drive or disk. "In this way," Gay explains, "teachers replicate the environment of the web without having to deal with the complications that often arise while using the web," such as slow modem or telephone connections, busy search engines, or busy servers at sites

These "weblets" are wonderful for geography, Gay maintains, "because they empower teachers to use the resources of the web. The images and information sources are truly world wide." Also, because students have had practice navigating cyberspace, teachers can then assign them geographic problems and "turn them loose" on the web to find the information they need to solve the problems.

Helping teachers create curriculum based on the geography standards is another way technology is proving to be an effective tool for teachers.

In many states, education departments are creating databases of the "best" geography lessons that teachers can access and download. A team of Minnesota teachers took that concept one step further and developed a CD-ROM called GeoLinks, which is designed to be an "alternative to a traditional curriculum."

"In Minnesota, local districts set their own curriculum, so the national and state standards are only models," explains Lanegran. With the GeoLinks CD, teachers can personalize and manipulate a collection of geography lessons and units to meet the specific needs of their students, knowing that they are still "teaching to the standards."

ENSURING ACCESS, EQUITY

Although Lanegran applauds the technological tools that enable teachers and students to more readily grasp geographic concepts, he worries that schools can't deliver on the promise of equal access to technology.

Other educators have the same concern. The use of technology in geographic education is not a major theme of the *1994 National Geography Standards*, says Roger Downs, geographer in residence at the National Geographic Society, and for good reason. At one stage, he explains, those working on the standards wanted to include a strong focus on technology, but some state commissioners of education worried that "if you write that [technology] into the standards, you will disadvantage our students because we simply cannot provide that level of technology in our classrooms."

The lesson in this, Downs suggests, is that as geographers and educators develop the technological tools to improve geographic education, they must also develop a way to ensure that these tools can be used by all teachers and students. "It's not good to invite people to do something they can't do," he says. If teachers don't have access to the technology, "you've just turned them off" to geography.

CHALLENGING HISTORY

The Past Remains a Battleground for Schools

Philip Cohen

The practice of teaching and learning history has changed dramatically over the last generation. Contentious, ongoing debates have led to reforms in both content and methodology. But experts still see the field as a battleground of political and pedagogical issues.

In the 1950s, California selected a textbook that reported of slavery: "Many of the slaves had snug cabins to live in, plenty to eat, and work that was not too hard for them to do. Most of the slaves seemed happy and contented."

By 1990, the state approved a textbook with a much different description: "Most of the slaves lived in drafty, one-room cabins with dirt floors. They slept on the ground on mattresses filled with corn husks." The text also notes the slaves' inadequate nutrition and seemingly endless hard work.

American Textbook Council Director Gilbert Sewall, who compiled these examples, says a generation of pressure has brought greater ethnic and gender diversity to history texts and curriculums. But, he believes, "Accuracy has been the first casualty of contemporary sensibilities, clashing ideologies, and pressures for inclusion." Proponents of new history curriculums and methods, however, say a more inclusive approach to history is inherently more accurate than the traditional, one-sided presentation.

The articles in this chapter were originally published in the Winter 1995 issue of ASCD's *Curriculum Update* newsletter.

Along with content changes, many teachers have also begun using new methods—including primary sources, oral histories, and investigative research—in their classes. As education merges with the "information age," these educators say, history should not just impart lists of facts. "You need kids who know how to deal with information, how to use it as a tool," says Bruce VanSledright, assistant professor of education at the University of Maryland–College Park.

Much of the discipline, however, remains steeped in traditional content and methodology. Most history teaching is still based on textbooks and lectures, centering on traditional political, economic, and military landmarks—often viewed through the lens of traditional interpretation.

A 1990 National Assessment of Educational Progress (NAEP) report found that while many high school seniors knew of basic historical events and people, fewer understood "the interrelationships among politics, economics, and culture." Half of high school seniors reported studying the Revolutionary War "a lot," but only one in five said they had studied the history of women and minority groups that much. As a result, most "failed to demonstrate an awareness of major elements of American social history, such as the women's movement."

"We're not really getting through to kids in terms of historical knowledge generally," says Thomas Turner, professor of holistic teaching and learning at the University of Tennessee at Knoxville. "If we don't do a better job of teaching history, of getting a sense of our historical identity, then we won't have a society."

The new guidelines from the History Standards Project may provide some direction to curriculum designers and teachers, but the debate over what to teach—and how to teach it—shows no signs of abating.

WHOSE HISTORY?

Ronald Takaki, professor of ethnic studies at the University of California at Berkeley, and the author of *A Different Mirror: A History of Multicultural America*, says the traditional curriculum was not only *Eurocentric* but *Anglocentric*, because it flowed from the experience of the original British colonists. In reaction, various marginalized groups produced curriculum that told "disparate stories." Previously excluded histories were told, but from a separatist perspective.

Takaki is seeking a "third way" in addressing the question. His "pluralistic and multicultural" approach is broad and comparative, "urging us to see the paths of history in the United States as crisscrossed over one another." Multicultural history, he believes, can show that "one culture" is nevertheless "rooted in the experiences of many different cultures."

With such an approach, for example, Takaki says students could learn how the experiences of such different groups as Chicanos, African Americans, and Navajos all led them to volunteer to fight in World War II, making it a "multicultural defense of democracy against fascism."

Takaki rejects the notion that this broadening of the history curriculum represents a political crusade. The criticism of "political correctness" is mostly "a red herring," he says. "Multiculturalism has an intellectual purpose. We're there because we want intellectual accuracy."

Some of the impetus for change in content comes from demographic trends. Non-Hispanic white children now make up less than half of all public school students in such states as Texas, California, New Mexico, and Mississippi. Many teachers have seen the faces of their students change and are looking for ways to respond.

The demographic trends alone have some critics worried that American society is fragmenting into disunited cultures, and they hope to see education combat this trend. Arthur Schlesinger Jr. has argued that "the republic has survived and grown because it has maintained a balance between *pluribus* and *unum*," but new multicultural history "is saturated with *pluribus* and neglectful of *unum*."

Columbia University history professor Kenneth Jackson acknowledges that "heterogeneity has made this land rich and creative," but he has written that "within any single country, one culture must be accepted as the standard."

How is such a standard defined? "Eventually we may need a unified cultural standard," replies Ali Mazrui, director of the Institute of Global Cultural Studies at Binghamton University, State University of New York. "But is the one we have now the right one?" The principle of unity is a good one, he adds, "but it doesn't mean whatever you have, keep it." The defense of a single culture is a "status quo argument," he asserts.

Mazrui is particularly wary of traditional history approaches that paper over conflict and oppression in America's past. "We have to be very frank about what has gone wrong in our society," he says. Such subjects as slavery and the destruction of Native American societies should be introduced "quite early" in school, he believes, with the explicit message that they "must never happen again."

The process of challenging traditional history content has grown out of changes in the study of history itself. "As the new social history spun out of African American and women's studies, we began not only to rewrite history, but to rewrite it in a different way," says John Duffy, who teaches history at Hinsdale (Ill.) Central High School. History content is moving toward the history of social life and daily struggles and away from a narrow emphasis on major political and economic landmarks.

For example, according to the National Women's History Project, to teach the history of women means to change the nature of history: "Women's history is social history. It focuses on the everyday lives of individuals of all walks of life."

With a thematic approach—making "a chain of connections"—educators can avoid the pitfalls of either excessively negative or purely laudatory history content, Takaki says. Takaki offers *cotton* as a theme. "If you follow the cotton," he says, it leads from Irish immigrant women in Massachusetts textile mills, to slave plantations in the South, on land seized from Native Americans, to the expansion into the Southwest and the eventual opening of trade through California to Asia. In the process, the struggles, ideals, failures, and successes of many different social groups can all be related. That gives students a deeper understanding of broad historical developments and elements of daily life.

A theme could also be an idea, such as *equality*. Advanced by the Founding Fathers, equality was at first denied to many in America; yet it remained a unifying concept, tying together not only national leaders such as Thomas Jefferson and Abraham Lincoln, but also activists from Frederick Douglass to modern women's movement participants.

Americans have different languages, religions, and group identities; and in that sense, Takaki believes, "we have a diversity of cultures." But "if we are talking about culture as a political culture, then I think we do have a common culture—the culture of equality."

In this view, American diversity is an accomplishment that nevertheless results from painful struggles. "It's a history of how we were forced to come together as a society," he says. "We are actors in this history."

Such content issues have a direct impact on the motivation to learn, many educators believe. Gail Hickey, associate professor of education at Indiana University-Purdue University at Fort Wayne, says students' feeling unconnected to the history material is a major reason for poor test scores.

That fits the experience of Deiadra Downes, K–8 multicultural consultant and social studies liaison at Highland Park (Mich.) Schools. When her 8th grade students, most of them African Americans, appeared frustrated after three years of pre-Civil War history, she asked them why.

"You just want us to be white," she recalls them saying. "Shouldn't we *not* like America? Hasn't America *not* been good to us?"

That experience helped her understand that "the kids really aren't getting it because they can't relate to it." Later she asked students to include personal histories as they researched a given period, interviewing their oldest living relatives, "so they could see the importance of history and relate it to themselves."

HISTORICAL THINKING SKILLS

In advocating a more multicultural curriculum, New York State's Social Studies Review and Development Committee in 1991 urged: "The subject matter selected for inclusion should give priority to depth over breadth." But Sewall believes that attempts to make history curriculums more diverse have resulted in textbooks' becoming broader, and more shallow. Teaching everything has never been possible, but with increasing pressure to *include*, something has to give, he says.

"All history is selective," says Takaki. The question is, "What do we select?" Multicultural history does not have to mean teaching less about more, he believes. Such common themes as revolution, industrialization, immigration, and civil rights can remain a focus, but with a new emphasis on connections among the experiences of different groups within these trends.

To broaden historical understanding without sacrificing depth, many educators advocate an emphasis on historical skills, giving students the ability to make meaningful comparisons and draw judgments on their own.

David Kobrin, clinical professor in education at Brown University, says historians often ask, "What is the content?" Teachers, on the other hand, are more likely to ask, "How is it that students learn?" Since different groups use history to define themselves, Kobrin says, teachers should not impose a particular perspective. "Who's got the right to define that for everyone else?" he asks.

So history should be seen as a "way of knowing rather than a content field," Kobrin argues. Instead of struggling over the content of the historical canon, then, schools should teach "learning how to think historically. You need to learn how to define a question that is answerable," he says, "to raise a question and deal with it with integrity."

"Can you ever escape teaching history from a dominant perspective?" asks Ohio Northern University Assistant Professor of Education Michael Romanowski. "I don't think you can." But teachers can "begin to talk about differences in the context of talking about similarities." And if schools "teach frame of reference," students will learn generalizable lessons they can apply to many cases.

In world history, for example, Mazrui believes students who learn how to see "simultaneity"—to "think across societies and across events"—will be better historical learners. When teachers avoid "putting societies into sealed enclosures," their students learn more from historical accounts.

In traditional history approaches, VanSledright explains, history was seen as a list of facts, and historians were supposed to observe those facts from a distance. The study of history now tends to put the historian at the center of the process—acknowledging that the interpretation of history is as important as the facts themselves, he says.

In schools, however, VanSledright says that most history teaching still "decenters the role of the historian. As a consequence, when kids learn it, it decenters them as well."

While some teachers are making great strides, "history teachers as a group have been the last to explore creative pedagogy," Duffy says. Students should learn how to "argue over evidence and interpretation." They won't absorb historical material, he argues, unless it is "innovative, engaging, critical, and student centered."

For example, Duffy's 11th grade American history students broke into three factions to study the buildup to the American Revolution. Each group took a different perspective and read original documents from the era, as well as secondary sources. They got beyond the simple question of freedom from Britain or not, he says, and looked at many internal divisions within the society. Then they acted on their understanding through role playing and public speaking.

"America was a very divided place in 1776," Duffy says. With the exercise, his students "have a new insight into the complexity of any major turning point in history." The most important element in that process, he believes, was students' "reaching some conclusions on their own."

In another unit, Duffy's students looked at pre-Civil War history from the perspective of different African-American groups—those advocating armed revolt, gradual abolition, immediate abolition, and repatriation to Africa. That exercise served as a springboard to a discussion of questions facing African Americans today.

Duffy emphasizes that not every unit of every year can delve so deeply. One dynamic project can lend excitement to the series of lectures that follow, however. And when he does cover a lot of ground in a lecture, he prefers to see it as a workshop: At times the teacher steps in and demonstrates while everyone observes, but then the teacher draws back and the students direct themselves.

Teachers are likely to be dissuaded from breaking old habits by the volume of information they feel pressured to get across. They often don't have time to really learn the material themselves, says VanSledright.

For students to develop historical thinking skills, teachers will need more freedom in the classroom, Romanowski says. He fears that a tendency to "teach toward the test" is encouraged by wide content standards. When teachers are under the gun to get content across, student-generated ideas become "sidetracks" from the *real* curriculum. That leads to staying on the surface of the material, and "you never get to what students are really interested in."

"If we continue to train students like this," he says, "we're going to have some great contestants on *Jeopardy*."

To get beyond a "learn more facts" approach and teach students to "connect those facts into a meaningful whole," VanSledright argues that more time needs to be devoted to history and thinking skills, especially in the early years of K–3.

HISTORICAL VALUES

The debates over content and methodology collide on the question of teaching values in history. In looking at westward expansion, for example, the content to be learned and the approach in the classroom both beg the question of values.

Was the expansion a victory for democracy and the birth of a new free society? Or was it a brutal military escapade launched against nonaggressive Native Americans? In terms of methods, should students learn about the daily lives of women on the frontier and the cultural practices of Native Americans? Or about the accomplishments and ideas of political and military leaders?

These sets of questions are directly related. From the viewpoint of some political leaders, the expansion was a triumph; from the viewpoint of many less famous individual women, African Americans, laborers, and so on, it was a mixed blessing or worse.

One view holds that values do not belong in a history classroom. "When you get into the teaching of values," says Sewall. "You're leaving history behind." Such topics are more appropriate for civics or self-esteem courses, "but that's a whole different curricular universe" from history, he says.

Turner disagrees. Because he sees all good history lessons as "rife with values," taking the values out amounts to "taking away the possibility of turning children on to history," he says. "It is only when we get to those things that make us think of what is right and what is wrong that we are into what is important" in history.

Romanowski attributes an absence of values in history classrooms to social trends. "We're in real turmoil right now, in our culture," he says. "It's a moral crisis," in which conflict over values has led to their abandonment for safer ground. When teachers try to focus on facts, without "at least allowing for dialogue" over values in history, they give up their role as "transformers" and become "technicians," he believes.

Some revisions of history take on a tone of debunking previously held myths, especially about heroes of the traditional curriculum. But an inclusive history can still find praise for old heroes, even when the truth demands a less-than-perfect picture, Turner says. "What made them great is there, in spite of what made them human, and therefore fallible," he adds. "We could find wickedness in every human being."

"The nature of history is, at its heart, about controversy," Duffy says. And even choosing what to study involves moral choices and conflicting interpretations.

While teaching critical thinking skills, Romanowski says teachers can operate "within moral frameworks of justice and equality," which are commonly held goals—even if there is little consensus on their definition. "I think teachers have to be moral agents," he asserts. "I think if a student in the back row is a racist, we have to deal with that."

Others point out that because teachers must insist on such values as responsibility, honesty, integrity, and fairness in their own classrooms, it would be hypocritical not to look for those values in the study of history.

Hickey believes that students should learn to read historical material with an eye for bias, propaganda, and purpose—rather than a simple emphasis on factual content. One way to explore issues of right and wrong while teaching critical thinking, she suggests, is to conduct mock trials of historical figures such as John Brown. That can lead students to see the same events from different points of view and tackle moral questions from an informed perspective.

Hickey argues that teaching values should not be relegated to its own class, but instead should be integrated into such areas as history. "Personal standards, cultural mores, and broadly accepted values have always played a part in historical decision making, and will continue to do so," she has written.

Bringing right and wrong into history lessons does not mean teachers have to dictate values to students. One of Duffy's students did a family history project on D-Day, in which she interviewed a friend of her grandfather's who had landed at Normandy. Her project turned into a short piece of historical fiction in which she explored "the bitter irony of a Jewish American soldier" fighting to drive Nazis out of France—only to find the society he helped liberate steeped in anti-Semitism. Since she explored the subject herself, Duffy says the student gained a deeper understanding of both the history and moral lessons involved.

The benefits of learning history are less tangible than some other curriculum areas—how does one measure the ability to act as a well-informed citizen? But historians and history teachers say the importance of the subject lends weight to the debates over its future.

The content speaks to the character of the culture in all its complexity. "The glue that holds a culture together is the history of that culture," Turner says. And the lessons in thinking and learning it provides are widely generalizable, so that "the skills of the historian transfer to almost any area of American life," according to Duffy.

As a social studies coordinator, Downes says, "I argue with my people all the time: *please* make it important."

STUDENTS AS HISTORIANS

PHILIP COHEN

The textbook is still at the center of teaching and learning history, but new methodologies are making significant inroads—bringing what proponents call a more engaging style of learning to the classroom and encouraging the development of higher-level thinking. Their aim is to lead students to think and act more like historians—to formulate their own questions, learn the interpretive process, and develop new research skills. These new methodologies include the use of primary-source documents and family histories.

"When you work with primary source documents, it just gets deeper and deeper, and you don't know where it's going to lead," says Leslie Gray, social studies department chair at Chantilly High School in Fairfax, Va.

Wynell Schamel, education specialist at the National Archives in Washington, D.C., conducts a two-week training course called Primarily Teaching, which introduces teachers to archival research and the use of primary documents in history classes. During the course, participants research a topic in the archives and then develop the documents they find into classroom materials.

The National Archives publishes primary source document kits on specific periods or events, such as the Constitution, the Bill of Rights, or Westward Expansion. Each has 40 to 75 facsimiles of sound, film, photographs or text documents; and the kits include context, background, and support materials. The archives contain government records—not only official documents, but also personal testimonials and artifacts, family Bibles, birth and death certificates, and eyewitness accounts.

When Gray went through the Archives training, she collected documents recording atrocities committed against African Americans during Reconstruction in the South. Her advanced placement students, who had read a novel about the period, wanted to know if the incidents in the book were realistic.

Gray says she found a "vast amount of information," most of it handwritten, detailing the incidents. Then she "just had the kids kind of pore over them and begin to weave together some of the stories themselves. It certainly made it seem real to them," she adds.

In another class, Gray's students had been studying immigration into Boston in the mid-19th century. She connected them with an AppleWorks database that contained a ship's manifest from an 1840 landing in Boston. Each student adopted a family, and—working with data about available jobs, housing, and transportation—tried to make a new start for them in historical Boston. After calculating a budget, "what they discovered was that they had to take one or two kids out of school and put them to work in a sweatshop," Gray says. Finally, the class looked at data from 1850 for the city and tried to update the lives of their adopted families.

HISTORY MADE REAL

Schamel calls the use of primary documents "a way of humanizing history, a way of dealing with those people who are actually experiencing the events."

Archival materials also lend themselves to inclusion and diversity in the history class, Schamel believes, because they make accessible a range of materials that go beyond the official story. In the archives on the Westward Expansion, for example, "you're going to find the women homesteaders and the black Buffalo Soldiers," she says.

Many teachers use family history as a readily accessible source of primary documents and oral histories. Jerome Sullivan, a social studies teacher at Highland Park (Mich.) Community High School, found that although students at first were "rather hesitant" to get into a family history project, once they began talking to relatives, "they were amazed," he says. "It was like a gold mine. Once they turned on the faucet, we couldn't get these people to shut up," he laughs.

Breaking away from the confines of his textbooks required "a mindset change," Sullivan remembers. He and his colleagues found that "the main problem was our addiction to talking." But the family history projects allowed him to "show people rather than tell them" about historical events and ideas—and students' learning became more meaningful as a result.

Gail Hickey, associate professor of education at Indiana University-Purdue University at Fort Wayne, proposes a "Different Sides of the Story" unit, which uses family history to develop critical thinking skills. Students interview family members about an event they all remember—a tornado, election, baseball game, or family landmark, for example. Then they compare the different perspectives and try to learn what "true facts," if any, can be determined. That exercise in turn leads to a discussion of what ends up in history books, press accounts, or official records—the process of how history is made.

TEXTBOOKS PLUS

Seventy to 90 percent of history teaching is "textbook driven and derived," estimates Gilbert Sewall, director of the American Textbook Council. Although many textbooks now include a collection of primary documents, the shape of the course is still largely decided by the textbook.

And because of the practical advantages that textbooks offer—organization, exercises, chronology, and information—they are not likely to be supplanted. "The textbook in the foreseeable future is going to be the dominant teaching and learning instrument," Sewall concludes.

But Tom Gray calls the use of primary documents "just one thing in the bag of tricks," rather than a replacement for a textbook. Schamel adds that the National Archives advocate combining primary documents with textbooks. "The materials we develop are supplements to the textbook," she says. And when teachers bring in primary documents, "students are more interested in what the textbook says."

For information about National Archives training or classroom materials, contact Wynell Schamel, Education Branch, National Archives, Washington, D.C. 20408. Phone: (202) 501-6729.

◆

SETTING STANDARDS FOR HISTORY

SCOTT WILLIS

If the new national standards in history have the impact their developers hope for, students will get a much more thorough grounding in both U.S. and world history than they do today. In U.S. history, they will study far more than the Colonial Period, the American Revolution, and the Civil War. They will also learn, for example, about "the characteristics of societies in the Americas, western Europe, and West Africa that increasingly interacted after 1450"; about "how the rise of big business, heavy industry, and mechanized farming transformed the American peoples"; and about "the Cold War and the Korean and Vietnam conflicts in domestic and international politics."

In world history, students will learn about a panoply of civilizations, empires, faiths, cultural encounters, and revolutions. For example, they will study "how major religions and large-scale empires arose in the Mediterranean basin, China, and India, 500 BCE–300 CE"; about "the causes and consequences of the rise of Islamic civilization in the 7th–10th centuries"; and about "patterns of global change in the era of Western military and economic domination, 1850–1914."

Besides learning this abundance of content, students will also develop historical thinking skills. They will learn to comprehend historical narratives, interpret historical evidence, evaluate conflicting historical perspectives and explanations, and pursue historical research.

The national standards are intended to "affirm the significance of history to the education of today's students," says Charlotte Crabtree, professor emerita at UCLA, who served as co-director of the project. In recent decades, history has faded from importance in schools, because students have recoiled from rote learning of the subject, and because educators, in their desire to deal with present social problems, have "lost touch with the need for historical context," Crabtree believes. The history standards, she hopes, will restore the subject to its rightful prominence.

The standards developers wanted to help educators understand "what excellence in history really entails," Crabtree says, as well as to promote the importance of historical thinking. Learning history should not be merely a matter of memorizing names, dates, and places, she emphasizes, but should require—and inspire—high-level thinking.

There are three standards documents. One covers U.S. history for grades 5–12. Another covers world history for the same grades. A third document sets standards for both U.S. and world history for grades K–4.

The content of the history standards is broader in scope than what most American adults learned during their school days. The standards aim to make history "more balanced and inclusive," Crabtree says, by "bringing forth histories that have been silent in the past."

According to the project's other co-director, Gary Nash, a professor of history at UCLA and president of the Organization of American Historians, the standards "weave together" traditional history—which focuses on political and military events—with newer social history. The latter encompasses the history of women and ethnic and religious minorities, as well as the lives of everyday people. This blending reflects the widespread conviction among historians that "it's proper to treat all peoples" in society when presenting history, Nash says.

Another aspect of the standards that is new, according to Diane Brooks of the California Department of Education, who served on the standards council, is the greater emphasis placed on the modern years. As the old joke has it, a typical survey course in U.S. history ends with the teacher shouting, "We won World War II!" as students exit the classroom. The standards pay more attention to recent history, Brooks says, so that students will find history more relevant to their lives.

Also new is the emphasis on using literature and primary documents in teaching history—an approach that encourages "a very active engagement of the students with the content," says Linda Symcox of the National Center for History in the Schools, who was the project's assistant director. Using primary materials, rather than relying solely on a textbook, gives students opportunities to interpret multiple perspectives, as a historian would, Symcox says.

Development of the standards was administered by the National Center for History in the Schools at UCLA. The project was funded in spring 1992 by the National Endowment for the Humanities (NEH) and the U.S. Department of Education.

The standards were created through an inclusive process that lasted more than two years. Development of the U.S. history standards, for example, involved hundreds of educators, including history teachers, state social studies specialists, and state school officers responsible for history; dozens of historians; and representatives from a broad array of professional, scholarly, and public interest groups. Among those who reviewed the standards were nine focus groups convened by organizations of historians and educators, including ASCD.

For the most part, the standards were developed without pitched battles over "whose history" would be presented, Nash and others say. Two guiding principles helped the developers steer clear of prolonged political wrangling, Crabtree says. These were (1) that the standards should be "inclusive and balanced," and (2) that whatever content was included had to be "grounded in evidence"—based on sound historical data.

The standards were developed through "a very democratic process," Nash says, but "in trying to forge a consensus, we didn't go to the very fringes." The groups that would have been most contentious, the most difficult to pull into the circle, "probably weren't represented." These include fundamentalist groups of many stripes—religious, ethnic, and racial—that are fixed at opposite ends of the political spectrum.

MIXED REVIEWS

Reactions to the history standards have been mixed, ranging from enthusiastic praise from some teachers to broadsides from critics. Lynne Cheney, former chair of NEH, writing in the *Wall Street Journal*, has complained that the standards slight traditional history and betray an anti-American bias. The U.S. history standards praise West African culture, she points out, but "such celebratory prose is rare when the document gets to American history itself. . . . We are a better people than the National Standards indicate, and our children deserve to know it."

Others reject this criticism. The standards are in line with prevailing opinion in the field, says Symcox. "You will find a lot of what's in these standards in the latest textbooks," she asserts. The standards may "push inclusiveness a bit further," she says—but without straying into "fringe" territory.

Most of the educators contacted for this article were supportive of the history standards effort, but had reservations about specific aspects of the standards.

Susan Shapiro, who teaches world history at the University of Chicago Laboratory Schools, served as chair of the Organization of History Teachers' focus group on world history. Shapiro "strenuously applauds" the world history standards, which she considers long overdue. Nevertheless, she is troubled by the standards' "overarching desire to accommodate the increasing [clamor] for multicultural content, at the expense of good history." The developers paid inadequate attention to Western culture, she believes. For example, the Renaissance and Reformation were lumped together, whereas an entire standard was devoted to just the Mongols. But, she adds, she is "so thrilled" to have the standards that "it's hard to criticize."

According to Symcox, the "dominant position" among those who developed the world history standards was to avoid creating a Eurocentric document. On the other hand, "we have not belittled the place of Europe or Western civilization," she says. "There's strong, strong European, Western Civ. history in there."

One of the most frequently voiced criticisms is that the standards are simply "overwhelming"—an avalanche of content that will engulf educators. Teachers' initial reaction may well be to use the standards document "as a doorstop and leave it somewhere," jokes Sherrill Curtis, chair of history/social studies at Providence Senior High School in Charlotte, N.C., who served on ASCD's focus group.

The emphasis on diversity is "a real strength," says Mike Radow, a teacher of U.S. and world history at Mercer Island (Wash.) High School, who also served on ASCD's focus group. However, that inclusivity "doubles or triples the amount of things mentioned," he points out.

So that students have adequate time to learn this ambitious content, the National Council for History Standards recommends that schools devote no less than three years of instruction *each* to world history and U.S. history, during grades 5–12. With three full years of instruction and a well-designed curriculum, schools should be able to teach the content and skills embodied in each set of standards, Crabtree insists. "That's not asking too much."

One member of the National Council for History Standards who argued against "the three-year assumption" is Warren Solomon, a social studies consultant to Missouri's department of education. In reality, Solomon says, schools have limited time to teach history—which, after all, is just one part of social studies. By positing three years of instruction, the developers evaded making the hard choices about what's most important to teach, he says. How, Solomon asks, will teachers make a judicious choice if they want students to examine something in depth?

This concern is shared by another member of ASCD's focus group, Karen Steinbrink of Bucks County (Pa.) Intermediate Unit #22. It's "impossible for teachers to figure out how to use the information," she says. Steinbrink fears the standards could lead to more cursory coverage of content; they might "exacerbate, not alleviate" this common flaw in history instruction.

Surprisingly, some educators dismiss the charge that the standards are overwhelming. John Pyne, social studies supervisor for the West Milford (N.J.) public schools, believes that teachers are staggered only because they are unfamiliar with the format. "If teachers actually sat down and listed everything they do over the course of a year or two years, that would be a substantial document itself," Pyne says. "You'd be amazed how bulky that is."

Rejecting the standards as overwhelming is "not a legitimate response," says Brooks. Standards are not necessarily approached one by one, she argues; they can be combined. According to Gloria Sesso, a high school history teacher in Dix Hills, N.Y., who served on the task force that wrote the standards, teachers can meet a number of the goals at the same time, by "combining things to create a coherent lesson."

The standards may "seem to be overwhelming," says Geno Flores, project coordinator for the National Board for Professional Teaching Standards at UCLA. But they are intended to set a high standard, he points out. They present a lofty—but not unattainable—goal. "It's an ideal, a challenge."

The concern about content overload raises the question: Should the standards be adopted wholesale or treated as a resource to draw ideas from?

Crabtree believes the document should be implemented as a coherent whole. The standards are "absolutely not" a cafeteria from which to pick and choose, she says. According to Sesso, the standards are meant to establish "a common core" of history knowledge. If teachers take pieces from them here and there, they will be missing the point, she says.

Originally, the developers intended that educators should "take the whole ball of wax," Symcox says. However, they "tacitly agreed toward the end" that it would be "a flexible document." And, she points out, use of the document is voluntary, not mandated. "It's no Bible," adds Nash. "It has to be a resource."

Alan Hall, social studies chair at Yarmouth (Maine) High School, says his school system is using the standards as a resource bank to support what it has already decided to do in history. "We're pirating pieces here and there" to meet local outcomes, Hall says. Solomon points out that the standards are not tied to funding or assessment, so there is no penalty for ignoring them.

WHAT IMPACT?

Nash believes the history standards will be influential in three ways. One, they will prod publishers to create better books for teaching history. Two, they will encourage schools of education to ensure that future teachers of history acquire adequate subject-area knowledge. Three, they should have "a big effect on the way teachers conduct day-to-day classroom activities."

Nash says he will be "tremendously disappointed" if the standards don't encourage active learning. He is hopeful that the abundance of activities suggested in the standards—almost none of which call for students to "memorize" or "list" something—will help make students active participants in learning history.

According to Brooks, the standards will influence education professors as they formulate courses to prepare future teachers. They will also influence states and districts as they develop curriculum frameworks and guidelines. Teachers will find the "lesson and resource ideas" useful. And school boards may be swayed by the standards to bolster history when they make resource and time allocations.

Crabtree is heartened by the "extraordinary support from classroom teachers" the standards have received. The standards will "take" only if teachers like them and can make them part of what they do in classrooms, she says. Symcox hopes the standards will "open up a national discussion." For each community to revise its own curriculum is renewing, she says. But it's also important to assess, at the national level, what the disciplines should encompass.

CIVIC EDUCATION

WHILE DEMOCRACY FLOURISHES ABROAD, U.S. SCHOOLS TRY TO REINVIGORATE TEACHING OF CITIZENSHIP

JOHN O'NEIL

As the seeds of democracy begin to take root around the globe, most notably in Eastern Europe, there is growing concern that students in the United States leave school with neither sufficient knowledge about nor the inclination to act upon the rights and duties of responsible citizenship here at home. "It is a crisis and a scandal," says John Buchanan, a former U.S. congressman from Alabama who now serves as president of the Council for the Advancement of Citizenship (CAC) and chairman of People for the American Way (PAW). "At a time when we celebrate the bicentennial of our rich political heritage, we find little knowledge [among students] of the content of the Constitution or the Bill of Rights. And at a time when the whole world is in ferment in a movement for democracy, we've got record levels of apathy" in the U.S. toward the everyday workings of democracy. Concludes Richard Remy, associate director of Ohio State University's Mershon Center: "There is a deep malaise in citizenship education K–12 right now."

Hardly anyone, if asked the purpose of the common public school, would fail to prominently mention its duty to help prepare students to be participating citizens. Yet some experts believe that far too many schools lose sight of that aim somewhere between reading, math, faculty meetings,

---

This article was originally published as two articles in the January 1991 issue of ASCD's *Curriculum Update* newsletter. The second article was titled "Civic Education: Schools Aim to Link Knowledge, Active Lessons in Citizenship."

and Friday night football games. "On the one hand, citizenship education is up there in neon lights," says James Leming of Southern Illinois University. But the worthy goal of education for effective citizenship often ends up translated into dry lessons on "How a Bill Becomes Law." "It's not taught in an engaging, connected way," says Todd Clark, executive director of the Constitutional Rights Foundation. "There's more attention to theory and structure as opposed to practice and action." When schools are ineffective in teaching students the knowledge and values required for civic participation, the consequences are readily apparent. According to statistics and anecdotal evidence, a disquieting number of young adults don't bother to vote, are unprepared to join in public policy debates, or are unwilling to take part in community-building activities that are the central components of civic participation.

For example, the percentage of American 18- to 24-year-olds voting in presidential elections has never topped the 50-percent mark, lags 20 percent behind the rate for those over age 25, and has declined since 18-year-olds were enfranchised in 1972. Further, *Democracy's Next Generation*, the results of a survey completed at PAW's request, suggests that many young adults have an incomplete view of responsible citizenship: they generally equate being a good citizen with being a good person. "To them, citizenship is more about compassion and practice of the 'golden rule' than about voting or taking part in national affairs," the report says.

Many experts are counting on projects such as CIVITAS, a joint venture of CAC and the Center for Civic Education with funding from the Pew Charitable Trusts, to help turn the tide. The project, its proponents say, represents the most comprehensive effort to date to spell out what graduates prepared for a lifetime of meaningful citizenship might look like, and how schools might organize to make developing such students possible. A curriculum framework for grades K–12, CIVITAS places equal importance on civic knowledge and skills, civic participation, and civic virtue.

Civic educators also are pleased with the recent passage of the National and Community Service Act of 1990, which authorizes more than $280 million over three years. Among other features, the Act will help to establish part-time community service programs for young adults through schools or community organizations, a focus bound to help raise students' civic knowledge, awareness, and commitment. Experts say such programs are vital to ensuring an informed and participating citizenry. As Buchanan puts it: "We have to reinvest our entire society in the high office of citizen."

STUDENT INVOLVEMENT

What started four years ago in Nick Byrne's 5th grade classroom as a lesson on the First Amendment has evolved into a student-led effort to amend the U.S. Constitution.

Byrne, who teaches at Tenakill Elementary School in Closter, N.J., was teaching about the First Amendment and wanted to help students understand how it applied in their lives. So he sent them home with a weekend assignment to clip newspapers and search for public issues that caught their interest. As fate would have it, the weekend papers were full of stories on the environment and the problems of pollution and waste, and the class unanimously adopted the issue.

Beginning with a letter-writing campaign to government officials and the media, students quickly came to realize that their letters would yield only modest results, says Byrne. So they formed a club called "Kids Against Pollution"—which proceeded to grow into an international network of some 900 students, teachers, and parents seeking a saner approach to environmental waste. For their efforts, they've racked up an array of awards and been named by *U.S. News and World Report* as one of the "thousand points of light." One of their latest efforts is to offer a pro-environment amendment to the U.S. Constitution, and U.S. Rep. Frank Pallone, Jr., from New Jersey has agreed to sponsor the plan.

Along the way, says Byrne, the students have learned a variety of important (and sophisticated) lessons about how public issues are debated and decided. And although the group's efforts have included boycotts against merchants using polystyrene containers (believed to be environmentally harmful), Byrne says students have also learned that public debates are often won by gathering information and negotiating behind the scenes, not necessarily by the adversarial tactics that attract media interest. "The kids now feel that they have the power to make change through their knowledge, not with super-confrontation," he says.

In classrooms like Byrne's across the U.S., teachers are struggling to address the age-old goal of preparing students to be participating citizens in a democracy. In the face of declining voter turnouts, apathy toward public issues, and other signs of an uninterested populace, many feel the time is ripe for citizenship education to re-emerge as a guiding force for schools.

"For years public schools have issued broad statements of their intention to educate for responsible democratic citizenship," says a draft version of CIVITAS. "However sincere these statements may have been, systematic programs to educate for civic participation have yet to appear, and no more than a few students ever emerge from schools with the knowledge, skills, and dispositions to monitor and influence the public policies that affect their communities, the nation, and the world community."

A NEW 'DARK AGE'

Failure to provide effective civic education programs could eventually help to take public decisions out of the hands of many and place them in the hands of a few, warns Ernest Boyer, president of the Carnegie Foundation for the Advancement of Teaching. "Unless we find better ways to educate ourselves as *citizens*, America runs the risk of drifting unwittingly into a new kind of dark age," Boyer wrote in the November 1990 *Educational Leadership*, "a time when specialists control the decision-making process and citizens will be forced to make critical decisions, not on the basis of what they know, but on the basis of blind belief in so-called 'experts.'"

At the heart of the CIVITAS project (for which Boyer serves as chair of its national review council) is an effort to build student competence in three areas—civic knowledge and skills, civic participation, and civic virtue. Many observers feel there is convincing evidence of shortcomings in each of these areas.

Reports by the National Assessment of Educational Progress in civics have revealed some troubling gaps in students' knowledge and skills. For example, although the vast majority of 12th graders tested in 1988 could display rudimentary knowledge of civics, only 6 percent could evidence "broader and more detailed knowledge of the various institutions of government" (for example, Congress' power to override presidential vetoes) and a "more elaborated understanding" of a range of political processes (such as the role of primary elections and public opinion polls).

Further, relatively few schools have as a primary goal that students should learn the skills needed to participate effectively as citizens in a democracy. That lack has resulted, some believe, in young (and older) adults who don't see the functions that testifying at a town meeting, volunteering to help senior citizens, or casting a ballot in a public election have in ensuring the civic health of our democracy. Schools "don't really develop a realistic view of the political system and how students can have an impact on it," says Charles Quigley, CCE's executive director.

"The way civics has been organized over the years is essentially a descriptive view of public life—the lives of mayors, governors, the president, and so on," adds Joseph Julian, director of civic education at the Syracuse University Maxwell School of Citizenship and Public Affairs. "Very little attention has been given to what the role of the citizen is in all of this." As a result, he says, students "are conditioned to think of citizens as being observers, not as policymakers."

Finally, the notion of civic virtue proposed by CIVITAS, some believe, addresses a vital concern not reflected enough in school curriculums or society at large. Richard Remy, associate director of the Mershon Center at Ohio State University, says such problems as juvenile crime and high dropout rates can be traced back to—among other factors—a sense among young people that they are disconnected from the core values that characterize community. "Many of our young people lack a sense of civic responsibility, a sense of commitment to basic core values that we hold important," he says.

Students need to be taught how to balance private with public good, and they need to learn—and care about—problems such as poverty and homelessness, Maxine Greene of Teachers College, Columbia University, told participants at a curriculum conference convened by ASCD last summer. "One of the most frightening things I see in schools . . . is not giving a damn," she said. She cited the example of a teacher who took a group of students to a New York City grocery owned by a Korean merchant who was attempting to outlast a prolonged boycott over an alleged racial incident. "That, to me, is as important as lessons in the history of justice or of modern democracy," she said.

A Balanced Approach

Effective programs to prepare students for informed democratic participation must address students' civic knowledge, participation, and virtue simultaneously—a tricky balance that some believe is typically the exception rather than the rule. Many civics programs are grounded in the didactic teaching of governmental functions without giving students a chance to experience civic debate; others offer occasional chances for participation but don't ensure that students master the knowledge and skills required to inform that participation. The developers of CIVITAS argued over the ordering of the three organizers in the K–12 framework, but each part is essential to an effective, cohesive program, says Diane Eisenberg, former executive director of the CAC.

Supported by a $1-million grant from the Pew Charitable Trusts, CIVITAS is the result of two years of work by a framework development committee, a teacher advisory committee, and a national review council. When published, it will provide a guide to curriculum developers and textbook publishers for planning civic education programs. "We hope that the state departments of education, especially, that are responsible for curriculum frameworks which have the most influence on textbook adoptions will be interested" in using CIVITAS, says Quigley.

Quigley compares CIVITAS to efforts of the American Bar Association to bring experts together, develop model penal codes, and make them available to various states and jurisdictions. CIVITAS, too, brought together experts from many fields to reach a consensus on the attributes of effective citizenship and how curriculums might be organized to help students become good citizens. Although the framework proposes scope and sequence, goals, and objectives for civic education, it is not a complete curriculum but instead should serve as a point of departure for curriculum deliberations, its developers assert. "This is not a national curriculum that's being inflicted on teachers," says Eisenberg.

PUSH FOR PARTICIPATION

While experts agree that civics programs need to continue to emphasize knowledge and skills, much of the attention in the field is being directed toward expanding opportunities for student participation. "If the point were just to get students to mature into voters who watch television news diligently and pull a voting machine lever every few years, traditional civics courses would suffice," reasons Benjamin Barber, director of the Whitman Center for Culture and Politics at Rutgers University. "But if students are to become actively engaged in public forms of thinking and participate thoughtfully in the whole spectrum of civic activities, then civic education and social studies programs require a strong element of practical civil experience—real participation and empowerment."

In New York State, for example, schools have looked to a variety of sources to fulfill a new state requirement that all students take a one-semester "participation in government" course before graduation (usually during the senior year). The aim of the requirement is to bridge "the gulf between knowing the structures and functions of government and being able to participate within it as a citizen," says Kenneth Wade, chief of the state education department's social studies bureau. Students in some schools, he adds, are serving as interns in political campaigns and participating in community service projects, among other activities.

Syracuse University's Julian, who helped to develop a course to fulfill the New York graduation requirement, says students learn how to study issues and policies and then apply the methods they've learned to a local issue. "Students seem to enjoy the process of examining local issues because it gives them a sense that they're shaping the public discussion of those issues," he says. Materials developed at Syracuse are being used with 25,000 students statewide, he said.

Byrne, the Closter, N.J., teacher, stresses that involving students in participatory experiences requires that they learn the civic knowledge and skills they would likely be asked to learn in a traditional curriculum. After studying environmental issues firsthand, his pupils often "became more knowledgeable than the people they were talking to," he says.

SENSE OF HOPELESSNESS

For a variety of reasons—ranging from changes in the ways public issues are debated to the realities of overcrowded and undersupported classrooms—many schools encounter difficulties in attempting to put into practice the ideas outlined in CIVITAS and other reports on civic education.

One important reason young people sometimes appear indifferent to democratic participation is the same one that adults cite: many Americans feel they can't make a difference. With the advent of PACs, innumerable "specialists" of every stripe, and misleading political campaigns, it's as difficult for students and teachers as for the public at large to make sense of complex public issues. "I think there's a feeling of hopelessness among young people, and also among adults, about their ability to make a difference in the democratic process," says Donna Fowler, issues director for People for the American Way.

Stephen Janger, president of the Close Up Foundation (a group that promotes citizenship education programs) says last fall's [1988] national budget fiasco is a case study on how difficult it is to follow public policy issues, let alone participate more fully in them. "Politically, people went back and forth so often, with the White House changing its mind, and Republicans voting with Democrats, and Democrats voting with Republicans, that maybe only Congressional staff really knew what was going on," he says. "If I were an 18-year-old, I might walk away from the whole thing in disgust."

Moreover, involving students in debating issues such as U.S. involvement in the Persian Gulf or the relative merits of allowing a controversial group a public forum is considerably harder for teachers than giving a lecture or assigning material in a textbook, some experts say. James Leming of Southern Illinois University notes that teachers are "under incredible pressure to cover content." Opening up the classroom as a forum to have students debate controversial issues sometimes ends up taking a back seat. "Teachers I know have taken six months just to establish a climate" where informed debate can take place, he adds.

Others note that given the tendency for assessment to drive instruction, programs will continue to focus on basic content more than hands-on experiences in participation. "It's much more difficult to assess if a young person's got the [requisite] skills to engage in consensus building or conflict management to lobby the city council to build a playground at 4th and Green streets" than whether that student has mastered some isolated facts about civics, Remy observes.

Further, Remy questions whether schools, as opposed to other institutions, are even in a very good position to teach students about coalition-building or effective lobbying. It may be, he says, that schools should focus on cognitive skills and knowledge and allow students to learn participation skills in other ways—for example, through an internship or service project.

Finally, a revamped program for citizenship will encounter the daily realities facing teachers: overcrowded classes, lack of parental support, and students who may rarely read newspapers, or who come to school malnourished or abused, notes Fowler. "When teachers see that, the idea of teaching kids about voting, or about participation in the community, must seem ludicrous."

SPARKING CHANGE

Those involved with the development of CIVITAS, however, believe the framework can help spark change that will overcome some of these obstacles. Eisenberg says she expects CIVITAS will have "great ramifications for the way that civics will be taught" in the years ahead. And Quigley notes that until this project, "nothing had been done as rigorously or comprehensively" to provide teachers and curriculum developers with a clear description of what might be done to help students become better citizens. Adds John Buchanan, president of CAC: "What we hope to do is to help reform civic education throughout the society, using this resource as a platform from which to build."

Whatever the success of CIVITAS or other efforts to boost students' civic competence, global events are providing regular reminders of why democratic government requires better-informed and participating citizens. Jan Urban, a Czechoslovakian teacher who lost his job in 1977 as one of two teachers who refused to sign a government statement condemning a human rights group, spent the next 10 years employed as a stable hand, a forklift driver, a construction helper, and a bricklayer.

Fresh from his work organizing Civic Forum (a pro-democracy group) during the 1989 revolution in Prague, Urban last fall told participants at a conference sponsored by the U.S. Education Department that Americans must not forget that democracy functions only with the sustained involvement of its people. "That beautiful right given by democracy, the right not to care" can only be kept, paradoxically, through an informed, active citizenry, he said.

SEEKING COHERENCE IN THE SOCIAL STUDIES

CHARTING A COURSE FOR A FIELD ADRIFT

JOHN O'NEIL

"One wonders what is left to be said of a field which uses a loose confederation of separate subjects for its content and has little or no agreement regarding its goals and objectives," concluded a book published by the National Council for the Social Studies in 1977.

If such a critique of the social studies still rings true, it's not from a lack of effort by would-be reformers. The past five years have been dominated by an array of proposals aimed at providing a new coherence to the social studies. While the field may have drifted from its traditional core of history, geography, and civics during the curricular reforms of the 1960s and '70s, these subjects have returned to prominence. Citing low student achievement in history and geography and increasing voter apathy, numerous scholars are now recommending a rethinking of the traditional content areas—with the understanding that new teaching methods, better materials, and greater integration of the social sciences are vital components of an updated model for the social studies.

As with any reform movement, attempts to reshape the social studies have sparked a spirited debate over such questions as what learnings are of most worth. In the opinion of some experts, however, prospects are improving that the field can navigate between both the formless, content-starved 'mini-courses' that punctuated the '60s and '70s and the arid parade of

This article was originally published in the November 1989 issue of ASCD's *Curriculum Update* newsletter.

names, dates, and places that marked traditional courses in the preceding decades. This article reports on projects attempting to do just that.

Of the many fronts in the social studies reform movement, perhaps none has captured more attention than the move to greatly expand the teaching of U.S. and world history. Led by such scholars as Diane Ravitch, historian at Teachers College, Columbia University, and Paul Gagnon, historian at the University of Massachusetts, the push to restore history to its preeminence in the social studies curriculum has resonated through several recent projects.

"This has been nothing less than a watershed in the history of social studies development," says Charlotte Crabtree, director of the National Center for History in the Schools, which is funded by the National Endowment for the Humanities.

A common charge of advocates for more history is that the curricular trends of the past few decades sharply curtailed the amount of time devoted to the discipline. Ravitch, for example, has argued that the study of history was frequently displaced by electives, an array of 'mini courses' on contemporary topics, and special interest programs in everything from consumer education to gun control. John Patrick, director of the Social Studies Development Center at Indiana University, says that the period from the late 1960s to the early 1970s was "a Golden Age for attention to the behavioral sciences in the curriculum, but since then it has receded."

A number of recent projects, however, seek to restore history—and its companion, geography—to the core of the social studies.

For example, California is now implementing a new history-social science framework that proposes, among other features, three years each of U.S. and world history between grades 4 and 12. The framework also departs from traditional survey courses in that the courses focus on different time periods (with some review), to minimize unnecessary repetition and encourage more in-depth study.

Last year, the Bradley Commission on History in Schools voiced a need for a "history-centered" curriculum in grades K–6 and at least four years of history instruction in grades 7–12. The knowledge and "habits of mind" gained from history study, the commission wrote, "are indispensable to the education of citizens in a democracy." Asserting that historical study must focus upon broad, significant themes and questions, rather than the memorization of facts without context, the commission went on to suggest several alternative frameworks and potential themes and topics of study.

While commissions and scholars debated the need for more history study, the school reform movement is credited with guiding more students into history classes. As evidence of this shift, federal data show that between 1982 and 1987, the number of students taking at least one U.S. history survey course increased from 76 to 87 percent, while the number of students taking a world history course grew from 33 to 44 percent.

Although many historians and educators are delighted with the prospects of a resurgence in history teaching, the trend worries others.

Writing in *The Social Studies*, Ronald Evans, education professor at the University of Maine at Orono, asserted that "the current revival of history is hopeful in that it may start a meaningful dialogue, but the general thrust of the revival so far has been wrongheaded, emphasizing more history, taught as history, as the chief means of ensuring adequate cultural knowledge among our youth. More history, taught as history, is not the answer. We must find a way to revise the teaching of history so that historical data are brought to bear directly on the larger questions facing our nation and the world, questions that impinge on students' lives."

Evans and other critics of the current movement for more history teaching say that if the subject is taught only as a chronological narrative, with teachers forced to cover enormous chunks of time without making connections to today's issues, students will continue to be ignorant of the past and the implications it holds for contemporary problems.

Francis Hunkins, education professor at the University of Washington, says the experiments in inquiry-based social studies during the 1960s and '70s—frequently the target of proponents of history-dominated study—were sound attempts to refocus social studies from an endless series of names and dates to a setting that enabled students to learn how historians and other social scientists approach problem solving. "The social studies should truly be history and the social sciences," he says. "I would hate to see social studies defined narrowly."

The National Commission on Social Studies in the Schools, in a report to be issued this month, attempts to resolve the tension by recommending that history, along with geography, serve as the "matrix" for the social studies, with topics and concepts from the social sciences woven into courses at all levels.

Geography Heats Up

Although debates over the teaching of geography have received less attention than those over history, by some measures it is geography that has experienced a more serious decline. While about 40 percent of all high school students take both a U.S. and world history course, only about 15 percent take one in geography. Gilbert Grosvenor, president and chairman of the National Geographic Society (NGS), asserts that the discipline "has all but disappeared from America's classrooms." As a consequence, a Gallup Poll last year found that Americans aged 18–24 ranked last of nine nations on a geographic literacy test.

Such recent projects as the California framework and the new guidelines from the National Commission on Social Studies in the Schools strongly endorse reestablishing history and geography as the pillars of the social studies. "History, placed in its geographic setting, establishes human activities in time and place," the California framework asserts. "History and geography are the two great integrative studies of the field."

One promising sign of a resurgence in geography study is that several disciplinary organizations have combined to provide a model of what needs to be taught. *Guidelines for Geographic Education: Elementary and Secondary Schools,* a joint publication of the National Council for Geographic Education (NCGE) and the Association of American Geographers (AAG), provides a blueprint for action. Since its release, the Geographic Education National Implementation Project (GENIP), which involves AAG, NCGE, NGS, and the American Geographical Society, has issued two follow-up reports that recommend "themes, key ideas, and learning opportunities" for grades K–6 and 7–12.

Last year, NGS launched a $40-million effort to boost geography study in the schools. The group's projects include a network of alliances in 27 states that provide opportunities for teacher training and classroom materials. By working with state officials, school administrators, and teachers, NGS hopes to "create a powerful force for broad systemic change" that will boost geographic literacy, says Grosvenor.

Beyond Civics

A primary goal of teaching history and geography, of course, is to help students make informed decisions as they participate in civic life.

Increasingly, educators are arguing that having students memorize the branches of government or the names of their state's senators is insufficient to prepare them to participate in democratic problem solving.

Education for Democracy: A Statement of Principles, issued in 1987 by the American Federation of Teachers, the Educational Excellence Network, and Freedom House, said civic education would be strengthened through "a more substantial, engaging, and demanding social studies curriculum," including the history of the United States and of democratic civilization, the study of American government and world geography, and at least one non-Western society in depth.

Paul Gagnon, an advisor to the Education for Democracy project and principal investigator of the Bradley Commission, suggests that "the increased pushes for history and for citizenship are complementary."

Although *Education for Democracy* was endorsed by educators and legislators across the political spectrum, it raised the ire of some who argued that following its tenets would result in a nationalistic, ethnocentric portrayal of America's involvement with other governments and cultures. The report urged that democracy be taught as "the worthiest form of government ever conceived," but that such an approach should not be misconstrued as promoting unbalanced discussion in social studies classrooms on topics about which "good democrats can and do differ." However, an article appearing in *Social Education* argued that the report represented "an avowedly nationalistic bias. . . . Clothed in the rhetoric of concern for democracy, the recommended concern for history is a narrowly defined portrayal of progressive democracy pitted against totalitarian oppression," a framework challenged by some historians, charged author William Fernekes, a Flemington, N.J., social studies and Spanish teacher and member of the research advisory committee of the National Council for the Social Studies.

In the citizenship arena, statements such as *Education for Democracy* appear to touch a raw nerve among both social scientists who dispute its heavy dose of classical history and global educators who worry about skewed treatment of issues that cross international boundaries.

A growing trend in civic education is toward "participatory citizenship," reports Walter Parker, associate professor of education at the University of Washington.

In one of a series of articles on participatory citizenship that appeared last month in *Social Education,* Benjamin Barber, director of the Whitman Center for Culture and Politics at Rutgers University, suggested that: "We need programs that require students to perform community service, that empower them in pertinent school decision-making processes, that give them practical political experience, and that make them responsible for developing public forms of talk and civic forms of judgment. These will not be found in civic courses alone."

Parker says that schools need to move on three fronts in civic education: (1) helping students learn not only the structures and procedures of local and national government but also those of political theories and debates manifest in the U.S. Constitution, (2) organizing school life to enhance civic virtue (the disposition to act on behalf of the public good), and (3) supporting sustained dialogue about public problems.

In 1985, New York heeded the call by mandating a "participation in government" course for high school seniors. An array of programs incorporating such strategies as community service and participation in public issues have been developed to meet the requirement.

Another sign of increased interest in civic education is the development of CIVITAS, a project sponsored by the Council for the Advancement of Citizenship (CAC) and the Center for Civic Education, and supported by the Pew Charitable Trusts. ASCD Executive Director Gordon Cawelti* serves on the project's national review council. Chaired by Ernest Boyer, president of the Carnegie Foundation for the Advancement of Teaching, the CIVITAS working group is developing a curriculum framework to advance citizenship in the schools. A report expected in 1991 will aid curriculum developers in integrating civics throughout the curriculum, says Diane Eisenberg, CAC co-director.

OTHER TRENDS

Besides the broad changes suggested for teaching history, geography, and civics, social studies experts point to several other trends. Among them:

---

*Gordon Cawelti retired from ASCD in June 1992.

• *A move toward more content in the early grades, and a weakening of support for the 'expanding environments' curriculum.*

Influenced by "test-driven nervousness about the three Rs," elementary schools have gradually reduced the amount of time devoted to social studies, says Parker. According to Jean Craven, co-chair of the curriculum task force of the National Commission on Social Studies in the Schools, social studies is typically taught in the elementary grades for only 11 minutes per day.

Crabtree and others assert that the "expanding environments" or "near-to-far" organizer in the early grades, which focuses on home, family, neighbors, and the local community, is needlessly repetitive and simplistic. Diane Ravitch of Teachers College, Columbia University, argues that the framework "persists today because it is the status quo," though it is unsupported by cognitive psychology research. Crabtree adds that because the "near-to-far" organizer brings many students into contact with things they already know—for example, the facts that they belong to a family or shop in supermarkets—"elementary principals have said: 'forget the social studies, kids know that anyway, and concentrate on skills.'"

Several curriculum models, such as the California framework, propose that appropriate myths, stories of heroes and heroines, and biographies be more widely used to enrich content in the early grades.

A 100-member committee currently reviewing the Shawnee Mission, Kan., social studies program was "influenced considerably" by such proposals, says social studies coordinator David Wolfe. The district plans to begin a new framework that emphasizes "people making a difference," moving between studies of "people of the world," biographies, and the local community in grades K–3.

Craven says that while "a lot of school people are not interested in changing these themes, which are serviceable, they are very interested in reorganizing and rethinking the content" of the early grades. The commission's new report "collapses several years of the expanding environments pattern into two or three, respecting the principle of teaching back and forth from what is familiar to what is new, but respecting also that children should not be taught the obvious."

• *Closer attention on content selection to allow greater depth.*

Experts from every conceivable vantage point have criticized the tendency in the social studies to sacrifice depth for coverage. The typical American history survey course, for example, comprises everything from Mayans to moon landings, says historian Gagnon. "We are, as far as I know, the only country in the Western world that tries to teach the whole of our history to students in a single year. It's just insane."

The Bradley Commission report, the California framework, and the curriculum task force report of the National Commission on Social Studies in the Schools all emphasize the necessity of choosing rich, integrative topics.

Parker concludes that, "the real challenge facing the social studies curriculum now is in the area of content selection." Simply dictating more history or geography alone won't decide what topics "will give us the most mileage," he says. Although professional groups and commissions are providing some models of what themes and topics are most worth pursuing, legislators and special interest groups also hold sway, and educators will be challenged to develop appropriate guidelines, Parker adds.

A corollary notion is that if schools succeed in selecting the best possible questions and topics, greater depth will provide more opportunity for critical thinking.

Fred Risinger, an Indiana University professor and president-elect of the National Council for the Social Studies, says there is a growing realization among social studies educators "that students need to do much more in the way of analysis and critical thinking."

Similarly, Hunkins says that, too frequently, social studies "is presented as a series of answers to be learned." Social studies, he adds, might model the tactics of good science instruction, which calls upon students to actively investigate problems or questions, gather and analyze evidence, and propose answers.

• *Infusion of a global perspective in the social studies curriculum.*

Fueled by technological and other changes that are diminishing national boundaries, many educators are proposing that more time be devoted to the study of other nations and their interrelatedness with the United States.

In a report issued early this year [1989], the National Governors' Association (NGA) said that international education "must become part of the basic education of all students." NGA called for a world history requirement for all students and more foreign language study.

The Study Commission on Global Education, a 19-member panel funded by the Rockefeller Foundation, has called for an infusion of a global perspective across subject areas. The panel's 1987 report concluded that "there is a strong connection between citizenship education, as a traditional and essential component of education in the United States, and a global perspective in that education. . . . The increasing internationalization of society and interdependence among peoples and nations brings a new dimension to the citizen role and places a special responsibility upon our educational institutions to develop citizens able to function effectively in that world."

• *Increasing emphasis on the study of economics.*

Economic literacy is an essential component of education for citizenship, points out Ronald Banaszak, vice-president of educational programs at the Foundation for Teaching Economics. However, too few students are sufficiently acquainted with key economic principles to make use of them in everyday life.

A survey of 8,200 high school seniors carried out last year by the Joint Council on Economics Education (JCEE) found that only 34 percent could correctly answer questions about such concepts as inflation or Gross National Product. Further, only 15 states require that students take an economics course, and just 28 states require economics to be taught in any form.

In releasing its findings, the JCEE recommended that all students take at least one course in economics, that economic principles be integrated throughout the social studies curriculum, and that teachers be better trained to teach it. Economics proponents must contend with numerous other topics for limited space, however. Says William Walstad of the University of Nebraska–Lincoln, who co-authored a report on the JCEE survey: "All too often economics is simply left out of the list of required subjects. . . . Our schools provide separate courses to make certain that kids learn math and science. The same will be necessary for economics."

TEXTBOOKS AND TEACHERS

Numerous experts contend that bringing about the rich discussion of important concepts in history, geography, civics, and the social sciences called for by scholars will require dramatic changes in the quality of school textbooks and in the training of the teachers who will use them.

Attempting to satisfy the skills and content guidelines of as many jurisdictions as possible, social studies textbooks all too often read like a two-minute review of the earth's history.

Gilbert Sewall of Teachers College, Columbia University, who reviewed 11 textbooks for a project sponsored by the Educational Excellence Network, charged that while "a riot of colors and compartmentalized content may excite textbook buyers . . . the atrophied, fragmented narrative in these textbooks signals their developers' belief that the story of the American past cannot by itself sustain the interest of today's students."

In the November 1989 issue of ASCD's *Educational Leadership* magazine, Harriet Tyson and Arthur Woodward suggest that students' lack of historical knowledge "can be attributed mainly to inaccuracies caused by excessive compression of text and by misconceptions fostered through the avoidance of controversial issues."

Proponents of the California framework claim that, because the state represents 10 percent of the textbook market, better textbooks will result from publishers' efforts to meet the framework's requirements. However, others argue that publishers are not willing to risk being stuck with a product that may not sell well outside California.

Patrick of the Social Studies Development Center notes that "pressures are being exerted that publishers cannot resist; these will perhaps lead to more academically sound products," but, he adds, given their limitations, textbooks need to be supplemented with other resources.

There are numerous obstacles, as well, to ensuring that the social studies are better taught. Teacher preparation, for example, has been criticized for failing to produce teachers competent in both content knowledge and teaching strategies.

Groups such as the Bradley Commission are suggesting that social studies teachers in middle and high schools be required to have earned at least a minor in history. In addition, the training required to transform content knowledge into skilled lessons shouldn't be neglected. The teaching of history "can't be the old history that was taught as dry facts," says Marjorie Wall Bingham, a Bradley Commission member and founder of the 400-member Organization of History Teachers.

Better selection of content and a broader repertoire of pedagogy are needed to reverse assessment results such as those reported by Diane Ravitch and Chester Finn, Jr., who found that more than two-thirds of America's 17-year-olds were unable to place the Civil War in the correct half-century. "We think students are taught such things," Craven says of these findings. "But if it wasn't tied to a big picture, it wasn't any more memorable than the 3 million other things they were taught."

NEED FOR BALANCE

According to many in the field, debates over the social studies curriculum are perhaps slightly less polarized now than in the past. The work of the National Commission on Social Studies in the Schools, a group composed of scholars and practitioners from every segment of the field, is viewed by some as a balanced set of guidelines on needed change in the social studies.

The recommendations of national commissions, though, are notoriously slow to reach the average classroom. Frameworks developed by the National Council for the Social Studies, the Bradley Commission, the State of California, and the National Commission on Social Studies in the Schools will be broadly distributed. When local curriculum developers begin work, says Parker, they want to know the recommendations of commission scholars, but they also "know how to hear advice without necessarily taking it."

The major groups associated with social studies reform will plow ahead, nonetheless. The Bradley Commission will soon issue a new book expanding upon its earlier work. The National Commission on Social Studies in the Schools plans to publish a book next year and will describe its new plan this month at the National Council for the Social Studies annual meeting. Also, the National Center for History in the Schools is working on an array of projects, including a description of essential learnings and national surveys of curriculum guidelines and teacher licensing. As Bradley chair and historian Kenneth Jackson suggests in the commission's new book, *Historical Literacy*, "the final decade of the 20th century may be more receptive to curricular reform than at any time in the past eight decades."

Section 4

SCIENCE

REINVENTING SCIENCE EDUCATION

REFORMERS PROMOTE HANDS-ON, INQUIRY-BASED LEARNING

SCOTT WILLIS

In Lisa Nyberg's classroom at Brattain Elementary School in Springfield, Oreg., 3rd and 4th graders are learning about simple machines. The classroom is a flurry of activity, as children take apart broken toasters and other household appliances, trying to identify the simple machines within. Students examine and test the mechanical workings intently, discussing their ideas with their partners. A child disassembling a tape recorder forms the theory that pushing a certain button works a switch. Another child is consulting the resource books scattered around the room, searching the index of *How Things Work* for "vacuum cleaners." When the children discover inexplicable components—such as electrical circuits and computer chips—they are eager to learn more.

Across the country, in Michele Bartlett's earth science class at Rundlett Junior High School in Concord, N.H., 8th grade students are participating in an international ozone monitoring project. Using filter-paper badges, students collect smog data locally and then share their findings via the Internet with students at 80 other schools around the world. Bartlett's students also graph and analyze the data. In the process, they learn vocabulary such as "nitrous oxide" and "parts per billion" without having to resort to rote memorization. Students also submit their

---

The articles in this chapter were originally published in the Summer 1995 issue of ASCD's *Curriculum Update* newsletter.

data to the Air Quality Board, the governor, and the National Student Research Center. Because they care about air quality, and because they are collecting real data to be shared with others, students take their work seriously.

If these students had been born only a few years earlier, their experiences in learning science might have been starkly different. Science education has traditionally followed the "teaching by telling" approach. Teachers have relied heavily on textbooks and lectures to convey large quantities of information, and students have been expected to memorize reams of facts and terminology. Hands-on experiences have typically been limited to "cookbook labs" with outcomes known in advance, not real investigations. In most classrooms, science has been presented as an inert body of knowledge to be assimilated, rather than a process of inquiry and a way to make sense of our world.

The traditional "telling" approach has allowed science teachers to cover a great many topics. But the quality of student learning that it has yielded has proven disappointing, experts in the field say. Many students can parrot what they've been taught, but their understanding of science concepts is often seriously flawed. Students' prior misconceptions, for example, stubbornly resist change.

Even on standardized tests, which emphasize recall over reasoning, student achievement has been lackluster. According to the most recent data from the National Assessment of Educational Progress, "Compared to 1969–70, average [science] achievement in 1992 was higher at age 9, essentially the same at age 13, and lower at age 17."

Perhaps worse, the "telling" approach bores and alienates many students, who stop taking science courses as soon as possible. As a cohort of students progresses through high school, the number enrolled in science classes drops by roughly half each year, experts say. And the students who typically stick with science courses and succeed in them—students who are highly verbal and have good memories—do not necessarily make the best scientists.

Faced with these problems, the science education community is working zealously to reform itself. Major organizations—such as the National Science Foundation (NSF), the National Science Teachers Association (NSTA), the American Association for the Advancement of

Science (AAAS), and the National Academy of Sciences—are vigorously promoting the kinds of hands-on, inquiry-based activities described at the beginning of this article.

Reformers have set forth, in detail, a new vision for science education. Strong themes in the reform literature include the following:

• Learning of concepts should be emphasized over memorization of terms and facts.

• Students should have ample opportunities for hands-on learning. Concrete experiences with actual phenomena should precede more abstract lessons.

• Science instruction should be inquiry-based, at least in part. Students should have opportunities to pose their own questions, design and pursue their own investigations, analyze data, and present their findings.

• Teachers should explain concepts thoroughly before introducing the terminology associated with them, to ensure real understanding rather than parroting.

• Teachers should teach fewer concepts, in greater depth, rather than covering a great many topics superficially. ("Less is more.")

• Students should have opportunities to *apply* science knowledge and to make connections between what they learn and their everyday lives.

• Teachers should build on students' prior understandings and prod them to rethink their misconceptions.

• All students should become science literate, not just the college-bound. Schools should prepare science-literate citizens, not just future scientists.

• Educators should begin to integrate the various science disciplines (biology, chemistry, physics), as well as integrating science with other subject areas.

The "overarching theme" of these reform ideas is constructivism, says Dennis Cheek, who coordinates mathematics, science, and technology for the Rhode Island department of education. The focus is on "allowing students to make meaning for themselves" through active learning experiences, rather than just barraging them with information.

These reform ideas are "absolutely vital," says Anthea Maton, a science education consultant from Oklahoma City. There's a big difference between teaching from the textbook and making sure students grasp concepts, she asserts. Students who only *know* the science they're learning and students who truly *understand* it are "poles apart."

Maton cites the example of a class she observed where a student incorrectly used the term *inertia* instead of *momentum*. If teachers introduce these terms without having students explore and discuss the associated concepts thoroughly, she says, students' understanding of the terms may be limited to "if something moves, it has it."

Inquiry-based learning yields deeper understanding because it focuses on the question "How do we know?" says Gerhard Salinger, a program director at the National Science Foundation. Although teachers can simply *tell* students facts—for example, that the earth has seasons because it rotates on a tilted axis—students will understand (and remember) such concepts better if they explore why we believe them to be true. Experimenting with a flashlight and tennis balls, he suggests, can help students truly understand what causes the seasons—and gives the teacher an opportunity to confront the misconception that, during winter, the entire earth moves farther from the sun.

These reform ideas are not new, experts in the field readily admit. Yet, from his visits to classrooms, Cheek has found "there's still an awful lot of 'chalk and talk' going on." Many teachers still place more emphasis on maintaining "control and quiet" than on using active, hands-on approaches that help students gain real understanding. Implementation of these ideas has a long way to go.

MAJOR REFORM EFFORTS

Several massive reform efforts are aimed at changing that situation. The National Science Foundation, for example, is funding statewide systemic initiatives to promote reform. Other high-profile efforts include NSTA's Scope, Sequence, and Coordination project, AAAS's Project 2061, and the new National Science Education Standards project.

Scope, Sequence, and Coordination of Secondary School Science (SS&C) is a reform effort of the National Science Teachers Association (NSTA). SS&C recommends that all students study each science discipline—biology, chemistry, physics, earth and space science—every year for six years (in grades 7–12).

This approach is a radical change from the prevailing "layer-cake curriculum," in which students study earth science in 9th grade, biology in 10th grade, chemistry in 11th grade, and physics in 12th grade. (More than half of all students don't take a science course after 10th grade, and only 19 percent take a course in physics, according to NSTA literature.) The SS&C approach spreads out the study of each science discipline over several years. It also features hands-on, inquiry-based instruction.

When students study each science discipline beginning in the middle grades, courses like chemistry and physics don't seem so "foreign" to them when they are juniors and seniors, says Thomas Sachse, executive director of the California Science Project, a statewide staff development network. And because students learn these disciplines gradually, without complex math at first, they develop "an affinity, not a fear" for them, he adds.

SS&C is "trying to provide a substantial level of understanding [in each science discipline] for all students, in a society where people believe that most students can't learn it," says Bill Aldridge, NSTA's executive director. Most people, including science educators, sincerely believe that science at certain in-depth levels can't be learned by everyone, he charges. Yet the evidence against this belief—from countries that teach demanding science to a far greater proportion of students than the United States does—is "overwhelming," he says.

Typical science courses put "all the abstractions at the beginning" and emphasize the memorization of facts and processes—an approach that "basically sorts people out," Aldridge says. By contrast, SS&C modifies the curriculum in accordance with the research on how students learn. As a result, "essentially all kids can learn it."

Since 1990, SS&C has been implemented at the middle-school level at six pilot sites. Now, a newly launched study of 15 high schools implementing SS&C will "put it to the test," Aldridge says. He hopes the independent evaluation will show "dramatic" results, especially for minority students. Just showing a positive effect will not spur broad-scale change, he believes.

Project 2061, a long-term reform initiative of the American Association for the Advancement of Science (AAAS), addresses science, mathematics, and technology, says Jo Ellen Roseman, the Project's curriculum director. It focuses on the curriculum, because curriculum is "central to the reform effort." The Project's philosophy is set forth in two major publications, *Project 2061: Science for All Americans* and *Benchmarks for Science Literacy.*

Science for All Americans, published in 1989, defines "a clear set of adult literacy goals in science, mathematics, and technology for everyone," Roseman explains. *Benchmarks for Scientific Literacy*, released in 1993, suggests concepts to introduce at grades 2, 5, 8, and 12 that would constitute "reasonable progress" toward the literacy goals. Where the benchmarks and the draft national standards for science education overlap (natural science and technology), they are "overwhelmingly the same," Roseman says, and thus mutually reinforcing. (For more on the national standards, see pp. 167–171.)

According to *Science for All Americans*, Project 2061 envisions a science curriculum in which

- the amount of detail that students are expected to retain is considerably less than in traditional courses, so that important concepts can be explored in some depth. Ideas and thinking skills are emphasized at the expense of specialized vocabulary and memorized procedures.
- boundaries between traditional subject-matter categories are softened and links are emphasized, so that students will appreciate connections among ideas.
- some topics rarely found in school curriculums are addressed, including the nature of the scientific enterprise, important episodes in the history of science and technology, and the major conceptual themes that run through almost all science thinking.

Project 2061 recognizes that curriculum reform is "necessary but far from sufficient" to transform science education, Roseman says. To support other aspects of reform, AAAS is producing computer disks of descriptions of recommended professional development resources and teaching materials. (The former will be available by the end of this year; the latter, by late 1996, Roseman predicts.) Two other publications, *Designs for*

Science Literacy and *Blueprints for Reform*, will help educators design K–12 science curriculums and pursue systemic reform, respectively.

WHAT TEACHERS NEED

The national science organizations are calling for reform, and teachers are listening. Do they like what they hear?

Teachers, as a group, have mixed feelings about the reform agenda. Those in the upper grades tend to be more resistant. The teachers interviewed for this article—all of whom have received Presidential Awards for Excellence in science—were enthusiastic about the reform ideas but described a variety of obstacles to implementing them.

To take a hands-on approach, teachers "constantly have to put together materials and activities," says Alfred Benbenek, who teaches 5th grade at Holt Elementary School in Whitman, Mass. Given small budgets for science materials, teachers have to "beg, borrow, and steal" materials such as cups, zip-lock bags, wires, batteries, and aluminum foil, he says. Because these things wear out, teachers are in constant need of them.

Teachers are eager to do hands-on activities, says Jane Carey, who teaches 2nd grade at Lancashire Elementary School in Wilmington, Del. Teachers are held back, however, by lack of direction about what to do, lack of materials (without scrounging), and lack of training, which makes them "hesitant to jump in."

Carey teaches a unit on "sinking and floating" in which students test a variety of objects to see whether they sink or float, then try to turn a "sinker" into a "floater" and vice versa. The class makes a chart of materials and their properties. Then students apply what they've learned by creating a classroom aquarium. "If teachers had the time and resources," more ideas like this would flourish, Carey says.

Judy Morlan, who teaches 6th grade at Brownell Middle School in Grosse Pointe Farms, Mich., finds it "very difficult" to put constructivist principles into practice in her science teaching. She is frustrated by "a tightly packed curriculum" that she is held closely to. Because she must cover all the objectives, Morlan can't take the time to teach certain topics in depth, as she would like to do. In addition, trying to identify the misconceptions of a classful of children, and then working to change them, is very time-consuming.

"I feel like I'm in the middle," she says, because she is forced to compromise. "I'm a part-way person."

Morlan uses active learning "to make an impression on kids with the important things." For example, she has her students pace out the relative distance of the planets from the sun. "They respond to this sort of thing," she reports. She feels her efforts have been worthwhile when, for instance, a student exclaims, "Oh, my gosh—I didn't realize Pluto was *that* far from the sun!"

High school teachers are reluctant to change because they still feel accountable to colleges and universities, says Margo Murphy, who teaches 9th grade environmental science at Georges Valley High School in Thomaston, Maine. Although Murphy herself doesn't teach from a textbook, most high school science is textbook-driven, she says. To create another kind of course demands "an enormous amount of work" from a teacher. It takes "a huge amount of time to convert" to an inquiry-based approach, she says.

Naturally, given these challenges, reformers are calling for more professional development for teachers of science. Teacher training is a big component of reform proposals, says Maton. "Nobody is advocating just *telling* teachers to teach this way."

Reform should *focus* on teacher education—both preservice and inservice, says Marvin Druger, chair of science teaching at Syracuse Univerity and president of NSTA. "That's where the action should be." Many reformers are urging that undergraduate science courses become inquiry-based as well. Future teachers who have learned science in 300-seat lecture halls will not know how to foster active learning, they assert.

TAKING ON TEXTBOOKS

In the reform literature, "textbook-driven" has become a pejorative term. Reformers of science education have criticized textbooks for abetting the "teaching by telling" approach.

Science texts in the United States differ from those used in other countries, says Senta Raizen, director of the National Center for Improving Science Education. U.S. textbooks "treat many topics in a scattershot fashion," whereas those in other countries treat fewer topics, in greater depth, and include far less review.

But U.S. texts are beginning to change, Raizen says. Textbook publishers try to follow state guidelines, she notes. "They're not nasties." But they can't prescribe how motivated teachers will be to encourage students' own investigations rather than lecturing from the textbook, she adds.

One 11th grade textbook that anticipated the reform movement is *Chemistry in the Community*, developed in 1982 by the American Chemical Society. Now in its third edition, the book is "still considered rather nouveau," says Sylvia Ware, director of the Society's education division.

Chemistry in the Community was designed to correct the "mismatch" between chemistry instruction and students, Ware says. Most high-school chemistry serves best as an introduction for those who intend to earn a bachelor's degree in the subject—"but of course most students won't do this," she points out. Instruction is too abstract and too mathematical, Ware charges. "Chemistry doesn't have to be a quantitative discipline from Day One."

Unlike a traditional text, *Chemistry in the Community* examines issues in the community, to teach "chemistry for citizenship." The book is designed around eight issues: water needs, conserving chemical resources, petroleum, food, nuclear issues, air, health, and industry and its role in society.

Students using the text make lots of decisions and apply chemical knowledge, Ware says. In the first unit, for example, a scenario describes a "fish kill" in an imaginary river. Students investigate why the fish died, then hold a town meeting, where the facts come out. Then they must decide how to handle the problem.

"We're trying to rehabilitate the utilitarian," Ware says. "Knowledge can be useful—that's not a negative! If knowledge were only abstract, we'd never have got out of caves," she jokes.

GOING TOO FAR?

Despite widespread enthusiasm for reform, some science educators fear that reform ideas may be taken to extremes.

"There seems to be a [misconception] that all science at all grade levels should be learned through inquiry," says Audrey Champagne, a professor of chemistry and education at the University of Albany (SUNY). Champagne finds this view too one-sided. In the early grades, inquiry-based learning can help students develop knowledge and reasoning skills that will enable them to learn in more traditional ways ("book learning") in the upper grades, she believes.

The heavy emphasis on inquiry may be an overreaction to the current overemphasis on facts, Champagne says. "Education in the United States is characterized by pendulum swings to the extreme."

Inquiry-based instruction is "a good idea in moderation," says David Haury, director of the ERIC Clearinghouse for Science, Mathematics, and Environmental Education. As students, "we all benefit from a *mixture* of experiences."

In today's climate of reform, there is a readiness to denigrate textbooks and lectures, Haury says. But when students' curiosity is aroused, they are receptive to reading or listening. And if students are to become science literate in 12 years of schooling, "some things must be told to them." Therefore, teachers should seek a "happy balance," Haury advises. "You don't have to throw away one [approach] to do the other."

Haury also has concerns about the "less is more" philosophy. Teachers embrace the idea, he says, but they are uncomfortable with having to defend the practice. Teachers are placed in an awkward position when they must respond to administrators or parents who ask, "Why aren't you teaching this formula or that set of facts?"

Paring down the curriculum in keeping with the "less is more" philosophy ought *not* to be done on an individual-teacher basis, says Carolee Matsumoto of the Education Development Center. It's "risky" for teachers to take a stand on their own; they are too vulnerable to attack. Instead, the school or district should develop a scope and sequence with input from science experts, teachers, parents, and others, she says.

Some science teachers are uncomfortable with the notion of de-emphasizing facts and terms. Paul Pomeroy, who teaches 12th grade physics at Archmere Academy in Claymont, Del., believes the reform ideas are "incredibly good in many ways." But he also thinks the heavy emphasis on teaching concepts is "a misguided notion." What started as a push to *include* hands-on activities and opportunities to conceptualize is being "misconstrued by many as the only good way to teach science," he says.

Pomeroy agrees with reformers that "memorizing and spitting stuff back is horrible science." But students still need to know terms, facts, and how to compute, he says. And "there are times you have to get into the theory and muck through it."

College-bound students still need to develop the skill to "regurgitate" information, says C. Ford Morishita, who teaches biology at Clackamas High School in Milwaukie, Oreg. Teachers of Advanced Placement (AP) courses *must* emphasize coverage and teach prescribed labs, he adds. "You can't cut content or you're cutting students' throats on AP exams."

Raizen also advocates using a mix of instructional strategies. "I'm someone who wants to make sure we don't throw out older styles of teaching," she says. However, most classes are still textbook- and lecture-oriented, she points out. "We're far from having the pendulum swing too far—yet."

The reform notion of extending science instruction to a much broader range of students also raises concerns.

Schools can't teach just a "literacy curriculum," says Morishita. "Bright kids need another level of opportunity." He worries that schools might phase out advanced single-discipline science classes and research opportunities. "We can't do 'science for all' at the expense of the high achievers," he says.

Pomeroy also fears that "in making sure every student gets some science, we may sell the top third of students short," by "diminishing the intensity" of their instruction. He is disturbed by the prevalent attitude that bright students will thrive, regardless of their school experiences. "A good student needs to be pushed too—and farther," he says.

"Science for all" is the subject of "a raging argument," Salinger of NSF says. One way of teaching that challenges *all* students—even "the really bright kids"—is to pose open-ended "design problems," he says. For example, a teacher could ask students to design a container to get a baked potato home hot from a fast-food restaurant. This problem requires students to set a standard for what "hot" is, measure the thermoconductivity of various materials, consider structural rigidity, and address environmental concerns. Different students could be encouraged to design their solutions under different sets of constraints, depending on their ability, Salinger adds.

MOVING BEYOND EXPERIENCE

The reform movement in science education is promoting many very good ideas that make logical sense, Haury says. But how do educators actually put them into practice? "None of us have experienced it," he says of the new vision of active learning.

"Trying to get large communities of people to think beyond the boundaries of their own experience—that's the challenge."

A SNAPSHOT OF THE FIELD

SCOTT WILLIS

How does science education play out on a day-to-day basis, in classrooms across the United States? Findings from the 1993 National Survey of Science and Mathematical Education, conducted by Horizon Research, Inc., with funding from the National Science Foundation, shed light on this question. The survey gathered data from approximately 6,000 U.S. teachers of math and science in grades 1–12 about their beliefs and practices. It also gathered data from department heads and lead teachers about their schools' science programs. Some illuminating findings follow.

SCIENCE INSTRUCTION

• Although use of hands-on activities has increased since the mid-1980s, science teachers still rely heavily on lectures and textbooks.

• The vast majority of science classes use one or more commercially published textbooks or programs, including 95 percent of middle and high school science classes. At the elementary level, 75 percent of science classes use published textbooks or programs, down from 86 percent in 1986.

• Looking across all science classes, the largest proportion of class time is devoted to lecture and discussion (38 percent), followed by hands-on or laboratory work (23 percent), individual seatwork (19 percent), and nonlaboratory small-group work (10 percent), with the remaining 10 percent of time spent on noninstructional activities.

• Sixty percent of high school science and math classes listen and take notes during presentations by the teacher on a daily basis; 94 percent do so at least once a week.

• More than 60 percent of high school science classes never take field trips, 54 percent never use computers, and 43 percent never work in class on science projects that last at least a week.

TEACHERS' GOALS

• According to teacher reports, the most heavily emphasized objectives in science classes are learning basic science concepts (heavily emphasized in 83 percent of science classes overall), increasing awareness of the importance of science in daily life (77 percent), and developing problem-solving and inquiry skills (74 percent).

• Approximately 20 percent of science classes in each grade range put heavy emphasis on preparing students for standardized tests.

• Teachers in classes with high proportions of minority students are more likely than others to emphasize preparing students for standardized tests, and less likely to aim toward preparing students for further study in science and math.

TIME DEVOTED TO SCIENCE

• In elementary classes, an average of only about one-half hour per day is spent on science instruction. This figure has increased slightly over the past 15 years.

• Students are typically required to take two years of science in high school.

DIVERSITY ISSUES

• Non-Asian minority students are particularly likely to "drop out" of science and math course taking.

• The proportion of science and math teachers who are themselves members of minority groups is very low—only about 11 percent in the elementary and middle grades and 7 percent at the high school level, at a time when roughly 30 percent of students belong to minority groups.

EQUIPMENT NEEDS

• Many science teachers indicated that certain kinds of equipment they need are unavailable. The most frequently cited needs were for running water, electrical outlets, gas for burners, and hoods or air hoses in laboratories, as well as videodiscs and CD-ROM players.

This article was adapted from *A Profile of Science and Mathematics Education in the United States: 1993,* by Iris Weiss of Horizon Research, Inc., 111 Cloister Court, Ste. 200, Chapel Hill, NC 27514-2296.

TEACHERS' ATTITUDES TOWARD REFORM

SCOTT WILLIS

Do teachers embrace the reforms in science education that national organizations are advocating?

The 1993 National Survey of Science and Mathematical Education provides some insights. Conducted by Horizon Research, Inc., with funding from the National Science Foundation, the survey asked approximately 6,000 U.S. teachers of math and science in grades 1–12 about their training, pedagogical beliefs, and instructional practices. Here are some highlights from the findings:

Teachers Support Some Reform Ideas . . .

• Nearly all teachers believe hands-on activities should be part of science instruction.

• Most teachers believe that science instruction should provide students with concrete experiences before exposing them to abstract treatments. About 84 percent of high school teachers, and more than 90 percent of teachers at other levels, hold this view.

• Most teachers believe that students learn best when they study science in the context of personal or social applications. More than 90 percent of teachers at the elementary and middle school levels hold this view, as do 86 percent of teachers at the high school level.

• Most teachers support the use of cooperative learning in science classes. More than 80 percent of teachers at the high school level, and more than 90 percent of teachers at other levels, hold this view.

. . . But Resist Others

• Teachers are divided on the idea of emphasizing "depth over breadth." Only about 70 percent of elementary and middle grade teachers, and fewer than 60 percent of high school teachers, agree that science and math instruction should provide deeper coverage of fewer concepts.

• Many teachers resist the advice of reformers to teach science concepts *before* teaching the terminology associated with those concepts. Nearly one-third of teachers in grades 1–4, increasing to more than half of high school science teachers, indicated that "it is important for students to learn basic scientific terms and formulas before learning underlying concepts and principles."

• Although the reform literature calls for de-emphasizing factual learning in science, many teachers report that they emphasize this objective in science classes. Half of elementary science classes, and nearly 2 out of 3 in the middle and high school grades, put heavy emphasis on learning "important terms and facts in science."

• Many teachers doubt that heterogeneous grouping is the way to ensure success for all students. Roughly 3 in 10 teachers of grades 1–4 believe that students learn science and math best when grouped with peers of similar abilities. At the high school level, more than 7 out of 10 teachers hold this view.

• Although reform advocates tend to be critical of science textbooks, most science teachers are pleased with the quality of their textbooks. About 3 out of 4 teachers rate their science textbooks "good" or better.

ATTITUDES DIFFER BY GRADE LEVEL

• Elementary teachers tend to be confident in their ability to use reform-oriented strategies such as cooperative learning. However, many do not feel confident in their ability to teach a number of elementary science content areas.

• High school teachers are more likely to have extensive preparation in their subjects, but they are less supportive of reform-oriented teaching techniques, less confident in their ability to use them, and less likely to do so in their classrooms.

This article was adapted from *A Profile of Science and Mathematics Education in the United States: 1993,* by Iris Weiss of Horizon Research, Inc., 111 Cloister Court, Ste. 200, Chapel Hill, NC 27514-2296.

THE IMPACT OF NATIONAL STANDARDS IN SCIENCE

NATIONAL STANDARDS SEEN AS A CATALYST FOR REFORM

SCOTT WILLIS

Science, like many other subject areas, will soon have a set of national standards to bolster the efforts of reformers. Developed by the National Research Council (an agency of the National Academy of Sciences and the National Academy of Engineering), the *National Science Education Standards* have been widely disseminated in draft form. The final version is expected to be published this fall.

Unlike some similar efforts in other subject areas, the science standards take a systemic approach. Beyond spelling out important science content, they describe the kind of teaching, professional development, and assessment the field should provide. The draft document also includes "program standards"—criteria for judging school science programs—and "system standards," which address resources and coordination at the state and federal levels.

Not surprisingly, the science standards promote the major themes in the reform literature. The standards document states the following principles, among others, at the outset:

• All students should have the opportunity to attain higher levels of scientific literacy than they do currently.

This article was originally published in the Summer 1995 issue of ASCD's *Curriculum Update* newsletter.

• All students will learn all science in the content standards.

• All students will develop an understanding of science that enables them to use their knowledge in personal, social, and historical contexts.

• Learning science is an active process.

• For all students to understand more science, less emphasis must be given to some science content and more resources must be devoted to science education.

Development of the standards began in 1992, with broad input from scientists and science educators. The fourth and last round of review began in December 1994. Close to 40,000 copies of the draft document have been distributed, half to individuals and half to focus groups of teachers, professors, businesspeople, and scientists.

"I am relieved to say that most of the responses are very positive," reports Angelo Collins, director of the National Science Education Standards Project. One complaint some reviewers have made, however, is that the draft document is too long. "No one has suggested something to take out, though," Collins notes wryly. Other reviewers have criticized the standards for failing to capture adequately the *quantitative* aspect of science—a concern that will prompt some revisions, Collins says.

The content standards focus on fundamental concepts—the "big ideas" such as motion, force, matter, energy, evolution, and genetics—rather than bogging down in numerous topics, factoids, and technical words, says Rodger Bybee, who served as chair of the working group on science content standards. Bybee is associate director of the Biological Sciences Curriculum Study (BSCS).

The content standards also attempt to broaden science learning beyond a narrow focus on life, earth, and physical sciences, Bybee says. Therefore, they include several other categories as well: science and technology, science in personal and social perspectives, history and nature of science, unifying concepts and processes, and science as inquiry.

According to the standards document, inquiry "involves making observations, posing questions, examining books and other sources of information to see what is already known, planning investigations, reviewing what is already known in light of experimental evidence, proposing answers and explanations, and communicating the results."

The content standards represent fundamental concepts that *all* students should grasp, Bybee says. "We're focusing on the question, 'What should all citizens know and be able to do?' not 'What do students need to know to get into graduate school?'"

The standards are "silent" on the question of how the curriculum should be organized, Bybee points out. They do not pass judgment on the layer-cake curriculum, interdisciplinary approaches, or AP courses, for example. States and districts must determine what form the curriculum should take, he says.

TEACHING STANDARDS

Although the science standards also address teaching, they *don't* say, "This is the one way to teach," notes Karen Worth, who served as chair of the working group on science teaching standards. Worth is a senior associate at the Education Development Center and a faculty member in the graduate school of education at Wheelock College.

According to the standards, teachers of science should plan an inquiry-based program for their students; guide and facilitate learning; continually assess their teaching and students' learning; create environments that provide students with the time, space, and resources needed for learning science; develop communities of science learners; and actively participate in the ongoing planning and development of the school science program.

Because the standards promote science as inquiry, they ask teachers to help students become inquirers who learn basic concepts in the context of investigations. Worth acknowledges that this role will not appeal to all teachers. "There are teachers out there who still do not believe philosophically in teaching for understanding rather than [dispensing] information," she says. "If you're in the 'they-really-should-know-these-facts' camp, you won't want to do this." Teachers who want students to construct their own understandings, on the other hand, will find the standards "an important validation," she believes. These teachers "tend to be viewed as the fringe," she says. "Now they will be validated as the center."

The bottom-line message of the assessment standards is that educators should collect information about what students understand for a *vari-*

ety of purposes—not just to assign grades, says Audrey Champagne, who served as chair of the working group on science assessment standards. Champagne is a professor of chemistry and education at the University of Albany (SUNY).

Currently, teachers think of assessment mainly in terms of high-stakes testing, where reliability and validity are important, Champagne says. But teachers can use creative ways to gather information to refine their teaching and planning, without worrying too much about reliability and validity. They can use various "tests" that collect data in different ways, such as short answer, extended response, and laboratory assessments.

The new emphasis on inquiry and reasoning skills poses a challenge for assessment, Champagne notes. It's relatively easy to assess whether a student can use a balance to measure mass, for example—it's harder to assess whether the student can figure out that she *needs* to use a balance. Yet both kinds of abilities are important to assess.

NOTHING NEW?

"To some degree, you could say there's nothing new in the standards," says Harold Pratt, who worked on the standards development team for more than two years. A former director of curriculum in Jefferson County, Colo., Pratt now directs an elementary science program for BSCS. The ideas reflected in the standards have been widely accepted in the field for many years, Pratt notes. Yet "they are far from being implemented," he says. Implementation has been "our Waterloo."

The standards should be neither slavishly followed nor dismissed out of hand, Worth says. "This is not a perfect document, and it should not be followed perfectly—but it should be seriously considered."

The response of many teachers to the standards, however, is "You must be kidding," Worth concedes. Teachers' resistance is not so much a reaction to the philosophy embodied in the standards as to the fact that assessments and resources are not yet aligned with that philosophy. Even some teachers who fully endorse the standards say, "I'm not going to touch these until the rest of the world agrees and provides the resources we need for implementation." Worth calls this attitude "a well-founded cynicism."

Educators should not expect that teachers will pick up the standards and use them directly, Pratt says. "This is not a document that tells you what to do in your classroom tomorrow." The standards are "not a how-to document," Worth agrees. Instead, they are "a guide for decision making"—a set of criteria against which to weigh policy decisions, from the school level to the national level.

Perhaps unfortunately, the scope of the national standards does not, for the most part, extend to higher education, Pratt notes. "That piece is yet to be done—and it's an important part of the system."

The standards are one strategy for moving reform forward—not a panacea, Pratt says. But they will serve as "a catalyst for improvement," he believes. "They will focus our attention." Science educators should get acquainted with the standards and use them as a focus of dialogue and discussion, he advises.

Although the standards document is only in draft form, "the signs are that it's already had a big impact," Collins says. The standards are exerting an influence on state curriculum frameworks, textbook publishers, and professional development offerings, she says. The major organizations in science education are all promoting their implementation, she adds. For example, NSTA has already published *A High School Framework for National Science Education Standards* to help educators create programs based on the standards.

"The harder task lies before us," Bybee cautions. "It was relatively easy to develop the standards. But translating them into programs to help all students achieve higher levels of scientific literacy will be a tremendous task," he says. The "scaling up" will require a concerted, national effort. States and districts will have to devote resources to the endeavor, as will the U.S. Department of Education, the National Science Foundation, organizations such as NASA, and private foundations. "It's their move now."

The final version of the standards, anticipated next fall, will be sold by National Academy Press. For more information, contact the National Science Education Standards Project, 2101 Constitution Ave., N.W., HA 486, Washington, DC 20418; (tel.) 202-334-1399.

Section 5

THE ARTS

LOOKING AT ART
THROUGH NEW EYES

$\blacklozenge$

VISUAL ARTS PROGRAMS PUSHED TO REACH
NEW GOALS, NEW STUDENTS

JOHN O'NEIL

Cutting pieces of orange construction paper to make pumpkins at Halloween. Making turkeys at Thanksgiving. So-called "holiday art." Those are the memories that many of us have of our art classes in school.

But art is conceived more broadly at Big Ridge Elementary School in Chattanooga, Tenn. Employing a philosophy known as Discipline-Based Art Education (DBAE), teachers at Big Ridge incorporate the disciplines of art history, criticism, production, and aesthetics into their curriculum. Art is also integrated with other subject areas. "Art is no longer 60 minutes on Friday" devoted to creating holiday art or crafts, says Principal Mary Uchytil. Instead, art is an integral part of many of the units that teachers develop; it's woven into history, literature, and even math.

Is the school's approach paying off? Uchytil thinks so. "Whoever thought you could discuss Matisse with a 2nd grader?" she jokes. Yet students are learning much about different forms of art, periods of art history, and how to look at art with a trained eye—in addition to producing art themselves. "The kids talk about art, which they never did before," says Cynthia Swope, who teaches 2nd grade. Several of her students who have attention deficit disorder seem to excel in art, displaying impressive critical thinking abilities, she adds. Moreover, some students are showing the

The articles in this chapter were originally published in the January 1994 issue of ASCD's *Curriculum Update* newsletter.

influence of art lessons in other ways. "Parents have told me that their children ask for art reproductions for Christmas," says Uchytil. One 3rd grader went to Washington, D.C., with his family on vacation and spent his $20 travel budget at the National Gallery of Art on a book about Impressionist painter Edouard Manet, she recalls with delight.

Art programs such as the one at Big Ridge are the silver lining in a very cloudy national landscape. Despite presidential endorsements, pronouncements from blue-ribbon panels, and polls showing the public's support of art, art educators in many areas are struggling to put into place comprehensive programs that equip all students with the skills and knowledge they need, advocates say. Although up-to-date national statistics are scarce, much of the available data is cause for concern. The amount of instructional time devoted to art in elementary schools declined between 1962 and 1990, according to a survey by the National Arts Education Research Center at the University of Illinois at Urbana-Champaign. A 1988 report by the National Endowment for the Arts found that only about half of all students in grades 7–8 take a visual arts course; and the participation rate drops to 21 percent in grades 9–10 and 16 percent in grades 11–12. Moreover, art supporters say many local art programs have been cut back: arts specialists have lost their jobs and funds for classroom materials and trips to art museums are drying up.

Education in the visual arts has never had a stronghold in the basic curriculum, and the school reform movement launched in the early 1980s did little to change that. Driven by concerns over basic skills and economic competitiveness, the reform movement barely addressed the arts (generally conceived of as music, theater, and dance in addition to the visual arts). Instead, mathematics, English, and science drew the interest of most reformers. "The arts have never achieved the super status of mathematics, science, social studies, and English," says Charles Fowler, director of National Cultural Resources, Inc., and a featured speaker at ASCD's upcoming Annual Conference. "People do not connect the arts to what they consider the purpose of education—to get a job, to get into college, to do well in life. They don't connect the arts with that."

Arts educators suffered a symbolic setback when former President Bush and the nation's governors unveiled national goals for education in 1990. One goal stated that students should demonstrate competence in challenging subject matter in mathematics, science, history, geography, and English—but the arts were ignored entirely.

Experts in art education would like to think the field is rebounding, however, and the national goals are a case in point. After the arts were omitted from the national goals, arts supporters went on the offensive, lobbying publicly and loudly for the benefits of good arts programs. As a result, Congress is now considering legislation that includes student competency in the arts in the revised national goals. In addition, national standards in the arts are expected to be issued this month. The new standards attempt to right the imbalance of visual arts programs that focus solely on producing art. "The potential impact of these standards is very large," says David O'Fallon, staff director of the Arts Education Partnership at the Kennedy Center and former director of the Arts in Education program at the National Endowment for the Arts. "At the very least, the document represents an enormous amount of good thinking" about what all students should know and be able to do in the arts, he says. "That is a major step forward."

Still, the articulation of standards is only one hurdle on the road to better art programs. Many experts believe that art educators must do a much better job of convincing policymakers and the general public that a solid grounding in art is as essential to a general education as the traditional basics. For that to occur, art educators must make a better case for the benefits of studying art, as well as make their programs more relevant to students who aren't "art stars," as one expert puts it. The way in which the visual arts and the other arts have been taught "has left the impression with parents and superintendents, and principals—the people who become the gatekeepers of the curriculum—that if you're not gifted or talented, there's no way for you to excel in the arts, and the arts are not relevant," believes Leilani Lattin Duke, director of the Getty Center for Education in the Arts, which promotes DBAE. "The arts have not been taught as cognitive subjects—subjects that have a base of knowledge that, like math and science, you can only get if you study these subjects."

"We have something unique to offer," Fowler agrees. "We do facilitate communication within and across cultures. And we teach a different kind of perception and understanding that you really can't get any other way. If you don't have the arts, you don't have a complete education." If art educators make such cases persuasively, experts hope, perhaps art education will overcome its rocky start and join the school reform movement as a full partner.

ARTS FOR ALL

The recent public furor over federal funding of controversial art projects may seem a world away from the typical art program in a local public school. But similar public attitudes about art influence both domains.

First, there is the public's tendency to view as exceptional those who are "good" in art. In public discourse about art, this means artists are often viewed somewhat suspiciously, especially when they seek taxpayer money to underwrite their controversial projects. In public schools, it has led art programs to be tailored to the relatively few students highly skilled at producing art.

Second, an attitude persists that art cannot really be taken seriously because artists themselves appear to have few standards or criteria for what is to be valued or worthy of academic study. Thus, in the big picture, art is considered a frill—something to entertain us, but not important enough to deter schools from their primary mission of preparing students for college or work.

These are the kinds of attitudes that art educators must counter if art education is to become a more prominent part of the school curriculum. Art educators have high hopes for more comprehensive programs that enrich the lives of all students. But even before the recent highly publicized debate over federally funded art, educators found themselves in a Catch-22. To gain public support, art educators need to broaden the scope of their programs and alter its focus. But without public support, art education will lack the resources (such as space in the curriculum and funding for staff development) to undertake such a transformation.

"We've gone through a terrible [period of] public attitudes condemning the arts," says Fowler, an arts education consultant who sees connections between events such as the controversy over grants awarded by the National Endowment for the Arts and the struggles endured by local school art programs. "We're in a position in art education where we've got to counter these influences and bring to the public a truer understanding of art and art education."

"The case is strong for art education," Fowler adds, "but I don't think the case is being made strongly enough."

IMPORTANT LESSONS

What *are* the benefits of a strong curriculum in the visual arts? Art educators point to several ways students gain from studying art.

Elliot Eisner, professor of education and art at Stanford University, suggests that art offers students an alternative to the "one right answer" approach so characteristic of some other subject areas. Spelling and computing, Eisner points out, emphasize conformity and single correct answers. In art, by contrast, "there's an opportunity for youngsters to recognize that there are multiple solutions to problems, that they can affix their own individuality onto their work in a way that many of the other subjects do not provide," says Eisner. "That is a very important lesson."

In addition, a good visual arts program literally helps children learn to "see" the world around them with new understanding and insight. "The ability to 'see' is not an automatic consequence of maturation," Eisner believes. Visual arts programs can help children see the world with an aesthetic frame of reference; recognizing the qualities of form, color, shape, and light in the surroundings, for example.

Moreover, Eisner and others point out that all cultures have used the visual arts to create and share meaning. All of the art forms, Eisner says, allow humans to say things that they could not say in other ways. Although it may seem esoteric, the ability to communicate through the arts—both as one who produces and one who is communicated to—is as vital as being able to spell or count. "What we're talking about is helping youngsters become multiliterate—literate in the sense of being able to access and create meaning from the variety of forms that humans have historically employed," Eisner continues. "That's one of the things that parents ought to want for their kids."

RETHINKING PRACTICE

For myriad reasons, such arguments have not yet won art education the status in the curriculum sought by its advocates. Many art educators believe that the field must be redefined if it is to play a larger role in the movement to transform schools. The task at hand, they say, must include rethinking who art education is for and how it is taught.

In many school districts, experts say, students receive a modicum of art instruction in elementary school (an hour a week or less), often consisting of brief lessons focused on producing art. Sequential curriculums that introduce students to other aspects of art—art history or criticism, for example—are rare. By the end of elementary or middle school, students with obvious talent in producing art are encouraged to continue taking elective courses. Generally, these are "studio" courses in which students use their creative abilities to make various works of art. Those students not talented or motivated enough to take studio courses are left by the wayside.

"The reality is that current practice is directed toward the talented studio kids," the "art stars," says Dwaine Greer, professor of art and director of the Art Education Program at the University of Arizona. Other experts point out that for every student who will, perhaps, earn a living in the art world, many more students need an education that will help them to become enthusiastic and knowledgeable consumers of art. "If the only goal of arts education is to identify and nurture talent, then the majority of students can't be expected to care much," Ruth Mitchell wrote in a recent issue of *Basic Education*. "On the other hand, students with talent need to learn as much as others about art history, criticism, and values, not to mention receiving training in their own field. . . . The aim of arts education must be to produce students as well educated in the arts as they are in mathematics, science, and other academic subjects."

Judith Burton, professor and coordinator of the program in Art and Art Education at Teachers College, Columbia University, decries the attitude that art instruction ought to be focused on students who possess obvious talent, and that art instruction for others is somehow a waste of time. "It seems to me as unthinkable to say we won't teach children art in secondary school or upper elementary school because they're never going to become Rembrandts as it would be to say we're not going to teach English because they're never going to become Wordsworths," she says.

But if *all* children are to be served by more comprehensive and substantive programs in the visual arts—programs that call upon students to do more than just produce art—what should their instruction consist of? Discussion of this issue has been fueled in recent years by a debate over the merits of a philosophy of art instruction called Discipline-Based Arts Education (DBAE).

ENTER DBAE

A decade ago, the Getty Center for Education in the Arts, a Los Angeles program operated through the J. Paul Getty Trust, was launched to promote DBAE and to support its implementation in schools. According to the DBAE philosophy, students should have broad and rich experiences with works of art in four ways:

- by making art (art production);
- by responding to and making judgments about the properties and qualities that exist in visual forms (art criticism);
- by acquiring knowledge about the contributions artists and art make to culture and society (art history); and,
- by understanding how people justify judgments about art objects (aesthetics).

Art production, art history, art criticism, and aesthetics are the "foundational disciplines" that comprise DBAE. In addition, the Getty Center suggests that art instruction be based on written, sequential curriculums, although it prescribes no single curriculum.

The DBAE philosophy existed prior to the Getty Center's formation, but the Center's efforts sparked a lively debate in the field over differing goals for art education. Some critics felt DBAE would water down instruction in art production; others believed it might stifle students' creativity or self-expression; still others felt that instruction for gifted art students might suffer. Such concerns continue to be directed at DBAE.

The Getty Center "has provoked a very important and very timely debate in the field," says Burton. "There is no doubt that art education as generally constituted across the United States and also in Western Europe is mostly made up of 'studio,' and often studio not very well taught." But Burton, for one, doesn't think that educators need to adopt the DBAE approach to improve art education. "We really need to rethink how studio is taught," she says. Studio art can be enhanced through the fluid integration of "acts of making and acts of appraising," in Burton's view. "Good art teachers have always done some version of making and appraising" art in their classrooms, she says. "They did not need DBAE to tell them what they were doing."

Bernadette O'Brien, facilitator of ASCD's Arts in Education network, also has concerns about DBAE, saying the approach is too focused on artists of the past, and that the studio part is not made important enough. "Personally, I think it's more academic than studio," and reflects the Getty Center's emphasis on developing future "museum-goers," says O'Brien, who also serves as executive director of Business and Industry for the Arts in Education, Inc.

Others are concerned that DBAE's emphasis on academics may turn off students who are drawn to art courses because they find the emphasis on creating art fun and motivating. "If I were teaching a different population, I would probably do more of the art history," says Toby Needler, assistant principal of an art magnet program at New York City's Washington Irving High School. But "most of our students have had trouble in the academics, and hands-on art is something that appeals to them," she adds.

Leilani Lattin Duke, director of the Getty Center, counters that some of the reservations about DBAE come from studio enthusiasts reluctant to change their approach to meet the needs of students not necessarily talented in producing art. Art educators trained in the studio method may feel that "any time taken for reflection, for reading, for non-production activities, is detrimental to students in their courses, because the students in their courses generally are the kids who want to go on to art school," says Duke.

But as long as talent in the visual arts is equated with talent in drawing or painting exclusively, "I think we can continue to expect kids to opt out of it," Duke says. The students not currently served by art instruction "are who we're most concerned about," she adds. "They're the kids who have been turned off to the arts, for one reason or another, because they don't feel they're talented enough or that the arts have anything to say to them."

Eisner, who supports the DBAE philosophy, notes that the goals of art education have changed over time. Following the Progressive Era of education, instruction centered on "the uses of art as a personally therapeutic exercise [for students], as a release from the intellectually demanding subjects. You gave them paint and clay, etcetera, and didn't interfere." DBAE, Eisner believes, takes advantage of many of the rich possibilities for student learning in all facets of art without restricting students' opportunities to express themselves creatively.

Getty Center officials suggest that the DBAE approach does *not* mean that art production will be minimized, or that teachers are expected to incorporate each of the four foundational disciplines of art into every lesson. According to the Getty Center, art production will continue to occupy a central place in the art curriculum, but the other art disciplines will be integrated in the course of a planned curriculum to ensure that students spend time talking about art as well as making it. Students' production activities are enriched by their broader exposure to art history, criticism, and aesthetics, Duke believes.

Many of the ideas behind the DBAE philosophy are influencing the field, says Duke. For example, at least 25 states have curriculum frameworks in the visual arts that reflect DBAE's more expansive view of art education. The new efforts to create national standards in the arts and to develop an arts framework for the National Assessment of Educational Progress also show the influence of DBAE, Duke says. Taken together, these efforts confirm "the trend toward accepting the redefinition of art education that we've been talking about; that if art's going to be for all kids, it needs to be broadened."

NEW STANDARDS

The new national standards for education in the arts—expected to be issued this month—are the culmination of the most important national effort in years to redefine the character of arts education, including instruction in the visual arts. The development process forced arts professionals to directly confront the issue of what students should know and be able to do in the arts, and, by implication, what school programs will need to prepare students to do. The standards will strongly influence the ongoing debate over the philosophy and methodology guiding school programs in the visual arts, proponents say. And the standards may help to lift the arts into a more prominent position in debates over the content of a basic education for every student, supporters believe.

Addressing student proficiencies in the visual arts, music, theatre, and dance, the standards represent the first joint attempt to reach consensus and communicate to the general public what's important for students to learn in the arts, says John Mahlmann, executive director of the Music Educators National Conference and project director for the standards effort. "These will serve as a guide" to inform professionals and the public, he says, and the standards are expected to influence the development of arts curriculums and assessments, as well as teacher training. The standards are being developed by the Consortium of National Arts Education Associations under the guidance of the National Committee for Standards in the Arts.

Although the standards were still in draft form at press time, some of the prominent features of the new standards document include:

• An emphasis on an arts education that provides students with a long-term, broadly defined, sequential program of study, not merely occasional exposure or access. For each art form, standards are organized according to three interdependent areas of competence: creating and performing, perceiving and analyzing, and understanding cultural and historical contexts. The weight accorded to each area will vary according to local considerations. There are standards for grades K–4, grades 5–8, and grades 9–12.

• Two types of standards are offered. *Content standards* specify what students need to know and be able to do. For example, one draft content standard for grades K–4 in visual arts is "Selecting and using visual arts media, techniques, and processes to effectively communicate ideas." *Achievement standards* specify the understandings that students will be expected to attain by the completion of grades 4, 8, and 12. For the content standard above, for example, a related achievement standard for the end of grade 4 is that students "are introduced to, become familiar with, and are able to safely use different art materials (such as pencils, paint, clay, fibers, paper, and wood)."

• One set of achievement standards is suggested for grades K–4 and for grades 5–8. All students are expected to attain these standards. The achievement standards for grades 9–12 are divided into two levels, "proficient" and "advanced." All students, the standards document suggests, should reach the proficient level in at least one of the arts. The advanced achievement level is more likely to be attained by students who have elected specialized arts courses in the various art forms.

MIXED REACTION

Reactions to the standards as they were being developed range from wholehearted endorsement to hopes that they will help increase the prominence of arts education to doubts about whether they provide the right direction for arts programs.

"Unless we have articulated what it is we want kids to learn, the parents haven't the foggiest notion of what's going on in arts programs," and teachers base the curriculum largely on their favorite topics or teaching approaches, says Richard Pioli, who recently became an arts consultant after 17 years as director of aesthetic education in the Montgomery County, Md., public schools. In fact, Pioli worries that because the standards are voluntary rather than mandatory, their influence may be too restricted. "We have been doing voluntary arts education programs for a long time, and that is one of the pitfalls."

The standards will be extremely useful to teachers and others planning curriculum for arts programs, believes Jennifer Davidson, arts education consultant for the Oakland (Mich.) Intermediate School District. In mathematics, she points out, standards have been integrated into textbooks and have guided curriculum development. "I think they're crucial," she adds, and "we'd be foolish not to participate" in developing them.

Others are more critical. Burton was not happy with the draft version of the standards circulated for comment last fall, saying that they ignore children's developmental needs and capacities. The standards, "if enacted quite literally would desperately and unforgivably underserve children," Burton charges. "They're even worse than where we've been, and I would not happily put my name to what I see is being done at the moment."

In addition, standards may be seen as largely irrelevant in situations where educators are struggling to make do with meager resources. "There's no point talking about skills if there are no art programs," says Needler. "My concern is that there *be* art teachers in the schools. Their problem isn't knowing what to teach, it's getting their feet in the door to teach it."

Needler says national standards are not among her priorities for needed changes to support art education.

Others who have seen the draft standards suggested that the development of national standards was important, although they disagreed with some aspects of them.

"Anything that gives us equity with the basic subjects in the curriculum will be helpful," says Fowler. The standards represent a broader conception of the arts than the public and general educators will be familiar with, he adds. But Fowler questions whether the standards might be overly detailed and complex, noting that "everyone's got their favorite things they want to see taught. . . . I haven't made up my mind about the standards," he says. "I hope they'll do some good."

Eisner believes that "if standards encourage people to think more clearly about what they're after, if they stimulate dialogue among professionals, that's wonderful." But if standards are used to justify a common curriculum or common national tests, they will have a damaging impact. Educators time and again struggle with the task of specifying common content and objectives for all students, Eisner says, "and what one winds up with are hundreds of these specified objectives that teachers cannot manage" or a document "composed of such general statements that they do not perform the function for which they were intended."

CREATING SPACE FOR ART

Although the ultimate impact of the standards is uncertain, they are likely to contribute to a greater degree of agreement (if not consensus) about not only the broad aims for art education but also the details needed to flesh out those aims, experts believe. Perhaps the biggest unresolved issue is whether the school curriculum will make room for art programs that would fulfill these aims and help all students reach necessary standards of performance.

In elementary and middle schools, the Consortium developing national standards suggests that at least 15 percent of instructional time should be devoted to instruction in the arts.

In high school, where students' courses of study become more specialized and diverse, the amount of time in the curriculum devoted to the arts is much more variable. For students to achieve the competencies set forth in the standards document, there must be *some* form of course requirement in the arts for all pupils, the Consortium believes. However, the Consortium leaves open what kind of course or courses students should take. What kind of coursework would prepare students to be proficient in not only the visual arts but also the other art forms? Does a year of band, even if it fulfills a graduate requirement, suffice to make one literate in the arts?

There are no easy solutions, experts admit. One option is to offer students a quarter of a year's study in each art form, says Pioli. Such programs might give all students some grounding in the various arts, but they are difficult to schedule, he says. Another option is to revamp the first year courses in each of the art forms to be more accessible to students who might not be interested in more than a brief exposure.

Another approach to including more art instruction in the curriculum for every student is to weave it into other content areas.

Teachers of the visual arts need to "build bridges" with teachers of other subjects, says Carol Sterling, director of arts education for the American Council for the Arts. It's important to keep the integrity of the visual arts intact, she says, but "when a theme or concept is *best* taught by cross-disciplinary strategies," art teachers should be prepared to work with their colleagues to take advantage of the content of the visual arts, she says.

Bill Horning, a former middle school fine arts teacher in Bloomfield Hills, Mich., spent several years in a high school helping teachers in other subjects integrate art into their curriculum. The purpose, he says, was to make art "an integral part of what [the teachers] were teaching, not just an enhancement." So when a teacher's lessons focused on early 19th century literature, for example, their approach was not to say "these are the paintings they also did in this era." Instead, the lessons prompted students to look at the social climate and attitudes that influenced both the literature and the artwork of the period, he says. Another teacher was looking at the Great Depression, trying to get students thinking about how people of that era *felt*, says Horning. So Horning helped to collect a variety of photographs of ordinary people from that period. The lessons also addressed the impact of the photos (for example, how published photos of children at work influenced the passage of new child labor laws).

Most of the classroom teachers came up with the topics or units, Horning says; they just needed help seeing where art could fit in and getting the actual art prints or other resources to weave it all together. The teachers said students "really enjoyed" the contribution art made to their lessons, Horning says, adding that some pupils even wrote private notes thanking him for the added dimension he helped to bring to their coursework.

The interdisciplinary approach does have its drawbacks, however. Greer, for one, worries that interdisciplinary strategies in the past have positioned art as "the handmaiden of other subjects." Students may encounter art only occasionally in their various courses and not receive the comprehensive and sequential grounding in the subject they need. In addition, some experts say classroom teachers aren't yet convinced that integrated lessons are valuable—and they currently lack the support they need to move toward interdisciplinary lessons.

"The art educators' fear is that they will become totally obsolete" if art is woven throughout the curriculum, says Harriet Fulbright, director of the Center for the Arts in the Basic Curriculum. Integrating art into other subjects "only works really well if the art teachers are active partners in the whole effort," she says. "Otherwise it becomes cutesy fun and games." But, properly executed, an integrated approach should make art instruction more comprehensive, not less, she says.

Making Connections

An interdisciplinary approach requires much more collaboration between arts specialists and others, experts say. But even without the goal of integrating the curriculum, art educators need to work more closely with teachers of other subjects, school administrators, parents, school board members, and policymakers if art is to become a stronger part of the school curriculum.

A number of signs suggest that arts educators in the various art forms are working more closely together, and that art educators are trying to reach those outside the field. Groups such as the Getty Center for Education in the Arts, the American Council for the Arts, and others regularly publish information for lay persons that make the case for the important contributions education in the arts (including the visual arts) make to students.

A major challenge to the field is to make that case even more strongly and to convince policymakers and the public that art education should be part of the movement to reform general education.

"You've got to step out of the art room, and into the principal's office, and into the school board meeting room," says Sterling. As an art teacher, "I was a nut about documentation and evaluation" of what students learned from their experiences in art programs, she says.

Educators must do a better job connecting the production of art to the academic study it requires, agrees Doug Herbert, director of the Arts in Education program at the National Endowment for the Arts. The student-created art parents see displayed at exhibitions or in classrooms is rarely linked to academic objectives. "No one explains the work behind the creation of the art," he says, "so parents don't intrinsically understand it." One art educator suggests that the artwork students create and take home should routinely be labeled in some way to describe the academic content and objectives linked to the work.

"The most important thing visual art educators can do is to become articulate spokespeople on behalf of their programs," says Sterling. If the case is made more persuasively, art educators believe, public attitudes about art and art education might finally begin to shift in a more favorable direction. And the prospects of a visual arts program firmly rooted in the basic curriculum will be better than ever.

TAKING CHANGE INTO THE CLASSROOM

JOHN O'NEIL

Most experts agree that visual arts programs must be broadened to reach more students and transformed to address more than the production of art. But how do such ideas play out in school classrooms? Those involved in trying to change classroom practice along these lines say that hurdles exist, but that the rewards are considerable.

Big Ridge Elementary School in Chattanooga, Tenn., is in its fourth year of using Discipline-Based Art Education (DBAE). Principal Mary Uchytil and several teachers have attended regular training sessions in DBAE organized by the Southeast Center for Education in the Arts. The Center's DBAE program is one of 7 regional institutes supported by the Getty Center for Education in the Arts.

Big Ridge now uses DBAE schoolwide, and Uchytil feels the program has greatly enriched the school's curriculum. "What this program has done for the curriculum is immeasurable," she says. Teachers weave art into interdisciplinary thematic units, and students write about and talk about art as well as producing it, she says. One of her regrets is that the benefits of DBAE are not obvious in achievement data, she says.

DBAE "has changed my preconceived notion of how to teach art" by demonstrating the advantages of a broad approach to instruction, says Kristi Bailes, a 3rd grade teacher. Her students have come to realize that art is more than just production—and they appreciate the chance to use their different talents. "If they don't feel good about their sketching, they may feel better about writing" about art, says Bailes. In addition, students like the idea that their knowledge of art history makes them somewhat special. "It helps build their self-esteem, because they're showing something that other people don't know," she says.

Teachers typically have two primary concerns about DBAE, says Jeffrey Patchen, director of the Southeast Center for Education in the Arts. One is that DBAE is "one more thing I've got to do" in a crowded curriculum, he says. The other is "getting their hands on materials" to teach DBAE.

Cynthia Swope, a 2nd grade teacher at Big Ridge, says she had reservations about finding the time to plan for and implement DBAE. But by using thematic instruction, she finds that she "can get more art done."

A key to success with DBAE is assembling the needed resources, Uchytil says. At Big Ridge, for example, each grade has a core teacher who can help other teachers trying to implement DBAE. And the local PTA chipped in to buy art reproductions for the program.

Uchytil is sold on the advantages of the DBAE approach. "It enriches the curriculum in a way that I don't think anyone can really fathom unless they've experienced it," she says.

◆

MIXED RESULTS

JOHN O'NEIL

Recently, the Getty Center for Education in the Arts concluded one of the largest research and development efforts ever undertaken to explore how to change schools' approach to visual arts instruction. The Getty Institute for Educators on the Visual Arts, a program established by the Getty Center in the early 1980s, illustrates some of the challenges of undertaking widespread change in visual arts instruction. A group of 21 diverse independent school districts in Los Angeles County, Calif., participated in the Institute, which spanned the years 1983–1990.

Teams of teachers and administrators from the participating districts attended three-week summer sessions to learn about DBAE, among the Institute's many features. Districts were expected to develop a written curriculum for DBAE instruction. And each district was required to form a leadership team to begin implementing its plan to establish DBAE programs.

More than 100,000 students received DBAE instruction from the 1,300 teachers who received training during the project, the Getty Center estimates. An evaluation of the program found that teachers and principals attending the summer programs revised their views about the place of art in general education and about the way art should be taught. Teachers who were trained in the Institute devoted more classroom time to art instruction, and they spent more time on non-production aspects of art than their colleagues who were not trained (although production remained the predominant activity in both samples), the Center found. In addition, students of teachers participating in the Institute earned higher scores than students of non-participants on tests of art achievement.

"When teachers are provided with substantive training, when there is a district-mandated written curriculum for teachers to follow, when there is effective and ongoing leadership supported by adequate funding and resources, and when leadership is committed and enthusiastic, it is possible to establish DBAE as part of a district's regular instructional program," a report on the Institute states.

Overall, however, the project's effort to revamp art instruction in all 21 districts—when examined at the Institute's conclusion—yielded mixed results. One of the districts ultimately rejected the DBAE program; another 9 districts "paid little more than lip service" to it, the Center's report states. Five districts showed moderate levels of support and 6 districts displayed an excellent level of support. One major constraint to the success of implementing DBAE is the lack of commercially available curriculums that reflect DBAE.

The Getty Institute for Educators on the Visual Arts is chronicled in a new publication, *Improving Visual Arts Education*. For ordering information, contact the Getty Center for Education in the Arts, 401 Wilshire Blvd., Suite 950, Santa Monica, CA 90401-1455.

MUSIC EDUCATION

EXPERTS TAKE NEW LOOK AT PERFORMANCE, GENERAL MUSIC

JOHN O'NEIL

Prize-winning orchestras and choral groups, marching bands a hundred strong or larger—these are arguably the most visible signs of music's prominence in the school program.

Ironically, the success of such groups obscures, and may even contribute to, the field's Achilles' heel: the vast number of secondary students who never participate in any formal music study. According to the U.S. Department of Education, only one student in three ever takes a music course in high school, almost exclusively in performance classes that have been attacked as overemphasizing entertainment at the expense of their educational value. And while general music lessons are standard fare for primary and middle grade students, the limited amount of time devoted to music and the number of students who need to be served by each music specialist at those levels make a comprehensive, sequenced program of music learnings difficult.

"I think the biggest issue in the field is to convince people that music is more than entertainment—it's a legitimate part of the curriculum," says John Mahlmann, executive director of the Music Educators National Conference (MENC), which has 57,000 members. Educators with diverse philosophies—from Mortimer Adler and William Bennett to Ernest Boyer and John Goodlad—share the view that music is an essential ingredient in a curriculum that helps produce culturally literate students. But accom-

The articles in this chapter were originally published in the June 1990 issue of ASCD's *Curriculum Update* newsletter.

plishing that aim has eluded many school music departments, with experts complaining that secondary school programs "teach the best and forget the rest."

Still, many music educators cite reasons to be cautiously optimistic about the prospects of a stronger foothold in the curriculum. States are increasing their support for the arts, including music, through new graduation mandates. The integration of technology in the music curriculum, efforts to build student awareness of the music of other cultures, and projects to develop sounder means of assessing student progress in music all resonate strongly outside the field and are winning support. According to Charles Hoffer, a music professor at the University of Florida and current president of MENC, such trends offer "tremendous opportunities" to enrich and expand music's role in the general curriculum.

BROADER ROLE SOUGHT

In Louise Gray's 7th grade general music class at Pittsburgh's Columbus Traditional Academy, students listen to everything from Igor Stravinsky's *Rite of Spring* to Robert Johnson's "Preachin' Blues." As part of the course focusing on contemporary composers, pupils learn to listen critically to a diverse range of music, do research projects on performers, and even build their own instruments. Through the course, students gain a vocabulary that helps them appreciate and think critically about music, says Gray. Students, some of whom otherwise experience music only on MTV and popular radio, "are more open-minded and willing to discuss" the general characteristics of various musical styles and their own impressions of them after taking the class, she adds.

Gray's class, one of the subjects of a research project sponsored by the National Arts Education Research Center at New York University, addresses one of the key questions confronted by music educators nationwide: How can music strengthen its role in the general education of all students?

For a variety of reasons, experts on music education assert, the goal of musically literate graduates has been more strongly endorsed than supported in practice. Particularly at the secondary level, they say, programs have failed to adequately balance musical performance with strategies to help students think critically about music of different genres and styles, make sense of music history and theory, or become otherwise musically literate.

"I think we're still attempting to overcome the perception that the arts are either for the entertainment of the general student or for the serious study of talented students," says Richard Bell, national programs director for Young Audiences, Inc. "The great middle ground of kids—who may not be exceptionally talented but are not without ability or interest—aren't being served at all."

WINDOW OF OPPORTUNITY

While reaching out to more students and strengthening music's position in the core curriculum has been an ongoing struggle for music educators, several factors have converged to raise the stakes.

First, the school reform movement of the 1980s raised academic graduation requirements in many states, putting the squeeze on elective subjects such as music. The new mandates hit especially hard in secondary schools with a six-period day, where college-bound students, in particular, sometimes had to quit music groups for other mandated courses. As a result, music educators more than ever must seek to attract not only the most musically talented students, but also those who may have interest but no previous training.

Dan Steinel, manager of information services for the Music Educators National Conference (MENC), says music enrollments overall have not suffered during the reform era, but pockets of attrition do exist, often where six periods a day is the norm. A loss of quality to music programs is harder to prove, he says; but the exodus of talented students meant that some music directors had to face "losing the 1st clarinet, the 1st trombone, and the 1st bassoon player—and maybe that was the only bassoon player you had." Moving to a seven-period school day, says Charles Hoffer, professor of music at the University of Florida and MENC president, can "almost double enrollments in elective courses" such as music.

A second reason, also the offspring of school reforms, is the passage in many states of graduation requirements in the fine arts. In 1979, only two states mandated a course in the fine arts for graduation. Twenty-nine

What Are the Goals?

The Music Educators National Conference recommends that, as the result of a K–12 music education program, every student should:

+ be able to make music, alone and with others;

+ be able to improvise and create music;

+ be able to use the vocabulary and notation of music;

+ be able to respond to music aesthetically, intellectually, and emotionally;

+ be acquainted with a wide variety of music, including diverse musical styles and genres;

+ understand the role music has played and continues to play in the lives of human beings;

+ be able to make aesthetic judgments based on critical listening and analysis;

+ develop a commitment to music;

+ support the musical life of the community and encourage others to do so; and

+ be able to continue musical learning independently.

Source: *The School Music Program: Descriptions and Standards,* Music Educators National Conference, 1902 Association Dr., Reston, VA 22091; $10.50 prepaid ($8.40 for MENC members).

states now require a fine arts course, or will phase in such a requirement by 1992, according to a recent report by the National Endowment for the Arts. Although some leaders in the music education field are disappointed that some of these new graduation requirements count courses not considered as the core fine arts (music, visual arts, theatre, and dance), there is virtual unanimity that the new requirements provide a golden opportunity to reach out to more students.

Finally, an issue framing the school reform movement's adding of academic requirements—deciding what core knowledge or skills within each discipline are most worth teaching—is forcing music educators to rethink their methods and curriculums. One result has been a push within the field to tighten its offerings, by more clearly articulating course objectives, learner outcomes, student assessment, and program evaluation methods.

"Unlike other disciplines in the curriculum, music does not seem to have clearly defined, measurable objectives," asserts Donald Corbett, associate chair of the school of music at Wichita State University. Only when music educators ensure that music "is taught in the same rigorous, sequential, and comprehensive way that other subjects are taught," he adds, will the field enrich its curricular role.

Numerous Obstacles

Restyling music education to take advantage of the current window of opportunity faces numerous obstacles, however, most experts admit.

At the elementary level, for example, instruction in music is typically required of all students, but in many instances without adequate time to permit a comprehensive, sequenced program. "If a math specialist saw students for 30 minutes a week, what kind of comprehensive math program would you have, and what would you expect students to know by the end of the 6th grade?" asks Hunter March, associate professor of music education at the University of Texas and chair of MENC's Society for General Music.

Especially at the secondary level, music educators also must fight the perception that their programs are designed more to entertain than to educate, a byproduct of the pressure to perform publicly. Though outside forces have doubtless influenced this dilemma, numerous music educators admit that the field must share the blame for sending the wrong message. An overemphasis on rehearsals and performances, fundraising drives and group trips to Disney World, the expanded number of performance groups and the opening up of musical repertoires beyond those considered traditional or classic, and the failure to attract the general student—all have contributed to a view of secondary music as more an activity than a basic subject.

Hoffer points out that music professionals strongly support the cultural and artistic outcomes of the discipline in making a case for enriching its position in the core curriculum. But those are sometimes being sacrificed to a beefed-up performance schedule filled by a dizzying array of school music groups, "In too many situations, especially at the secondary school level, the impression can be easily gained that the purpose of music in the schools is to provide pleasant activities for the students and entertainment for the community," Hoffer cautions.

While acknowledging the important contributions of performing groups such as band, orchestra, chorus, and other ensembles, many leading music educators worry that the pressure of rehearsing for frequent performances and (in some cases) competitions can divert attention from producing educational outcomes. Because enrollments in performance classes far outdistance those for nonperformance courses, an opportunity to produce more well-rounded music students is lost, they argue.

Moreover, the fact that rehearsals and performances frequently occur outside class time may undermine music's position as a curricular basic. "As music educators, we are constantly waging a battle to convince others that music is part of the curriculum," asserts Judith Delzell of Ohio State University. "Yet, when we have a heavy schedule of extracurricular activities, we imply that the music program is indeed extracurricular."

"There is a musical and artistic heritage that we need to pass along," Corbett concludes. "It's not an entertainment heritage."

'BEYOND PERFORMANCE'

The questions raised about the emphasis on music performance parallel a debate in the arts field generally. The Getty Center for Education in the Arts, for example, has been influential in vigorously fighting the notion that arts study need only focus on what students can "produce" or perform. The National Endowment for the Arts outlined a similar thesis in Toward Civilization, its 1988 report mandated by Congress. And former Education Secretary William Bennett, in James Madison High School, his 1987 report outlining his views on the secondary core curriculum, advocated a music program for all students strongly grounded in the historical and cultural roots of music.

Such views have provoked sharp debate within the music education field. Many educators say that well-managed performance groups accomplish such objectives; others argue that emphasizing history, for example, might drive students away from both performance groups and the music electives needed to attract general students.

"The last thing that's going to turn on the students we're trying to reach is a [music history] course that starts with the Middle Ages and ends in the 19th century," warns March.

"We need to question some of the assumptions underlying the 'beyond performance' movement," says Robert Cutietta, coordinator of music education at Kent State University. While lectures about music history are probably out of place in band, orchestra, or choral choruses, these classrooms do offer a chance to help students analyze and critique their own performances, thereby enriching their command of critical listening, he points out. Another way of expanding the performance group is suggested by a recent high school group's spring concert that Cutietta attended. A different student preceded each selection by explaining to the audience what the group tried to achieve in performing each piece.

"Students in performing groups should learn the historical and theoretical bases of the repertoire they perform," concludes Paul Lehman, senior associate dean of the school of music at the University of Michigan. "All courses in music," including the traditional performance classes and general music offerings for the nonperformers, "need to do that to some extent. But when kids study band, they're doing it to play an instrument."

GENERAL MUSIC

Deciding the role that performance, music criticism, history, aesthetics, and other topics should play in the music curriculum is equally important outside the traditional performance groups. Although band, orchestra, and chorus groups serve the majority of secondary students who take music, numerous music educators stress that more needs to be done to provide some comprehensive framework of music instruction for the general student.

Whether students elect a music course to fill one of the new fine arts requirements, experts say, largely depends on the field's success in reaching out to students who may want to learn about music, but not necessarily join a performance group. "More kids might be taking [music], but what do you teach them?" asks John Mahlmann, MENC executive director. "You can't give a trumpet to everybody."

The answer, some music educators believe, lies in initiating or expanding a diverse range of general music courses at the secondary level that capitalize on adolescents' natural interest in music without requiring the time commitment of performance groups.

"The goal should always be [students who are] musically educated, whether they're in a performance group or not," says Leon Burton, an education professor at the University of Hawaii and former president of the island's ASCD affiliate. He adds that, while 85 percent of secondary students are not currently enrolled in a music course, "there's more attention being given to that 85 percent [today] than at any time in the history of music education."

The payoff from this interest is a modest number of unique general music courses aimed at broad student outcomes. March says that what unifies the diverse array of general music offerings is a way of teaching rather than a common course of study. General music teachers, he says, use a variety of methods to motivate students of differing skills and interests to build musical understanding through such activities as "listening, performing, analyzing, and creating." Teachers also attempt to help students "realize that basic music elements are present in all styles and genres and exist in music of all cultures and historical periods."

One trend having its greatest impact on general classes is the growth in the applications of such technologies as personal computers, synthesizers, and electronic keyboards to composing and producing music. Formerly, March notes, "general music used singing as its only performance medium." The low cost of keyboards, however, has increased their popularity and availability.

Musical Instrument Digital Interface (MIDI) technology, for example, standardizes the output from various musical instruments so that the computer can record, notate, and play it back. This has considerably enhanced the ability of students, particularly general students, to compose music, says Sandy Feldstein, former president of the Music Industry Conference and currently president and CEO of CPP/Belwin, a print music publisher. "This means that a student can compose music in four or five parts by putting in one line" and adding extra parts. Further, MIDI can be used with many of the personal computers schools previously have bought for other subjects, he says.

Some guidance on how to build general music offerings may come from a recommended course of study for general music expected to be issued this fall by MENC. Part of a project that will suggest courses of study in the areas of band, orchestra, choral, and general music, the guide will give direction to teachers by suggesting sample objectives in general music K–12, according to Linda Mercer of the Ohio education department, who is coordinating the general music task group's effort.

One challenge in developing general music courses will be finding and training teachers for them. Music educators typically are trained with an eye toward helping students learn to play an instrument and perform. And some are wary of teaching general music students, who may be less motivated or musically talented. "Finding ways to teach the general student, for teachers who've been prepared to do something else, is a real challenge," says Mary Palmer, a music education professor at the University of Central Florida. "For some people, it may not be as satisfying and rewarding."

Despite a growth in interest in secondary general music offerings among educators, only 2 percent of high school students ever enroll in a nonperformance course—and some of these are students also taking performance courses. Some educators complain that an opportunity to capitalize on new arts requirements is being squandered. "Everybody in music fought for those [fine arts] requirements," says Burton. "But once they were there, the band director said: 'I'm not going to teach that group.'"

AN UPHILL BATTLE

Music educators are going to have to better resolve such issues, most experts agree, to strengthen the field's place in the curriculum. Approaches to teacher training, curriculum development, and the policy arena need to be enhanced; progress in these areas will help determine if music is seen as a frill or a basic.

But while music may seem to be fighting an uphill battle compared with the support given disciplines viewed as more "practical," the ability of the arts to foster the human side of learning will always be in demand.

Lehman quotes John Naisbitt, who points out that every new technology ("high tech") introduced into society must be counterbalanced with a humanizing influence ("high touch"). "As society is increasingly overwhelmed by technology," Lehman asserts, "we feel an even greater need to express ourselves." Music, he says, is an ideal means for expression through participation.

GENERAL MUSIC COURSES OFFER DIVERSITY

SCOTT WILLIS

Four selected general music courses highlight very different approaches to providing music learnings for all students.

THE GREAT WORKS

Students taking Music Perspectives, a course offered in Baltimore County (Md.) high schools, study music from around the world and concert pieces from Bach to Bernstein. All high school students who do not elect chorus, band, or orchestra take the course.

Music Perspectives begins with roughly four weeks devoted to "music of the world's cultures," including music of Africa, India, and the Orient, as well as a variety of folk music. Then follow six units on Western art music, from the Baroque era to the present.

The course emphasizes music history and appreciation. "Every student should have some exposure" to great works of music, says Rebecca Silverstein, who teaches the course at Woodlawn High School. By studying pieces such as Handel's *Messiah* and Stravinsky's *Rite of Spring*, students learn about tone color, melody, harmony, rhythm, and polyrhythm. They also learn about the cultural contexts in which the works were created.

To keep students motivated, the course uses participatory activities. "We try to make it as active a course as possible," says James Wharton, who teaches Music Perspectives at Catonsville High School. For example, students act out the first scene of Mozart's *Don Giovanni* in a transplant, updated versions before listening to the same scene in the opera.

The course is "going over very well," says Silverstein. While about half of her students, she estimates, are resistant to the musical selections at first hearing, end-of-course comments indicate that many of these students broaden their tastes.

Contact: Rebecca Silverstein or James Wharton, Baltimore County Public Schools, 6901 N. Charles St., Towson, MD 21204.

COMPUTERS AND ROCK

Students in Music Lab, offered at Shoreham-Wading River High School in Shoreham, N.Y., use computer music systems to create compositions in rock and top-40 music styles. About 12 percent of the school's students take the course.

Students who are interested only in contemporary music get "locked out" of traditional music courses, says Tony Messina, who teaches at Music Lab. "I pick up the rockers."

In a dramatic departure from the "conservatory model" of teaching music, Messina's students work with computers, synthesizers, sequencers, and drum machines. They also learn to compose using this equipment—without first learning traditional music theory and composition techniques.

Messina requires his students to keep music journals, in which they write music and describe their reactions to music they hear. He tries to help his students become "more selective" in their musical tastes and stresses tolerance of others' preferences.

Some Music lab students may parlay their new knowledge of audiotechnology into jobs in radio, television, or film. "I'm pushing [my students] to make serious job and career choices," Messina emphasizes.

While some parents only tolerate his efforts, Messina says, other parents are supportive. The students in Music Lab, he adds, love the course. In fact, many more students wish to take the course than can be accommodated.

Contact: Tony Messina, Shoreham-Wading River High School, P.O. Box 337, Shoreham, NY 11786.

BASIC MUSIC SKILLS

Music in Our Lives "gives students an avocation" by teaching them to play guitar, keyboard, or recorder, says Ann Trombley, who teaches the course at Monticello High School in Monticello, N.Y. Approximately half the school's students take the course.

Music in Our Lives emphasizes playing and composing music, although Trombley gives basic information about the historical and social dimensions of pieces she introduces to the class. The course includes listening, performing, composing, and evaluation activities to give students a wide range of experiences.

Trombley's students may not become proficient enough on their instruments to perform publicly, but they do develop basic music skills they can build on throughout their lives. "I put the emphasis on process," Trombley says.

Besides learning to play, students compose an original blues piece over the course of the year, so they have a "finished product" when the course ends. They also do special projects on topics of their choice and keep journals of their progress.

"Students are very positive" about the course, Trombley says. "They take pride in playing an instrument, and they like to hear their music performed." Many students wish to continue their musical studies, she adds. "They ask me if there's a second class they can take."

Contact: Ann Trombley, Monticello High School, Port Jervis Rd., Monticello, NY 12701.

A CULTURAL BLEND

At Leon High School in Tallahassee, Fla., students who take Selected Musics of the Western Hemisphere study the musics and cultures of the United States, the Caribbean, and South America, and the role of African influences on them. "I'm trying to make music education relevant to all cultural segments of the school population," says Nancy Marsters, who teaches the course.

Through lectures, listening, and hands-on activities, Marsters' students learn how the fusion of three major cultures—African, Native

American, and European—has given birth to the varied musical styles of the Americas. "All of it is a mix," she emphasizes.

In the course, students learn to recognize different instruments and styles, and to "listen with their brains," says Marsters. Students also learn about the peoples who made the music. "There is no way to understand the music without understanding the culture and the times" that produced it, Marsters explains. At the end of the course, students do research on music they like and then make presentations to the class.

Selected Musics of the Western Hemisphere capitalizes on the liking most students have for the blues and reggae, but also expands their experiences and tastes. For example, many students develop "a great love of the music of the Indian peoples," says Marsters.

Contact: Nancy Marsters, Leon High School, 550 E. Tennessee St., Tallahassee, FL 32308.

Source: *Promising Practices: High School General Music*, Music Educators National Conference, 1902 Association Dr., Reston, VA 22091; $14.00 prepaid ($11.20 for MENC members).

PUSH FOR GREATER CLARITY DRAWS FIRE

JOHN O'NEIL

In making a case for a broader curricular role for music education, proponents need to do a better job of specifying objectives, learner outcomes, and assessment techniques and results, numerous educators agree. Still, others see dangers in shaping music after other disciplines, saying that aesthetic outcomes of music programs are difficult to measure.

The question of how structured and measurable a music program should be has been raised anew by a move to shift the arts away from a singular focus on production (or, in the case of music, performance). The Getty Center for Education in the Arts, through its support of discipline-based arts education (DBAE), and others argue that such a move will help build enough support for the arts to increase the number of students served by balanced, general programs.

More than ever, music programs need to articulate not just what activities were completed, but what learner outcomes were reached, notes Donald Corbett of Wichita State University. "Once we define our objectives in terms of what musically educated students should know and be able to do, we will receive the recognition and status we deserve from the education community. . . . We must start by insisting that music be taught in the same rigorous, sequential, and comprehensive way that other subjects are taught."

Student evaluation also needs to be overhauled, some experts suggest. Charles Hoffer, president of the Music Educators National Conference (MENC), says a 1987 survey conducted by the group found that only about half of music teachers are involved in student evaluations other than giving grades. And many in the field say grades are often based heavily on attendance. "The lack of adequate evaluation hinders the development of strong music programs," Hoffer asserts. "It is difficult for music teachers to ask for more time in the school day or more funds without having some clearly specified objectives and a means of assessing the achievement of those objectives."

Other caution that in the rush to state and measure outcomes, music educators must be careful not to sacrifice the field's strengths, such as its "hands-on" nature and its potential to motivate.

"Music is not like studying science or history," Mary Palmer, a music education professor at the University of Central Florida, says, in what has become a recurring criticism of DBAE. "We certainly don't want to take away the appeal of the subject matter" by downplaying performance. "When kids study band, they're doing it to play the instrument," adds Paul Lehman of the University of Michigan.

Robert Cutietta of Kent State University admits that music educators are "a little guilty" in not developing better means to measure student progress. But he worries that more assessment might lead to a greater emphasis on skills easily tested; note reading, for example, rather than skill in improvisation. "Music making is the real joy of music. That can't be measured by paper and pencil."

Many think that greater clarity about music education's goals and standards of performance is essential, however, for making the field a basic subject. "Until music is approached as a discipline of knowledge, I don't think that will begin to happen," says Leon Burton of the University of Hawaii.

Section 6

WORLD LANGUAGES

NEW GOALS, NEW WAYS OF TEACHING

LEARNING TO COMMUNICATE IN THE REAL WORLD

SCOTT WILLIS

If teachers of foreign languages have their way, never again will adults have reason to complain, "I took two years of French (or German or Spanish), but I can't speak a word of it." That cliché will become obsolete, as the focus of foreign language instruction shifts from grammar and vocabulary to communication.

This change is already well under way, experts in the field say. In U.S. schools, the study of foreign languages has moved off the workbook page and into the real world of language use. No longer do students merely learn *about* a new language and how it works; now they must also develop the ability to *use* the language to communicate. Therefore, vocabulary lists and grammar drills are giving way to activities that allow students to use the new language for real purposes. Consider these classroom scenarios:

• High school students learning Spanish write, produce, and videotape a 20-minute news program that includes news events, an on-the-scene report, weather, sports, and commercials—all presented in Spanish.

• Eighth graders studying French use the Internet to correspond with 13-year-olds at a school in southern France. The students ask their French counterparts about a typical school day, life in French communities, and what students there do for fun. They also share this information about themselves in French.

The articles in this chapter were originally published in the Winter 1996 issue of ASCD's *Curriculum Update* newsletter.

• Second-year students of Chinese prepare for a Chinese New Year's celebration, which they have read about in English and Chinese. The students design cards and invitations for the celebration, paying special attention to words and colors appropriate for the event. They also learn the words to a New Year's song.

These scenarios—all actual lessons devised by teachers—are included in the newly released *Standards for Foreign Language Learning: Preparing for the 21st Century*. These national standards are a collaborative effort of the American Council on the Teaching of Foreign Languages (ACTFL) and the national associations of teachers of French, German, and Spanish and Portuguese. Thousands of teachers had input into the finished product, which represents "a very strong consensus" of the field, says Christine Brown, director of foreign languages for the Glastonbury (Conn.) public schools, who served as chair of the Standards Task Force.

The standards emphasize that *communication* should be the organizing principle for foreign language study. "While grammar and vocabulary are essential tools for communication," the document states, "it is the acquisition of the ability to communicate in meaningful and appropriate ways with users of other languages that is the ultimate goal of today's foreign language classroom."

AIMING FOR PROFICIENCY

In promoting communication, the standards reflect the "proficiency movement" that has been making inroads in foreign language classrooms for more than a decade. The proficiency movement focuses on what students can *do* with what they know, explains Myriam Met, coordinator of foreign languages for the Montgomery County, Md., public schools.

In the past, teachers assumed that if students knew grammar and vocabulary, they could use a second language. The heavy emphasis on grammar, however, often did not equip students to interact with native speakers in real-life situations. After two years of study in high school, most students could function only as "polite tourists, if that," Met says.

"You don't really learn to speak by learning the grammar," says Nancy Rhodes, codirector of foreign language education and testing at the Center for Applied Linguistics.

By emphasizing grammar over communication, teachers turned out students who were "good at declensions but who couldn't speak spontaneously."

Over the past 15 years, researchers have been examining how students build competence in a second language, Brown says. Researchers have found that the study of grammar alone, through rote dialogues and drills, is not the best way to develop proficiency. When students are given opportunities to use the language in meaningful contexts, they develop proficiency faster—and are more eager learners. Therefore, rather than belaboring grammar, teachers should provide learning activities that "mirror real-life situations," Brown says.

"If the goal is for students to use language in real-life situations," Met says, "then teachers need to provide real and simulated conditions that allow students to communicate in authentic ways."

What makes classroom communication "authentic"? According to Met, authentic communications have a purpose. As in real life, language is used to get something done—to make a purchase or to express an opinion, for example. Authentic communications involve a true exchange of information—unlike contrived classroom talk, which often revolves around display questions such as "What is this?" or "What's the weather like?" And in authentic communications, the communicators have a shared sense of the context of their interaction.

In the past, classroom activities were contrived and "far from reality," says Lynn Sandstedt, excutive director of the American Association of Teachers of Spanish and Portuguese. Dialogues recounted the less-than-gripping adventures of "Anita y Tomas en la biblioteca," for example. Or students would practice using the conditional tense all week. Now classroom activities are more realistic: Students might role-play they are lost in downtown Madrid and ask a police officer for directions to their hotel, for example.

Compared to their peers of a decade ago, students in today's foreign language classrooms have many more opportunities to communicate in authentic ways, experts say. Students interact more with one another as they work in pairs or small groups. Classroom exercises convey real information, unlike the contrived dialogues and drills of the past. Students use authentic materials drawn directly from other cultures, such as magazines and menus. Extensive use of video, such as television newscasts, exposes students to authentic language use, as well as adding a visual context. Other technologies also provide a real purpose for communication. Through the Internet, for example, students can visit overseas Web sites and communicate with "keypals" in other countries.

Students should spend a large part of each class period expressing and interpreting meaning in authentic ways, Met advises. Group work makes this feasible. In a typical activity, a teacher might ask student pairs to find five foods they both like, or three things they will each do next Saturday. Such activities put the focus on meaning, with no teacher control over output. The exchange will be unpredictable, like communication in real life.

"Peer-to-peer interaction has a lot of benefits for language growth," Met maintains. Besides giving students more opportunities to speak, group work requires students to negotiate meaning—to make sure their language is understandable. (Teachers are often so good at "making sense out of nonsense" that students don't have to work very hard to convey meanings to them.) For novices, peer interactions may actually be better than interactions with native speakers, whose language proficiency is much too advanced, Met says. And contrary to myth, peers *don't* learn each other's mistakes, she adds.

A NEW ROLE FOR GRAMMAR

Although all agree that communication should be the overriding goal of foreign language instruction, experts are quick to point out that grammar, accuracy, and pronunciation should not be slighted. "These traditional elements are still there—but as means, not ends," says June Phillips of Weber State University, who served as project director for the standards. "We're not saying students should communicate with bad syntax and poor pronunciation," she emphasizes.

Nevertheless, some in the field worry that grammar, once dethroned, will be neglected. Some educators have misinterpreted the proficiency movement as saying "grammar is out," observes Rebecca Oxford, coordinator of foreign language education at the University of Alabama.

Many students need their teachers to present grammar in an orderly fashion, Oxford says. Teachers "have to lay it out in an organized way," she asserts. "It can't be seat of the pants or 'go home and read about it.'" The new standards acknowledge that structure is an integral part of communication and that accuracy is important, Oxford notes. "A very fluent person making a lot of mistakes won't be taken seriously."

"In German, grammar matters to communication," says Barbara Hogan Ingram, who teaches German at Pinckneyville Middle School in Norcross, Ga. "Every single ending makes a difference to meaning," she says—indicating who did what to whom, for example. Therefore, teachers need to intermingle grammar instruction with other activities. "I'm still free to teach grammar under the standards," she says, "but not as the focus of the lesson."

Scaling back grammar in teaching Chinese would be a mistake, says Madeline Chu, executive director of the Chinese Language Teachers Association. The Chinese language is "totally different" from English, she points out. But she agrees that grammar should be taught for a purpose—to serve communication—not for its own sake.

Some in the field have proposed changing the sequence in which grammar concepts are taught to better support the goal of communication, Met notes. Traditionally, grammar concepts are presented in order of difficulty, from simple to complex. Instead, teachers could present them based on their frequency in authentic speech or their flexibility and versatility—so that beginning students would not be mired in the present tense for months, for example. This idea has not yet won many converts. "What most teachers are doing is still very similar to the traditional sequence of grammar topics in the curriculum," Met says.

Teachers have made some changes, however. Some grammar concepts that are not extensively used in real speech—such as double object pronouns and certain uses of the subjunctive mood—used to be heavily emphasized by teachers, Met says. Today, such concepts receive less emphasis or come later in the syllabus. These shifting priorities reflect the acceptance that in teaching grammar, less may be more. Instead of teaching students a lot of grammar that they can't use, teachers are making sure students can use what they know in meaningful ways.

"Students can't internalize seven tenses in just two years of study," Met says. As a result, "they often speak using only one."

How much to focus on accuracy (in the use of grammar, for instance) has always been a dilemma for foreign language teachers, says Kathleen Riordan, director of foreign languages for the Springfield, Mass., public schools and past president of ACTFL. "There are times when accuracy is important," she says, "so you teach and test for it." But accuracy may be less important than communication in a role-play or interview. Teachers need to consider the goal of the particular activity, she believes.

In the past, only the accuracy goal counted, Riordan says. Now communication is taking pride of place. "We should not go off the deep end in either direction," she cautions. "What we need is moderation."

ATTRACTING STUDENTS

A prime advantage of the communication emphasis, experts say, is that students find it engaging. Students enjoy interacting with real people, reports Ingram, who teaches German. "Which is more motivating: picking apart sentences or communicating with a peer in another country?" she asks rhetorically. "Motivation is extremely important to learning a language."

Motivating students is also important because, in the past, foreign language courses have attracted only a minority of students, typically the college bound. According to ACTFL survey data from 1990 (the most recent available), only about 38 percent of students in U.S. public high schools were enrolled in a foreign language course. Most of these students take a foreign language for only two years. Only one state—New York—requires foreign language study for high school graduation.

At the middle school level, only about one-third of U.S. public schools offer a yearlong foreign language course. In 1990, only about 12 percent of students in grades 7 and 8 were enrolled in a foreign language course. On the bright side, a growing number of elementary schools are offering foreign language programs.

The most striking trend in enrollments today is the increased interest in Spanish. Enrollments in Spanish classes are "skyrocketing," says Sandstedt—a fact he attributes to the opportunities for real use, given the great influx of Spanish-speaking people into the United States. Spanish is "a very practical language," he points out. "You can step outside the classroom and use it." By contrast, "the practicality of French seems more remote—a situation that is reversed in Canada."

CHANGING ASSESSMENT

With the emphasis on communication comes the challenge of *assessing* students' ability to communicate. Foreign language teachers are rising to this challenge, experts say.

Unlike many other subject areas, the field of foreign language teaching has a history of performance assessment. "We've already been looking at alternative assessment through the '80s," Phillips says. Teachers have been experimenting with face-to-face interviews, reading and writing tasks, video clips, dialogue journals, teacher observations, student demonstrations, and portfolios of student work. "Assessment needs to be more holistic and open-ended—with all the challenges that entails," Phillips believes.

Although achievement tests are still valuable measures of what students know, teachers can test real-life proficiency—what students can *do* with the language—better through other means, Sandstedt says. For example, teachers could ask students to write a letter home as if from abroad, describing where they're living and what they did last week. To do this, students would have to use their knowledge of vocabulary, the past tense, and gender and number agreement of adjectives.

Assessment has been leading the way in the foreign language field, says Charles Stansfield, a former director of the ERIC Clearinghouse on Languages and Linguistics, who is now a testing consultant. In 1986, the ACTFL Proficiency Guidelines were published, he notes. This scale for assessing high school and college students defines four levels of foreign language proficiency: novice, intermediate, advanced, and superior. A trained tester can use an Oral Proficiency Interview (OPI) to rate a student on the proficiency scale. The OPI is a face-to-face conversation that lasts from 10 to 25 minutes.

Because the OPI requires extensive training and is expensive to administer, Stansfield developed an alternative: the Simulated Oral Proficiency Interview, or SOPI. Unlike the OPI, the SOPI is a tape-recorded test. Questions are posed on the tape. During a brief pause, the student records an answer to each question. Because the test is tape recorded, the teacher needs to be trained only to rate the student's performance, not to administer the test.

Among other tasks, the SOPI asks the student "to give directions to someone using a map; to describe a particular place based on a drawing; and to narrate a sequence of events in the present, past, and future, using drawings in the test booklet as a guide," Stansfield explains. The SOPI has been shown to correlate highly with the OPI, he adds, and more than 2,000 teachers have been trained in its use.

JOINING THE REST OF THE WORLD

Promoting communication is not the only goal of the new national standards for foreign language learning. Other major goals include learning about other cultures, making connections to other disciplines, developing insights into the nature of language and culture, and participating in multilingual communities. The standards also set forth a vision of K–12 foreign language programs for all students.

Learning a second language takes a long time, says Brown, the Standards Task Force chair. The standards "dispel the myth you read about in airline magazines—that you can get some tapes and learn another language in two weeks," she says.

To expect students to gain proficiency in a year or two of study at the high school level is "ludicrous," Brown says. Could students learn the entire corpus of K–12 mathematics in two years? she asks. Foreign language study ought to be part of the core curriculum from kindergarten through 12th grade, Brown says, to put U.S. students on a level playing field with students in other countries.

Through the standards, "we hope to show the American public what can be done with extended study," says Phillips. In other nations, students routinely begin to study foreign languages at age 10 or 11. "That's the norm in the rest of the world," she emphasizes.

Teachers of foreign languages express concern that the United States lags behind other nations in preparing its citizens to understand other cultures and to use other languages. Those in the field hope that the new standards—and the emphasis on communication—will win more people to the cause of foreign language study and help shake the public out of its complacent belief that the United States can remain a nation of monolingual citizens. Time will tell whether the public will indeed adopt the view that, as the new standards assert, "the United States must educate students who are linguistically and culturally equipped to communicate successfully in a pluralistic American society and abroad."

MAKING A CASE FOR FOREIGN LANGUAGE STUDY

KATHY CHECKLEY

Bryan Ingraham is a 5th grader enrolled in a Japanese immersion program in a Fairfax County school in Virginia. Knowing how to speak Japanese, he says, "will help me get a good job someday."

Donna Christian is president of the Center for Applied Linguistics. Learning another language teaches us to value cultural differences, she contends, which, in turn, promotes social harmony. "If we want communities to get along, people in those communities must have an appreciation for others' perspectives."

Marty Abbott is the foreign language coordinator for the Fairfax County Public Schools. Studying another language boosts cognitive ability, she asserts, basing her claim on data collected in a 1991 evaluation of Fairfax County's partial-immersion programs. The data revealed that after two years, immersion students achieved higher test scores in English language arts than did their nonimmersion peers. Says Abbott, "It backed up the research we had coming out of Canada—that just having the experience of learning a second language helps you better analyze and reflect on your own language."

To improve employment opportunities, to learn to value other cultures, and to enhance mental capacity—all are compelling reasons for studying foreign languages; all are valid rationales for promoting the study of foreign languages in public schools.

COMPETING ON A GLOBAL LEVEL

As young Bryan Ingraham is already aware, future employment options will be governed by an international marketplace, and his ability to communicate with people in other countries prepares him to compete for jobs created by a global economy.

Economic competitiveness is one of the reasons people should learn a foreign language, says Ronald Walton, deputy director of the National Foreign Language Center (NFLC).

Other experts agree. "We Americans are starting to see that knowing languages other than English is important to do business," says Abbott.

"Our economic and global stature is dependent upon our citizens' knowing other languages," adds Christian. "In the future, countries that have high-level language resources will have an advantage."

Developing and strengthening language resources in the United States is one of the goals of NFLC. The U.S. work force, Walton states, must have the skills necessary to deliver the services that "people all over the world" want. Providers of those services must be able to communicate with their international clients—clients who may not necessarily know English.

"In many countries, those who learn English are the elite," Walton explains. "If you want to provide services to people who work in the factories and live in the villages—where English is not so widely spoken—you need a basic level of understanding of the language."

Walton suggests that those with a basic level of understanding are those that possess skills that enable them to exchange information and ideas with people of different cultures. Scholastic study of foreign languages has its place in academia, he maintains, but the most critical attribute for tomorrow's workers is interactive communication.

"We don't think the name of the game is to know a language per se. What's important is cross-cultural communication—and language is a tool for that," says Walton.

CULTURAL CONNECTIONS

Effective cross-cultural communication is impossible if we don't understand the cultures of the languages used. The task force that developed new standards for foreign language educators recognized this premise and established goals that emphasize cultural awareness. As pointed out in the standards document, students who don't understand the cultural contexts in which languages are used will never truly master the languages they study.

Still, studying other cultures has benefits beyond improved global communication and a mastery of languages. Learning about other cultures helps develop citizens who embrace diversity. That attribute, says Bernadette Morris, is especially important in the United States, "a country that's so diverse culturally and racially." Morris, a foreign language consultant in North Carolina's Department of Public Instruction, agrees with other experts that learning a foreign language helps students accept different points of view. "When you learn another language, you become aware that there are many ways of looking at things."

Examining other cultures also helps students better understand their own culture, says Jose Sendra, a Spanish teacher at Plainville High School in Plainville, Conn. "We find a new appreciation for our own society and standards because we are forced to look at our culture through new and far more objective eyes," he explains. Exploring other cultures also allows us to see beyond the differences among people and recognize the similarities. All people, says Sendra, "need food, family, shelter, and love."

SHARPENING OUR WITS

In addition to the social benefits, experts say those who study other cultures and the languages of those cultures are more agile thinkers.

Cognitive flexibility, explains Marcia Rosenbusch, director of the National K–12 Foreign Language Resource Center, comes when students are able to separate words from the objects they represent.

"Take a pencil, for example. When you study another language, you come to understand that it could be called something different, according to the language you're studying." A language, she explains, reflects societal agreements made about which words will identify which objects, and when students understand this, it's "the first step they take in being open to other ideas."

A study of French immersion programs in Louisiana supports the assertion that foreign language study boosts brain power, says Rosenbusch. Research revealed that 5th and 6th grade students who received 30 minutes of French instruction every day, "significantly outperformed" students in the control group in English language arts. Other surveys of immersion programs in the United States and Canada have reported similar results.

Even studying classical languages, such as Latin and Greek, has a positive impact on academic achievement, says Robert Pamos, assistant principal at Holmes Middle School in Arlington, Va. "Knowing Latin may not enable students to communicate with other people in the world, but it gives them a fundamental understanding of the structure of language and can be a stepping-stone for learning other languages."

Pamos, who taught Latin for nine years, adds that studying Latin can also enhance students' understanding of the humanities because the language is linked to the Greco-Roman society. Abbott agrees. Knowing Latin, "helps you reflect across those centuries. Analogies and references to the myths become clear." Students may not be able to draw these connections, she says, if they don't have a Latin foundation.

A NEW BASIC?

Although foreign language educators and experts in the international arena offer convincing evidence that studying foreign languages is in our national and personal interests, the case must still be made to the public, whose majority is skeptical.

"People seem to think, 'Well, if you aren't going to use the language, why learn it?'" says Christian, and this attitude puzzles her. "I'm not sure why languages are different than other subjects," she says. "We don't expect to use high-level math and science in some occupations, but people don't suggest that studying these subjects in school was a waste of time."

This notion—that studying foreign languages should come second to studying the "basics"— was made all too clear in North Carolina.

In 1985, the state adopted a Basic Education Program that made foreign language instruction essential to a basic education. The program mandated second language study in grades K–5 and required that students have opportunities to study second languages in grades 6–12.

Some schools in North Carolina, however, have delayed complying with the mandate, says Morris, who attributes the failure to implement the standards to funding constraints as well as to a political climate that supports a basics-first emphasis in public schools.

"Schools are being judged and evaluated on how students are achieving" in reading, writing, and math, she explains. When students did not test as well in these areas as expected, foreign language study took a back seat to these "basics." What's more, local schools were given the authority to determine whether to provide foreign language programs. "There is no accountability system in place for foreign languages, and there are no penalties if schools don't implement the mandate," says Morris.

Still, Morris is hopeful that foreign language instruction will make a resurgence in North Carolina. She is heartened by recent reports that the state governor believes a focus on foreign languages should be included in the state standards for K–12 education. For her part, Morris intends to present her argument to a dubious public. "We obviously haven't done a good job of convincing others of the importance and benefits of learning a foreign language," she explains. "We always need to make that connection to the basics. We need to show that knowing a second language can help students in reading, writing, and math as well as in helping them accept other cultures."

IMMERSED IN JAPANESE

KATHY CHECKLEY

At first glance, the room resembles most 1st grade classrooms in the United States—brightly colored posters and samples of children's artwork adorn the walls; large, construction-paper numbers stretch across the blackboard; and the letters of the alphabet are posted on the bulletin board.

Wait a minute. Those aren't the ABCs most U.S. 1st graders learn! In this room, it's the Japanese alphabet that's displayed, and the language being spoken is Japanese. If the classroom feels like a foreign place to a visitor, imagine what students experience the first time they walk through the door.

Welcome to the Japanese partial-immersion program at Fox Mill Elementary School in Fairfax County, Va. The program is one of 13 such programs offered by the Fairfax County Public Schools (FCPS). The 240 students enrolled in the program at Fox Mill join more than 32,000 other U.S. students who receive part or all of their schooling in a language other than English.

"At the partial-immersion schools, students spend half their school day in classes with other immersion students," explains Marty Abbott, foreign language coordinator for FCPS. "For that portion of the day, for those curriculum subjects, everything the students see or hear is in the target language."

At Fox Mill, and indeed at all the Fairfax County immersion schools, math, science, and health are taught in the target language. "The reason those subjects were chosen is that in the primary grades, teachers make heavy use of manipulatives and hands-on activities. A teacher can take these materials and demonstrate to students what he or she is saying by using the objects," says Abbott.

When they can assign meaning to the concrete objects foreign words represent, students can make sense of what's being said. In Nahoko Nakayama's 2nd grade class, for example, students are studying mammals' body parts. Nakayama displays the tails of various mammals—such as a monkey and a donkey—and uses the Japanese word for *tail*, while students watch and repeat. Through this process, students learn Japanese and cover the content all 2nd graders at Fox Mill study. That, says Principal Dennis Nelson, is an important point to remember: "This isn't a school within a school—all students here receive the same curriculum."

Nelson also points out that the program is not targeted solely to gifted and talented students. "You'll see the same range of ability in an immersion class that you'll see in other classrooms," he says. Because of

Keys to Successful Immersion Programs

✦ Administrative, community, and parental support

✦ Qualified teachers who have near-native proficiency in oral and written forms of the target language

✦ Appropriate materials and time for teachers to prepare such materials in the target language

✦ Ongoing staff development

Adapted from *Foreign Language Immersion Programs*, by Myriam Met. Published by the ERIC Clearinghouse on Languages and Linguistics, October 1987.

this diversity, immersion teachers employ the same strategies as teachers in other heterogeneous classrooms, such as presenting the material in a variety of ways to reach more students.

This challenge is greater for immersion teachers because they must often create the materials they use. "It's difficult to find materials in Japanese that are age-appropriate, so teachers have to translate many of the materials into Japanese," says Abbott. And, although the Fox Mill program enjoys an unusual amount of support from the Japanese government and business community—namely books and technology—the bulk of the work still falls to the Fox Mill teachers. To ease the burden, Nelson compensates teachers who use their summer months translating the materials they'll need.

Immersion teachers must also cope with cultural differences. "Communication problems do exist," admits Nelson. "It's important, therefore, for administrators to understand the culture of the target language."

This point was driven home to Nelson when parents complained that one of the immersion teachers failed to keep them informed of their children's progress. "Our parents want a lot of feedback from their children's teachers," but the teacher didn't understand what all the fuss was about, explains Nelson. In Japan, where teachers are highly regarded public officials, parents seldom question teacher practices. Japanese teachers, therefore, must adjust to the expectation that they will communicate with students' families. "All the while, they're wondering why everybody is questioning what they do," says Nelson.

Immersion school principals must also be accountable to parents. If a student doesn't achieve as expected, parents are likely to blame the difficulty on the student's participation in an immersion program, "but problems persist beyond language barriers," insists Nelson. In fact, students in immersion programs usually outperform nonimmersion students. Still, Nelson agrees that keeping parents informed is critical to the program's success.

Abbott is satisfied with the success of the FCPS partial-immersion programs. Test scores are on target, and the anecdotal information she receives from parents convinces her that immersion students develop more global perspectives. "For example, in one Japanese class, a teacher asked students to figure out as many ways to say 14 as possible." The teacher expected students to offer mathematical expressions, such as 7×2 or $12 + 2$. Instead, students wanted to say the word *fourteen* in different languages. Says Abbott, "The students already realize that English is not the center of the universe and that people have different ways of saying things that mean the same thing."

But perhaps it's students who can best describe the value of programs like the one at Fox Mill.

"It's good to learn another language," says Andria Ortega, who has been studying Japanese at Fox Mill since 1st grade. Ortega recently visited Japan with her mother and several other students from Fox Mill. There for eight days, she "actually got to use the language."

Ortega, who next wants to learn Spanish, says mastering Japanese gives her a good foundation for further study: "I'll already have the experience of learning another language." And that, she believes, will make it easier for her to grasp a new language while maintaining fluency in the other language she's studied for six years. "I'll continue to speak Japanese," she says. "I'll find someone to tutor me if I have to."

EMPHASIZING WHAT LEARNERS CAN DO WITH LANGUAGE

AS ENROLLMENTS CLIMB, A NEW FOCUS ON 'PROFICIENCY'

JOHN O'NEIL

Following a bleak period of declining enrollments and a weakened national commitment during the 1970s, the study of foreign languages is enjoying a burst of popularity among students, educators, and the public. The field's strengthened position comes as leaders attempt to recast instruction from a heavy focus on grammar and translation to move toward "proficiency," which emphasizes the ability to communicate functionally in the second language.

"I came away from four years of Spanish afraid to speak it," David Edwards, executive director of the Joint National Committee for Languages (JNCL), says in explaining the popularity of proficiency-oriented foreign language programs. "Now it's not all boring grammar and word-for-word translation" exercises. "It's exciting for students to know that they can go to France and order in a restaurant or read a bus schedule."

By numerous measures, the study of foreign languages is riding a wave of popular support. The American Council on the Teaching of Foreign Languages (ACTFL) reports that the number of students in grades 7–12 enrolled in foreign language classes jumped by more than 1 million between the council's surveys in 1982 and 1985. States such as

This article was originally published in the January 1990 issue of ASCD's *Curriculum Update* newsletter.

Texas, Florida, New York, and Oklahoma have experienced 50-percent increases in student enrollment since 1983, the JNCL reports. And a study of high school transcripts by the U.S. Department of Education shows that while only one of two students in 1982 had received any foreign language credit, two of three students had received credit in a comparable survey taken in 1987.

"We're enjoying a boom cycle now—and hoping it's not just a cycle," comments ACTFL Executive Director Edward Scebold. Spanish has been a primary beneficiary of increased support, according to the U.S. Department of Education, as 36 percent more secondary students enrolled in a Spanish course in 1985 than in 1976. Twenty-seven percent more students took French over the same period, while the number of students taking German, the third most common language studied, declined by 12 percent.

Experts cite a variety of reasons for the upswing in popularity of foreign languages. *Strength Through Wisdom*, the 1979 report of the President's Commission on Foreign Languages and International Studies, may deserve some credit for building awareness of the critical importance of the field. It charged that "Americans' incompetency in foreign languages is nothing short of scandalous, and it is becoming worse." The commission recommended considerably broader commitment to foreign language studies, including expanding programs in elementary schools.

One factor behind the trend for greater investment in foreign languages is that the United States itself is becoming increasingly diverse. "There are more Puerto Ricans in New York City than in San Juan," notes Charles Stansfield, director of the ERIC Clearinghouse on Languages and Linguistics. Los Angeles, he adds, has become one of the largest Spanish-speaking cities in the world. Such trends have created a high demand for citizens able to communicate in a foreign tongue.

Many policymakers link the need for increased study of foreign languages to concerns about economic health and national security. Sen. Paul Simon (D-Ill.), who has helped drive home the importance of foreign language study to policymakers, points out that in so-called developing nations such as Botswana, "the average fourth grader has had more years of foreign language study [four] than has the average college graduate in the United States."

For the college-bound, a more pragmatic argument exists for taking a foreign language—they may not have a choice. The Modern Language Association, in surveys of institutions granting B.A. degrees conducted in 1982–83 and 1987–88, found that the percentage of institutions with a foreign language requirement for entering students climbed from 14 percent to 26 percent. Over the same period, the number of institutions requiring some foreign language credit for B.A. recipients rose from 47 percent to 58 percent. At the state policy level, the number of states requiring students to take a foreign language for entrance into some colleges rose from only three in 1979 to 18 in 1989, preliminary data from a JNCL survey suggest.

As foreign language professionals have lobbied for greater support for their field, they have pointed to an array of tangible benefits. For example, students who have taken foreign languages perform better on the verbal portion of the Scholastic Aptitude Test (SAT) than those who haven't. Students, too, are seeing that developing proficiency in a foreign language might be a ticket to a better job. Businesses "probably won't hire a French major over an M.B.A., but they'll hire an M.B.A. who has studied French over one that hasn't," the JNCL's Edwards comments.

FOCUS ON PROFICIENCY

Edwards and others believe that one trend that has helped foreign language programs attract more students is the growing influence on programs, from the elementary to the high school level, of "proficiency-oriented" instruction.

"Teachers are recognizing that proficiency is a very important concept," says Myriam Met, foreign languages coordinator for the Montgomery County (Md.) public schools, which have integrated a focus on proficiency into their foreign language programs. In a chapter on foreign languages in ASCD's 1988 yearbook, *Content of the Curriculum*, Met writes that, "unlike previous goals of language instruction, proficiency-oriented instruction focuses on what the learner *can do with language* rather than what the learner *knows about language*."

The focus on communicative proficiency is partly a reaction to what many leaders in the field claim are flaws in the popular grammar-translation and audio-lingual (ALM) methods of instruction that held sway previously, and which continue to influence many classrooms. "Neither one of them really added up to any kind of free communication," Rebecca Oxford, of the University of Alabama, says in what is a recurring criticism of the grammar-based and ALM programs.

In the proficiency-oriented curriculum, students learn to use four skills—speaking, reading, writing, and listening—to communicate in an authentic context. Grammatical accuracy, though important, is not the primary goal of instruction from the start. While some critics worry that an emphasis on proficiency may signal less commitment to grammatical accuracy, others say that as students need to use the language in increasingly sophisticated contexts, accuracy will play a stronger role. "You can't go on forever using 'me-Tarzan, you-Jane' language," says Met.

"Determining the grammar content of the foreign language curriculum should be based less on tradition and more on the communicative purposes of the learner," Met writes in the ASCD yearbook. For example, teachers have typically introduced the present tense much earlier in the curriculum than the past tense; real use might require knowledge of both from the start.

The evolution of proficiency-oriented instruction from its forerunner, "communicative competence," has been driven and underscored by the development of new assessments of foreign language proficiency. The proficiency guidelines, while providing new standards for foreign language professionals, have also provoked controversy.

Rooted in proficiency measures used by the Foreign Service Institute, the proficiency guidelines developed by ACTFL and the Educational Testing Service during the 1980s were intended to provide a common yardstick to measure proficiency in a foreign language. The guidelines feature descriptive statements of varying levels of ability in the skills of speaking, writing, reading, and listening, from nonspeakers through native speakers of a foreign language.

The development of the proficiency guidelines has been closely watched, and several authors of a series of articles published in the *ADFL Bulletin* warn against leaning too heavily on the guidelines in developing foreign language programs.

Barbara Freed of the University of Pennsylvania asserts in her article in the series that "despite the enthusiasm related to proficiency-oriented teaching and the enormous funds and energies invested in promoting proficiency standards, proficiency-based teaching, proficiency tests, and proficiency texts, members of the profession have recently started to voice concern about various aspects of the proficiency movement. . . . Has it, in fact, been the bandwagon many feared, with catchy slogans and empty balloons?"

Others urge caution in applying the guidelines to curriculum and instruction. "The use of proficiency tests may produce language programs that focus entirely on the tests and that even redesign their curricula and instruction to match the ACTFL guidelines," Kenneth Chastain of the University of Virginia writes in another article in the *ADFL Bulletin* series. "As a result, 'quick-fix,' simplistic solutions may be applied to complex, creative phenomena, which may lead to greater misunderstanding of the true nature of communication."

Edward Scebold, ACTFL executive director, stresses, however, that the guidelines are not intended to directly guide curriculum development. *Defining and Developing Proficiency,* a book ACTFL helped to publish, asserts that proficiency "considers the extent to which an individual can combine linguistic and extralinguistic resources for spontaneous communication in unpredictable contexts free from the insistent prompts and prodding of the classroom. This curriculum-free nature of the proficiency guidelines limits their direct transportability to curriculum and instruction either as learner goal statements or as learner achievement indicators."

Further, as Freed admits in her article, "When properly understood [the guidelines] have permitted a welcome and responsible escape from the tyranny of grammatically organized texts and the legacy of traditional approaches to foreign language instruction."

As experts continue to debate the advantages and potential pitfalls of proficiency-oriented instruction, many educators worry about large barriers to greater adoption of the method, such as the need for proficiency-oriented curriculums and the training of teachers in new methods. "It's what everybody thinks needs to be done," Richard Lambert, director of the National Foreign Language Center at Johns Hopkins University, says of the proficiency emphasis. But "whether it will take hold is a very tough question to answer."

Despite the widespread appeal of proficiency-oriented instruction, "it's a lot easier to write about such a curriculum than to produce one," says Met. And numerous experts say teachers who have used grammar-based curriculums for years need help to learn new methods.

Other signs are more promising. The push for proficiency-oriented instruction "has fostered a dramatic change in textbooks," Scebold believes. "There simply wasn't a market before" for such texts. "More and more, we're seeing good textbooks coming out—that's a big step," Oxford agrees.

ELEMENTARY PROGRAMS GROW

A second trend influencing the field is the growing expansion of foreign language programs in elementary schools.

"Things have really mushroomed in the last decade," Met says of the growing interest in offering foreign languages in elementary schools. "There's been a veritable explosion of foreign language enrollments at the elementary level."

There are sound reasons for beginning language study early, experts say. "Like any other subject, the earlier you start, the better off you are," says Nancy Rhodes, a research associate at the Center for Applied Linguistics and chair of the National Network for Early Language Learning. In addition, she says, it is generally difficult to learn to speak a foreign language fluently without an accent after the onset of puberty. Moreover, beginning the study of a foreign language during the teenage years has the disadvantage of catching children at their most self-conscious age. "Younger kids are not intimidated at all about imitating strange sounds," Rhodes points out.

Elementary foreign language programs are generally classified as FLES (Foreign Language in the Elementary School), FLEX (Foreign Language Experience), and immersion. FLES classes, taught all or partially in the foreign language, attempt to give students limited listening, speaking, reading, and writing skills and some cultural awareness. They typically meet two to five times per week for 20–40 minutes, and may begin as early as kindergarten or as late as 4th grade. The goals of FLEX programs, usually taught in English, are to introduce students to foreign languages, and they focus on cultural awareness and limited language skills.

Immersion programs, generally considered the most ambitious, involve teaching all or part of the curriculum in a foreign language. According to many advocates, immersion provides the greatest fluency in the foreign language and does not interfere with students' mastery of other subjects. "The bottom line is that children in immersion programs, compared to students in English-speaking programs, score as well or better in English," says Rhodes. Across the U.S., immersion programs in 10 languages are available ranging from the more common Spanish and French to the less common Arabic or Russian, according to the CAL. More than 16,000 students in 93 schools in 20 states are enrolled in such programs.

Despite the fact that immersion programs have proven the most successful at developing foreign language proficiency, FLES and FLEX programs, which are seen by many as less demanding on school programs, will probably continue to be more popular. As elementary schools begin to offer more opportunities for foreign language study, "the majority of them will probably go to some FLES-type" arrangement, Rhodes predicts. A survey conducted by Rhodes and Oxford in 1986–87 found that of elementary schools offering a foreign language component, 57 percent had regular or intensive FLES programs, 41 percent offered FLEX classes, and 2 percent used immersion.

Of more immediate concern than program type, perhaps, is increasing the overall proportion of elementary schools with any foreign language component. According to the study by Rhodes and Oxford, only 17 percent of public elementary schools nationwide offer any opportunity for foreign language study.

With a greater emphasis on early language programs, improving articulation between the elementary and secondary grades has become more important. Too many school districts that offer elementary foreign language programs, some experts say, fail to take advantage of the skills students learn in these programs and enroll many of them in a first-year middle or high school language course.

According to the national survey by Rhodes and Oxford, 31 percent of schools report that students who have studied a foreign language in elementary school must begin at the first level upon their arrival in a middle or high school. "It is wasteful of both human (teacher and student) and material resources for students having studied a language for up to six years to start at the beginning," they conclude.

"No FLES program should be started without consideration of the options open to those students who want to continue at the secondary level," Jo Anne Wilson notes in a "digest" on articulation prepared for the ERIC Clearinghouse on Languages and Linguistics. "At the outset, both elementary and secondary staff need to be involved in any planning committee," she adds, and "such planning should set realistic program goals and develop a sound curriculum."

INTEREST IN 'LCTS' RISES

A third trend influencing the reshaping of foreign language programs is a growing diversity in the number of languages offered and a commensurate increase in the number of students interested in the "less commonly taught" (LCT) languages. Among the LCTs enjoying increased popularity are Japanese, Chinese, and Arabic. In 1979, according to the JNCL, no state reported any local precollegiate program in Arabic, four reported having a program in Chinese, and three reported one in Japanese. Three states now report programs in Arabic, 18 states have them in Chinese, and 23 report having at least one program in Japanese.

While the sum total of student enrollments in these languages pales in comparison to the number of students taking Spanish or French, some school districts have gone to unusual lengths to expand offerings. At one middle school in Cincinnati, for example, immersion programs are offered in Arabic, Chinese, Japanese, and Russian, as well as the more conventional Spanish, French, and German. The program involves 16 teachers and more than 500 students, according to a CAL survey.

The study of Latin has not recaptured the prominence it once enjoyed, but it "has made an incredible comeback," adds Stansfield, director of the ERIC center. From 1962 to 1976, the number of secondary students taking Latin dropped from 700,000 to 150,000, he says. Although comparable figures are not up to date, one indicator of interest—the number of students taking the National Latin Examination—has increased from 9,000 in 1978 to 60,000 in 1986.

Schools adding less common offerings to their foreign language curriculums frequently have difficulty finding qualified teachers, several experts say. "We have a severe shortage of foreign language teachers in the U.S., and many teachers have not been able to put programs into place," says Madeline Ehrlich, founder and past president of Advocates for Language Learning.

Moreover, in the absence of better data on what works best in teaching LCTs, the growth in interest may only perpetuate ineffectual teaching and learning, worries Lambert, director of the National Foreign Language Center. To help provide some answers to key questions about the successful teaching of less common languages, the center has embarked on dual studies of how Japanese and Chinese are taught as foreign languages in the U.S., he says.

BUILDING A COMMITMENT

While foreign language educators are enjoying the current surge in popularity of their programs, many leaders in the field caution that much needs to be accomplished to make programs more comprehensive. The launch of Sputnik, they note, brought a similar increase in foreign language study that faded all too quickly.

One obvious barrier to a goal of greater proficiency in foreign languages is, simply, that students don't study them long enough. Two years of foreign language in high school and two in college, a typical arrangement for college-going students, doesn't provide nearly enough time for them to become proficient, experts warn. According to an analysis of the federal government's "High School and Beyond" study, moreover, only 60 percent of all students who take a first-level course in French, German, or Spanish continue to a second year, and only 21 percent of them go on to a third.

"The public has some very serious misconceptions about what can be accomplished in a foreign language course," Met comments. "Two years of a foreign language doesn't prepare you for any kind of usefulness any more than two years of math would prepare you to be an engineer."

The capacity of schools to increase course offerings, however, is limited, some experts admit. For example, Tennessee, which last fall mandated that students complete two years of a foreign language before entering the state's public university system, has seen enrollments in second-year language courses shoot up 150 percent between 1986 and 1988, notes June Phillips, executive director of the Tennessee Foreign Language Institute. "Frankly, that has taxed schools to the limits" she says.

The curriculum jam at the high school level may be as good a reason as any to begin language study earlier, New Jersey Governor Thomas Kean argued in a paper delivered to the ACTFL meeting last fall. "Two years of required foreign language study in high school or college barely enables the student to locate a 'Biergarten' in Bonn," he said. "What's more, we must consider the problem of curriculum sprawl—there are only so many courses that can be squeezed into a six-hour day. Therefore, it is not sensible to wait to offer languages to students until the secondary level."

The wave of interest in foreign languages over the past decade has been punctuated by "a series of small victories," Sen. Simon told ACTFL conferees at the group's annual meeting last fall. But to overcome the barriers that have created the "tongue-tied American," as he titled his book on foreign languages, "we have a substantial distance to go."

HEALTH AND PHYSICAL EDUCATION

PHYSICAL EDUCATION

PREPARING STUDENTS TO BE ACTIVE FOR LIFE

KATHY CHECKLEY

Ask physical educators to identify the most important aspect of their jobs and you'll likely be told that, first and foremost, they are responsible for helping young people acquire the skills and self-confidence they need to participate in a wide variety of physical activities—while in school and beyond. Whether students choose basketball or biking, hockey or hiking, they must make a lifelong commitment to engage in some form of regular exercise, experts say.

Physical educators can help students make that commitment by aligning instruction with the national standards for physical education and by creating curriculum and activities designed to instill within students a desire to be active for life.

EXERCISE FOR LIFE

The research is clear on this point: People who exercise on a regular basis are healthier than those who don't. Yet, despite numerous studies linking such health problems as heart disease, high blood pressure, and obesity to a sedentary lifestyle, the latest Surgeon General's report indicates that too many young people in the United States aren't getting the message and don't take part in the kinds of activities that contribute to good health.

The articles in this chapter were originally published in the Fall 1996 issue of ASCD's *Curriculum Update* newsletter.

Physical educators believe they can play a key role in reversing this trend by designing programs that (1) teach students the motor skills necessary to participate in a wide variety of physical activities, (2) help students understand the link between physical activity and health, and (3) convince even the most skeptical, least athletic of students that physical activity is fun.

"In physical education, we need to concentrate on movement," says Judith Young, executive director of the National Association for Sport and Physical Education (NASPE). "Physical education is not basketball, baseball, volleyball, or any other sport—these are the applications of what physical education is," she explains. When physical education programs focus on teaching students how to hone their motor skills, they learn "how the body works and how to keep it working," Young says.

When physical education programs also focus on fitness, students who are not high-performing athletes, "are finally finding a reason for physical education," adds Elaine Lindsey, chair of the health and physical education department at Dulaney High School in Timonium, Md. It's difficult to convince students to participate in a sport in which they do not perform well, she observes, but when the emphasis is on personal fitness, everyone succeeds, and many students, once excluded, "are finding a niche that they had not had before."

"The main idea is that it be fun—physical, but fun," says Dolores Albers, physical education teacher at Green River High School in Green River, Wyo. Albers often takes her students to the great outdoors for a sampling of "as many activities as I can possibly give them." From kayaking to rock climbing, she wants students to find an activity they will enjoy for a lifetime. "I have to plant the seed," she explains. "Then I have to give them the skills they need to pursue their activity of choice."

MOVEMENT BASED, FITNESS FOCUSED

A physical education program with a sole focus on fitness is incomplete, as is a program with an exclusive emphasis on movement and motor skills development, say experts. Therefore, the best programs stress both.

"Fitness, yes, but students also have to understand movement," insists Bonnie Mohnsen, coordinator of physical education and integrated technology for the Orange County (Calif.) Department of Education. Mohnsen helps teachers in her county develop curriculums that are aligned with the national standards for physical education.

Such curriculums, she maintains, should help students learn to analyze movement objectively. "If a student attempts to do a handstand and can't, that student should realize that his form was probably off—that his hands were too close together, perhaps, and he couldn't balance," explains Mohnsen.

Such curriculums should also help students see how fitness and movement are related, and teach them to assess what fitness-related factors might prevent them from successfully doing handstands. The student who can't do a handstand should consider the possibility that "he isn't strong enough and needs to develop more upper body strength," she says.

"Movement education helps kids discover how things work," agrees Jim Ross, a K–5 physical education instructor at Orchard School in Ridgewood, N.J. Only by understanding how their bodies move can students improve their physical performance, he contends, and often "students are not successful at skills because they aren't fit."

As a result, Ross spends a good deal of time in his classes discussing the levels of fitness required to perform well in a variety of activities, from gymnastics to baseball. Students who wish to participate in these activities are then encouraged to set their own goals for fitness improvement. "Goal setting is a great motivational tool," says Ross. "It allows kids to move at their own pace and enjoy success at their own rate."

Goal-setting and "helping students take responsibility for their choices" also guides assessment in today's physical education classroom, adds Leslie Lambert, chair of the department of education and physical education at Roanoke College in Salem, Va. She cites new uses for physical fitness testing as an example. "Instead of being used for grading, these tests are now used for diagnostic purposes," Lambert says. Students who are tested at the beginning of the school year can then set goals to improve their performance when tested again later in the year.

At first glance, says Nancy Raso-Eklund, some of the physical fitness tests used in today's schools look the same as those administered in the past, but there are differences. Probably the most significant change is that students learn why they're being tested before the test is adminis-

Getting Students Moving

Adolescents and young adults in the United States don't get enough vigorous exercise, and schools need to combat the problem, according to *Physical Activity and Health*, a 1996 report of the Surgeon General. Here are some of the report's key findings:

✦ Nearly half of American youths between the ages of 12 and 21 are not vigorously active on a regular basis.

✦ About 14 percent of young people report no recent physical activity. Inactivity is more common among females (14%) than males (7%), and among black females (21%) than white females (12%).

✦ Participation in all types of physical activity declines strikingly as age or grade in school increases.

✦ Only 19 percent of all high-school students are physically active for 20 minutes or more, five days a week, in physical education classes.

✦ Daily enrollment in physical education classes dropped from 42 percent to 25 percent among high-school students between 1991 and 1995.

Physical Activity and Health highlights the role that schools can play in encouraging young people to get off the couch and into an active lifestyle. "School-based interventions have been shown to be successful in increasing physical activity levels," the report states. Therefore, "every effort should be made to encourage schools to require daily physical education in each grade and to promote physical activities that can be enjoyed throughout life."

By "maintaining the habit of physical activity throughout the school years," educators can help students develop healthy habits that will last a lifetime, the report contends. "Childhood and adolescence may be pivotal times for preventing sedentary behavior among adults."

tered, says Raso-Eklund, a physical education teacher for two elementary schools in Green River, Wyo.

"Take the 'sit and reach,' for example. Before students take this portion of the test, they're told that it's to measure their flexibility," she explains. Students learn exactly what flexibility is (the ability to stretch, twist, and bend with ease) and the health consequences of not being flexible enough (back problems, muscle tears). Then, if the physical fitness test reveals that students need to improve in this area, students are encouraged to select activities that will improve their flexibility, such as adding stretching to their daily routines.

As long as fitness tests truly measure fitness and not performance, they play an important role in physical education programs, says Raso-Eklund. Such tests give students valuable data about their personal fitness, and they can use that data to create their own programs for improvement. And, she insists, it's not the test scores that motivate most students to improve, it's the knowledge that doing so will result in long-term health benefits.

MAKING MORE CONNECTIONS

Physical education programs today do more than help students understand the connection between physical activity and health. With proper planning, such programs can also help students discover connections between physical activity and other disciplines, experts contend.

"We're all responsible for making [interdisciplinary] connections," says Raso-Eklund, who, for the past six years, has teamed with other Green River elementary school teachers to create theme-based units. The most recent Olympic Games, held in Atlanta, provided an excellent opportunity to overlap concepts, she explains. While students in physical education classes recited the Olympic creed and discussed the meaning of sportsmanship, they explored the cultures of the competing countries in their social studies classes. In language arts, students examined the word "commitment" and discussed how it might be used to describe Olympic athletes.

Throughout the school year, teachers have many opportunities to connect subject areas—and it's important to do so, says Raso-Eklund. "When we look at how kids learn, we find that they need to understand the relationship between disciplines," she explains. "We need to make the sum bigger than the parts."

"I think all of education needs to come together more," agrees Cindy Kuhrasch, the K–12 physical education teacher in the Barneveld (Wisc.) School District. "In our current system, kids come to see the world as little blocks of time, and they get confused when they have to put it together in real life."

Kuhrasch encourages other teachers in her small district to collabo-rate with her by setting up a chalkboard in the teachers' lounge and ask-ing colleagues to identify their themes and lessons. She then develops activities based on their comments. "I make it known to teachers that I'm a resource," says Kuhrasch. "I'm there to provide a bodily-kinesthetic activity to complement what they're teaching."

According to Lambert, teachers faced with limited time and a "knowledge explosion" become strong advocates for integration, but most schools are just beginning to venture into the interdisciplinary realm. As a result, many first efforts are superficial. Still, Lambert acknowledges that "we're beginning to see intermediate steps, where people are looking at violence in our society, for example, and designing curriculums to help students understand social norms." Physical education can be used in this context to develop self and social responsibility, she says, because many of the activities used in physical education classes are designed to help students learn how to work together.

Ross agrees. "We try to set up problems that have . . . many solutions so students can use their problem-solving skills," says Ross. "We try to emphasize critical thinking and to concentrate on the process students use to solve the problems together."

In a group juggling activity, for example, students must use a two-handed chest pass to pass a basketball around to the other students. "Everyone must receive the ball once before touching it again, so students have to think about patterns and communication," Ross explains. Then, as more balls are added to the mix, the problem becomes more complex. "We ask students to explain what happens if they don't communicate when we add more balls. And the students answer, 'The balls go all over the place.' This activity teaches them how to communicate on a project and how to work with each other."

Improving communication and trust among students is the aim of the Project Adventure program Kathy Thornton uses with her 6th grade students. Thornton, a physical education teacher at Edgewood Middle School in Edgewood, Md., was trained in the program's trust-building activities before she introduced them to her students. Her experience convinced her that what students will learn about cooperation in the concentrated, 12-day unit can be applied throughout the year. "Students must bond together and problem-solve as a group," she explains.

A typical cooperative activity, for example, is the Spider Web. To successfully complete this low-rope element, each team has to get its members through the web without touching any of its sides. To make it even more challenging, students can only pass through each hole in the web once. Students who can't work together can't finish the exercise, claims Thornton. "Students learn that they really need to work together, and we hope they also learn that there are peaceful solutions to problems," she says.

Efforts to link physical education to other academic areas are applauded by experts in the field who agree that making such connections leads to deeper understanding in all subject areas. These same experts admit, however, that such integration is often easier at the elementary and middle school levels. "High school is still the hardest nut to crack," says Lambert, because many high schools are still so compartmentalized with rigid schedules. Teachers must be given time to plan together if "deeper models of integration" are to succeed, she maintains.

One such model can be found at Bell Gardens High School in East Los Angeles. In Second to None, a program with a school-to-work focus, juniors and seniors who have completed two years of core classes can then take courses related to a specific career path. Carolyn Thompson, physical education teacher at Bell Gardens, teams up with the health occupation, science, and English teachers to teach the health careers path. (Students go out of the path for such electives as mathematics or foreign languages.) In this model, physical education is viewed as no less important than the other disciplines. "The physical education teacher has a classroom and has access to computers, textbooks, and other resources—as do the other teachers," Thompson explains.

The course is divided into four, 9-week "highly interdisciplinary" units. In a unit on fitness, for example, students examine the principles of fitness in physical education classes while studying the digestive system in science; they discuss nutrition and metabolic rate in health while reading books that focus on cultures and food in English. Through these thematic units, students "understand the links between disciplines and are able to transfer that knowledge from one class to another," Thompson says.

The collaboration at Bell Gardens works, she adds, because teachers have a common prep time to discuss how best to integrate the subjects. "It's wonderful to be on a team, to talk and share ideas," she says. "Students really enjoy the integrated units, and other teachers have a new respect for physical education because we show how we're part of the total education of a child."

FAMILY FITNESS

The family also plays a part in the total education of a child, and this is of particular concern to physical educators.

"We can teach the value of fitness and proper nutrition at school, but we need to have families reinforce the concepts at home," says Raso-Eklund. This is especially difficult if reinforcing concepts means the family must make major lifestyle changes, she adds.

"We are challenged to convince adults that exercise is worthwhile—some recognize it, others don't," says Ross.

To inspire families to "recreate together," Ross has incorporated family activities into the Orchard School physical education program. Through family dances and hikes, he hopes parents will come to appreci-ate—and model—a healthy, active lifestyle.

According to Betty Reid, a specialist in health and physical educa-tion at the Maryland State Department of Education, involving parents and the community in physical education programs is a positive nation-wide trend. "Physical activity has not been historically emphasized in our country as a national goal," she explains. This neglect "puts us at an increased risk for disease." Reid hopes that outreach efforts by physical educators will help all citizens enjoy physical activities throughout life—to prolong life. "It's a matter of our own preservation," she claims. "Inactivity can reduce our lifetimes."

Thornton agrees. "We've got to get the community involved. Only then will we get the kids involved," she says.

For her part, Thornton plans to post a large sign at her school for all—students, their families, teachers, and other community members—to see. "It's going to say, 'Warning: The Surgeon General has determined that inactivity can be hazardous to your health.'"

Using Technology to Transform Physical Education

Kathy Checkley

The future is now in many of today's physical education classes, as students use technology to explore fitness concepts in ways that personalize the curriculum more than ever before.

Technology enables students to gather information about their bodies and apply it, says Leslie Lambert, chair of the department of education and physical education at Roanoke College in Salem, Va. "Heart rate monitors, anatomy and physiology computer software, equipment to measure body-fat composition—when students use these tools, they understand how data relates to their bodies," she explains. "Students can then take the information and set goals that will help them maintain, and possibly improve, their health."

Heart rate monitors are a wonderful tool for integration, says Susan Kogut, a physical education teacher at Seven Oaks Elementary School in Baltimore County, Md. Kogut has developed a curriculum that introduces students to the monitors and shows them how physical activity affects their heart rate. Students are then asked to record data at each stage in the exercise cycle, noting their heart rates during the warm up, at various points throughout a 20- to 30-minute cardiovascular activity, and then after they cool down. When students later plot their data, Kogut explains, "this becomes their math lesson," and analyzing the graphs becomes part of their science lesson.

Video cameras, computers, and the World Wide Web are all tools used by students in Orange County, Calif., says Bonnie Mohnsen, coordinator of physical education and integrated technology for the Orange County Department of Education.

For example, when students create multimedia presentations on their favorite sports, they use the World Wide Web to gather information. Video and computers allow students to analyze their movement and improve performance. First, students videotape a movement pattern or skill and then use software to digitize the images so they can be transferred to a computer. After students have practiced the skill, they can videotape the movement again, digitize the new images, and then compare the before and after movements. These images can then be stored in each student's electronic portfolio.

Such technology can transform physical education classrooms into cutting-edge, personal fitness centers, says Mohnsen. Still, in the rush to supply students with these innovations, she advises teachers to remember their own educational needs, and to take time to develop proficiency in using technology.

Toward that end, Mohnsen has created a three-step staff development program designed to bring Orange County teachers into the technological age. "Teachers must feel comfortable using technology," she says. "We have to teach teachers how to use these tools so students can."

MOVING PHYSICAL EDUCATION INTO THE FUTURE

SCOTT WILLIS

Physical education in U.S. schools will place far greater emphasis on skill development, if the vision set forth in *Moving into the Future: National Standards for Physical Education* is realized. These national standards, developed by the National Association for Sport and Physical Education (NASPE) in Reston, Va., call on teachers to help all students master a variety of movement skills.

"I really felt terrible about my achievement with students who came in with low skills and left with low skills," says Marian Franck, a physical education specialist from Lancaster, Pa., who taught for 34 years. The standards aim to rewrite that scenario, says Franck, who served on the task force that developed them.

Traditionally, physical educators have moved students "right into the total activity, playing the game, assuming that everyone can," Franck says. The standards, by contrast, emphasize the need to teach students motor skills such as throwing and catching—skills that transfer from sport to sport.

The skills-development approach calls for lots of repetitive practice. Therefore, students might work in small groups to practice dribbling, passing, and shooting, rather than playing a game of basketball. When students play games, only the skilled athletes handle the ball frequently, and "the very students who need the practice don't get it," says Shirley Holt/Hale, who served on the standards task force. Holt/Hale, coauthor of the book *Children Moving,* has taught physical education at Linden Elementary School in Oak Ridge, Tenn., for more than 20 years.

Holt/Hale individualizes instruction by giving her students a task, such as dribbling a ball and then she watches them. Typically, "four [students] could do it blindfolded, four can't dribble at all, and the rest are somewhere in the middle." She aims most of her teaching at this middle group, but she goes quietly to those who have mastered the skill and gives them a more challenging task. She also adjusts the task for students who are having difficulty.

Focusing on skill development is "not the easy way to teach," Holt/Hale notes. To teach throwing, for example, a physical educator must know levels of progression for the skill, develop a series of lesson plans, and individualize instruction. "You have to plan," she emphasizes. "You can't do that on the drive to work Monday morning."

Lack of preparation poses another challenge. Physical educators "haven't had textbooks that told how to break down skills and teach them to kids," Holt/Hale says. Moreover, physical educators are usually former athletes, and "the hardest thing to teach is what you're best at doing."

Fears that students will have less fun practicing skills than playing games are groundless, experts say. "It's just the opposite," Holt/Hale reports. "Instead of just your very elite being successful, all of a sudden everyone is successful at learning the skill." She speaks warmly of "seeing the joy in children's faces when they realize they can catch or kick."

Teachers can prevent repetitive practice from becoming boring by "changing the nature of the challenge" often enough to keep it exciting,

Holt/Hale says. Practice in a given skill can also be distributed throughout the school year, she suggests. Each time the skill is revisited, "you bump students up a notch." Students can also play games they design themselves in which they practice certain skills intensively, she adds.

ASSESSING STUDENTS' SKILLS

Moving into the Future also places heavy emphasis on the need to assess skills. The assessment component is "very new" in physical education, Holt/Hale says. Assessment requires "getting into what the skills are really about." Can the student dribble the ball without slapping it? Can she hold a balance for 30 seconds?

In the past, physical educators have tended to assess only the "product," such as how far a student could throw a ball, Franck says. "We have not done much assessing of process." In assessing how well a student serves a tennis ball, for example, the teacher could provide feedback on such elements as the movement of the racket, the speed of the serve, and the angle of the racket face to the ball.

Assessment should not become overwhelming for the teacher, Holt/Hale says. With guidance, students can do self-assessments, and they can assess their peers. ("They don't cheat," she reports. In fact, "students are more critical of themselves than adults would be.") Students can also play a major role in record keeping, maintaining records in their portfolios, for example.

When physical educators take a skills-development approach, academically inclined students "blossom as athletes," Franck says. These students "have wonderful minds that can control their bodies," when their teachers help them analyze movements. This approach "really turns kids in high school around," she says. Students stop seeing themselves as "klutzes" and "motor morons"—self-perceptions that discourage them from choosing to be active.

When students develop good movement skills, they are more likely to maintain an active lifestyle into adulthood, experts maintain. When students learn skills that can be applied in a wide range of physical activities, they are "set up for having fun for the rest of their lives," Franck says. "That's where the standards are taking us."

Special Needs, Regular Classrooms

Angelika Machi

Physical education teachers today are being trained to meet the needs of *all* students in their classrooms, including those with special needs, experts in the field say. Each child in the classroom, regardless of ability, should be exposed to the same experiences as his or her peers, these experts believe.

This method of teaching—where the teacher takes each child's needs, skills, and learning style into account while developing and delivering the physical education curriculum—is considered "developmentally appropriate," says Clersida Garcia, assistant professor of motor development and pedagogy at Northern Illinois University in Dekalb, Ill. When this concept is implemented on a daily basis in the regular physical education classroom, students with disabilities can be integrated into the classroom with ease, Garcia asserts.

Some major organizations agree with this view. The Council on Physical Education for Children (COPEC) and the Adapted Physical Activity Council (APAC) state that "all adapted physical education is simply good physical education."

Offering Choices

Experts stress that a high-quality physical education classroom offers students many choices. For example, when teaching children basketball skills, physical educators should place several hoops at different heights, permit nonconventional methods of throwing the ball, and allow the rate at which the game is played to vary, says Martin Block, assistant professor of adapted physical education at the University of Virginia.

Choices in equipment should also be available, says Lauriece Zittel, assistant professor of adapted physical education at Northern Illinois University in Dekalb, Ill. When teaching dribbling skills, for instance, a variety of balls should be offered to meet everyone's needs and ability level, rather than using only a basketball. A basketball may be difficult for some students—disabled and nondisabled—to hold, bounce, and control, thus hindering their ability to learn basic skills, Zittel explains.

"Balls come in every size, shape, color, and texture—from leather to soft, spongy balls," says Kathy Thornton, a physical education teacher at Edgewood Middle School in Edgewood, Md. Thornton even found a special ball that allows a legally blind student to participate in a game of catch. "When we play, I use a softball that has a beeper buried inside. As the ball moves closer to the student, it beeps louder. So, although she can see slightly, the equipment allows her to use another sense in catching the ball."

ADAPTING THE CURRICULUM

In addition to providing a wide array of equipment options, teachers must also make curricular modifications to ensure that the needs of disabled students are being met, without sacrificing the needs of nondisabled students, Block says. The degree of these changes will depend on the nature of the disability.

One level of modification that Block describes is the "curricular overlapping" approach. This variation is intended for the student who has a moderate to severe disability, such as confinement to a wheelchair or dependency on crutches. In this situation, the student should be presented with a viable activity that emphasizes skills similar to those his or her nondisabled peers are developing, Block says.

For instance, while some students are practicing soccer skills—an activity a student in a wheelchair cannot fully participate in—another group of students can be engaged in developing handball skills. Both activities build strength and flexibility, he notes, but in different ways, using different parts of the body. Students can rotate between the two groups throughout the class period, allowing the student in the wheelchair to practice skills continuously with nondisabled peers.

One teacher, for example, successfully introduced curricular overlapping in her class by announcing, "Today we will be doing two activities, tumbling and throwing." It is not necessary, Block observes, to single out special-needs children by asking, "Who will work with Johnny today?"

The next level of modification that Block describes is the "alternative activity," which is geared to the student who "just doesn't fit in at all," because of severe disabilities, health problems, or fragility. Again, small groups work on separate skills, but the disabled child now plays a different role. He or she can assist other students with lacrosse skills, for example, by rolling the ball down a ramp while classmates scoop the ball up with their sticks. Although the disabled child may not be practicing the same skills as his or her classmates, the student is still included in the process of skill development.

Block emphasizes that modifying the curriculum enables teachers to meet the main goal for including special-needs students in regular physical education classes—to increase flexibility and strength, develop motor skills, and teach the importance of lifelong exercise and good health.

THE IEP PROCESS

Modifying the curriculum is made easier when physical education teachers are involved in developing the disabled student's Individualized Education Plan (IEP).

An IEP is required for any student who has been classified as having a disability. The process begins with an IEP meeting, where the teacher(s), parents, administrators, and specialists meet to determine what special needs and services the child requires. Subsequently, the IEP is written, which includes the short-term objectives, the long-term, annual goals, and the program modifications and adaptations necessary to meet those goals. Essentially, the IEP is a tool that allows teachers, administrators, specialists, and parents to plan the child's curriculum collaboratively in order to meet the child's needs.

Too often, however, physical educators are not included in the IEP process because of scheduling and time constraints. Still, every effort should be made to work around those barriers, Zittel says. "Presently there is too much separation; there is not enough continuity between who designs the IEP and who implements it," she says.

If the physical educator *cannot* be present at the IEP meeting, he or she should make every attempt to discuss concerns, goals, and expectations with the classroom teacher before the IEP meeting, Zittel suggests. The classroom teacher can then take that information back to the team, so the recommendations of the physical education teacher can be integrated into the IEP.

There "truly has to be a team approach, it cannot be isolated," agrees Ginny Popiolek, an itinerant adapted physical education teacher at the John Archer School in Bel Air, Md. "There must be an interdisciplinary approach," and a "good relationship among all of the individuals involved with the success of the student," she says.

BENEFITS FOR EVERYONE

Including special-needs students in the regular physical education classroom benefits every student in many ways, experts say. Special-needs students in the inclusive classroom are independent, motivated, and have feelings of self-worth, belonging, and achievement, says Kathy Brinker, an adapted physical education instructor for the Cooperative Association for Special Education (CASE) in Lombard, Ill., who has worked with disabled students in both self-contained classrooms and inclusive classrooms.

The experience in the regular classroom provides the disabled student with "a replication of real life," where there are large crowds and high levels of noise, Block adds.

Nondisabled students benefit from the inclusive setting, Block explains, in that they learn about various disabilities, become empathetic toward others around them, and develop a new understanding of the value of being a helper and a friend. Inclusion also allows nondisabled students to "develop tolerance and respect for each other, which carries over to other aspects of the school day," says Donna Harris, a physical education teacher in Covington, Ga.

Nondisabled students also learn that interaction with disabled peers is a part of life, adds Zittel. "They are always going to be exposed to different ethnic groups, people of different ability groups." Inclusion teaches students at an early stage in life to embrace those differences, and to be more accepting of everyone, she says.

Physical education teachers benefit from their experiences with disabled students as well, Popiolek says. It allows them to employ a wider range of instructional techniques, and rewards them by confirming that "they are good at what they do and that *all* students can learn," she says.

HEALTH EDUCATION

A CRISIS-DRIVEN FIELD SEEKS COHERENCE

SCOTT WILLIS

Health education used to mean learning that germs cause disease, memorizing the four food groups, and—after you had reached puberty—labeling the parts on a diagram of the reproductive system.

That kind of program may have been adequate in a safer bygone era, but today's students need to learn much more if they are to navigate through the serious health risks that surround them. And merely adding a new unit on the latest health crisis, be it AIDS or steroids, won't suffice.

In essence, that is the consensus view of experts in health education, who believe that today's students need a comprehensive, sequential K–12 program to teach them the facts—and skills—they need to stay healthy.

Such instruction is vitally needed, these experts insist. Today's young people face a greater array of threats to their mental and physical health than did any previous generation—among them, alcohol and drug use, alcohol-related accidents, unplanned pregnancies, violence, depression, suicide, and sexually transmitted diseases, including AIDS. The high incidence of risk-taking behaviors among school-age children has created "a sense of urgency" among health educators, says Becky Smith, executive director of the Association for the Advancement of Health Education.

The recently completed *National Adolescent Student Health Survey* (NASHS), funded by three federal agencies, shows why students must receive comprehensive health education, says Smith. The survey, which

---

The articles in this chapter were originally published in the November 1990 issue of ASCD's *Curriculum Update* newsletter.

was administered to more than 11,000 8th and 10th graders nationwide in 1987, reveals some troubling attitudes and behaviors.

Of the students responding to the survey, only 40 percent had worn a seat belt the last time they had ridden in a car; one-third had "seriously thought" about committing suicide; more than half indicated that it is acceptable for people their age to have sex with someone they have dated for a long time; one-quarter did not know using condoms is effective in avoiding sexually transmitted diseases; and fewer than half perceived a great risk from having five or more drinks once or twice each weekend.

To help today's students develop healthier habits and avoid risks, schools need to provide a comprehensive program that addresses students' physical, mental, emotional, and social health, Smith believes. Topics covered in a comprehensive program typically include injury prevention and safety, presentation and control of disease, substance abuse, nutrition, family life (sexuality), consumer health, mental and emotional health (including self-esteem), and community health (including health resources in the community). If health education begins early, Smith notes, it can concern itself "not with behavior change but with behavior formation," helping students develop healthy habits that will last throughout their lives.

The delivery of health education today reveals "no consistent pattern," says Donna Lloyd-Kolkin, co-author of *The Comprehensive School Health Scourcebook*. Most often, it is part of physical education or family life courses, she notes, although some high schools may offer a one-semester course. Approximately three-quarters of the students who responded to the NASHS survey had completed a course in health education. The topics most often covered, the students reported, were drug and alcohol abuse, nutrition, and injury presentation. Fewer than half the students had received instruction on AIDS and other sexually transmitted diseases.

Health education is too often taught as an add-on or relegated to a single course or separate unit, says Gene Wilhoit, executive director of the National Association of State Boards of Education, which co-sponsored *Code Blue*, a report released in July by the National Commission on the Role of the School and the Community in Improving Adolescent Health. "Short-term, segregated approaches haven't worked," he says.

A comprehensive, sequential program is necessary to keep health education from reeling from crisis to crisis in a fragmented "disease-of-the-month approach," says Dana Davis, executive director of the American School Health Association. Some schools' programs bring in outside educators to address the burning issue of the moment but fail to provide coherent structure. "They're too busy with crisis intervention to make children healthy for the rest of their lives," she says.

A coherent structure is important, agrees Smith, because it allows new information to be incorporated logically into the curriculum. AIDS education, for example, can easily be made part of a unit on communicable diseases, she notes.

TEACHER TRAINING

In addition to a comprehensive program, experts in health education are pushing for better training for those who teach the subject, at both the elementary and secondary levels.

Davis fears that teachers who are not trained in health education but assigned to teach the subject nonetheless "just give a bunch of facts and don't really *teach* health." One of the battles, she says, is to improve teacher training at the elementary level, where good inservice programs are sorely needed. Elementary teachers are "lucky if they get one course" in teaching health issues during their preparation, she adds.

Smith believes that elementary teachers need ongoing support from a health education expert, while, at the middle and secondary levels, health education should be taught by a specialist in the field. More than 20 states have separate certification for health educators, she notes.

While experts agree on the need for better teacher training, they differ on whether health education should be infused throughout the curriculum or taught as a separate course.

Infusion is the only feasible option at the elementary level, Smith believes. At the middle and secondary levels, however, she recommends a separate course, perhaps lasting half a year. Infusion is not feasible at the secondary level, she contends, because the content is so sophisticated and in-depth that it "needs a focus of its own." As a former teacher of the subject, she knows that it demands a concentrated block of time. "I couldn't find enough time, and I was teaching an hour every day for the entire year," she says.

Wilhoit, however, contends that a separate course may not be practical or the most effective approach. He believes that health education content should be integrated into core subjects, especially science. Infusion helps students "see health as an integral part of their lives," he argues.

Davis advocates using both approaches. While she thinks the subject "definitely" deserves a separate class, she believes it is also important to integrate health-related content into other coursework.

CHANGING BEHAVIORS

More than most academic subjects, health education aims to change students' attitudes and behaviors—in particular, "to get kids to take fewer risks and to take preventive measures," says Lloyd-Kolkin. To achieve this goal, experts say, health education must do more than just impart knowledge; it must also give students the skills they need to behave in "health-enhancing" ways, including decision-making skills and refusal skills.

With this goal in mind, experts urge that health programs be skills-based and highly interactive. "It's not enough just to tell kids about risks," says Wilhoit. Strategies typically used to teach these needed skills include role playing, open discussions, and modeling how to make good decisions and resist peer pressure.

Opinions vary about whether health educators, in addition to imparting these skills, should merely inform students of the consequences of various behaviors or explicitly tell them how to behave.

Wilhoit believes schools should avoid a "dogmatic approach." But he also believes teachers should stress the consequences of risky behaviors. "In a way, that *is* directing and guiding," he points out.

"The public would be the first to admit that you can't change someone's behavior by telling them what not to do," adds Davis. The programs that are most successful at changing behavior, she says, are those that teach decision making and how to resist peer pressure, help students examine their own values, and involve parents.

Health education shouldn't end as soon as students cross the classroom threshold, experts contend; instead, the total school environment should reinforce classroom lessons. A school that teaches about nutrition, for instance, shouldn't set up a candy machine to raise money, Wilhoit says. Instruction "needs to carry over into all aspects of school life," agrees Davis. She warns that classroom instruction can be undermined if students are served greasy cheeseburgers for lunch or observe a teachers' lounge full of smoke.

NOT A PANACEA

Do health education programs actually produce changes in students' behaviors? A survey of more than 4,500 3rd–12th grade students in 200 schools, commissioned by the Metropolitan Life Foundation, found no distinct differences between the behaviors of students with no health education and those who had received one year of it. But after three years of health education, the survey showed, significantly fewer students drank or smoked "sometimes or more often," took drugs "a few times or more," or rode with a driver who had been drinking. The survey report concludes that continuous health education over several years does influence behavior patterns.

Despite the evidence that health education can be effective, experts agree that schools can't be the only players in the game. Health education is "not a panacea," cautions Smith. Schools need to work with other agencies to meet the broad needs of children, she says. Wilhoit stresses the need to involve parents and communities in the campaign to help young people stay healthy, saying, "It's impossible for schools to do this alone."

SEXUALITY EDUCATION

SCOTT WILLIS

Like their colleagues in general health education, experts in the field of sex education are pushing for a more comprehensive approach to their subject, one that goes beyond the presentation of clinical facts about anatomy and reproduction. As part of that effort, they have encouraged use of the term "sexuality education" to emphasize that their subject also includes the social, emotional, and psychological aspects of sexuality.

A focus on anatomical "plumbing" does not inform students about what they really want to know, says Debra Haffner, executive director of the Sex Information and Education Council of the United States (SIECUS), a national organization that promotes sexuality education and advocates "the right of individuals to make responsible sexual choices." Students, she says, are absorbed by questions such as "When will I be ready for sex?" and "How can I say 'no' and still be popular?" To help students with concerns like these, sexuality education must deal with issues such as sexual development, interpersonal relationships, intimacy, and gender roles.

Sexuality has too often been seen as a medical or health issue, adds Mary Lee Tatum, a sexuality education consultant from Falls Church, Va. Besides anatomy and physiology, she recommends that sexuality educators address topics such as identity, sexual orientation, the place of sexuality in human life, and media depictions of sexuality.

Despite these broad aims, far too few U.S. students receive sexuality education that goes beyond the anatomical basics, experts say. Fewer than 10 percent of students receive a comprehensive program in the subject, Haffner estimates. Sexuality education is often taught to secondary students in a 10-day block, usually in physical education, home economics, or biology class, adds Tatum. Ideally, most experts say, students should receive sexuality education from kindergarten through 12th grade, within the context of general health education.

The sexuality education program in the Alexandria, Va., public schools is unusual in that, in the amount of time devoted to the subject and the range of topics covered, it approaches the ideal proposed by experts. In grades K–6, classroom teachers handle the program, explains Jean Hunter, a teacher-specialist for family life education. In grades 7 and 8, students participate in the district's health program. In grade 9, students enroll in a required course called "Fundamentals of Human Growth and Development," in which they receive detailed information about sexual issues. A one-semester "Human Sexuality Seminar" is offered as an elective for students in grades 11 and 12. Alexandria's program, which was developed with input from the community, is designed to give a clear message of community values, Hunter adds.

As in general health education, one serious problem in sexuality education, experts say, is that the subject is often taught by teachers without the appropriate training—or sometimes even the desire—to teach it.

At the elementary level, whatever sexuality education occurs typically comes from the classroom teacher. At the secondary level, sexuality education is taught by teachers of a variety of subjects—physical education, health, home economics, biology—and sometimes by school nurses. Few of these teachers have received specific training in teaching about sexual issues, experts say. Michigan, Ohio, and Utah are the only states that require teachers to complete a course in human sexuality to be certified to teach sex education, according to the Alan Guttmacher Institute, a nonprofit corporation for research, policy analysis, and public education on sexuality issues.

Most curriculums and materials on the topic are well done, says Sandra Cole, a professor at the University of Michigan's medical center and president-elect of the American Association of Sex Educators, Counselors, and Therapists. "The abyss that occurs is mainly in the preparedness of the teachers," she says. "The best curriculum can fall on its face if the professional is not adequately trained."

In Alexandria, elementary teachers receive "careful training," Hunter says, while teachers of the 9th grade course are required to take two graduate-level courses to learn factual content and how to teach it appropriately. The training includes "lots of practice, and lots of peer critique," as well as examination and discussion of personal values.

Teachers of sexuality education need to be committed to their task, experts say, to weather the difficulties involved: students' embarrassment or reluctance to admit ignorance about sexual matters, outdated policies that emphasize teaching about reproduction over pregnancy prevention, the need to keep up-to-date with a large and evolving body of knowledge, and a perceived lack of support from the community.

This last concern, however, may exist more in educators' fears than in reality. More than 85 percent of U.S. adults favor sexuality education, with support running even higher among parents of school-age children, according to data from the Guttmacher Institute. "Parents want sexuality education," emphasizes Haffner.

Nevertheless, "in certain communities, the teaching of sex education is still a hot potato," notes Dana Davis, executive director of the American School Health Association. Richard Miller, executive director of the American Association of School Administrators, says he hears few complaints from administrators about sex-ed controversies, but he does hear reports that "there are still a number of parents out there who object to schools being involved in sex education." Successful programs typically involve the religious community and parents in developing the curriculum, he notes.

Parents' broad support for sexuality education has been reflected in action by state legislatures. Twenty-three states have mandated sexuality education, and 23 others explicitly encourage it, according to SIECUS. However, state mandates and encouragement do not necessarily produce local programs. According to Haffner, one-third of school districts in the United States offer no sexuality education, and many of the others provide only a minimal program.

ADVOCATING ABSTINENCE

Many sexuality education programs seek first and foremost to curb students' sexual activity, and teachers of sex education are more likely to teach about abstinence than almost any other topic, according to the Guttmacher Institute. Some experts believe that teachers should give students a strong abstinence message, while others believe that being explicitly directive is inappropriate and likely to backfire.

Haffner believes that abstinence should be promoted, particularly for junior high school students. Tatum, however, believes that giving an abstinence message is the parents' role. The school's role, she says, is to "help kids arrive at decisions that are positive," not to maneuver them toward absolute values. Cole believes in giving students a "menu" of choices, "weighted with facts, not with 'shoulds'." She advises that teachers present abstinence as a "strong option" and as the best way to prevent pregnancy and sexually transmitted diseases.

Many sex education programs skip over four topics feared as lightning rods for controversy: masturbation, homosexuality, contraception, and abortion. Skirting these subjects is ill-advised, experts say, because most students already have some knowledge about them—and probably misconceptions as well.

Teaching about contraception is a "red flag" to some parents because they believe that doing so sends a message to students that sexual activity among their age group is expected, acceptable, and perhaps even the norm. Some parents believe that giving students information about sexuality—and especially birth control—will increase the level of their sexual activity. Experts dismiss this notion as a myth.

"Numerous studies have demonstrated that sexuality education causes neither an increase nor decrease in ages and rates of sexual intercourse among teens," states the SEICUS report *Sex Education 2000: A Call to Action.* "Some studies do suggest, however, that teens are more likely to use contraception if they have had sexuality education courses." Despite these data, only about 45 percent of sexuality education teachers "discuss where and how to obtain birth control," the report points out. Teachers often shy away from potentially controversial issues like contraception, experts say, because they fear objections from the community.

Most experts agree that, while it may be desirable to deliver an abstinence message, educators must face the fact that, by high school, many students are sexually active. Therefore, all students should also be given information about preventing pregnancy and sexually transmitted diseases. While critics complain that doing both conveys a mixed message, most experts see the approach as a practical compromise between the ideal and reality.

Homosexuality, another of the four sensitive topics, needs to be addressed in ways that combat homophobia, experts say. Gay students make up approximately 10 percent of the student body, and in light of evidence that suggests young gays are more likely to commit suicide than their peers, it is especially important to affirm a range of sexual orientations, Haffner says, and to provide gay students with information about support services in the community. The Alexandria program aims to "get rid of the myths" about sexual orientation, says Hunter. "We make a real effort to say, 'You have a right to your personal beliefs on this issue, but you cannot abuse others.'"

Experts stress the importance of informing parents of what is being taught in a sexuality education program. "Absolute, full disclosure" of course content helps to defuse objections, says Haffner. Experts also recommend activities such as homework assignments and child-parent nights that encourage parental involvement in instruction. When parents strenuously object to the content of the program, the only practical solution, experts say, is to allow them to "opt out." Only about 1–3 percent of parents actually take this option, according to SIECUS.

Those who argue that topics related to sexuality should be discussed only in the home are naively optimistic about parent-child communication, experts say. Only 25 percent of U.S. adults report that they learned about sexuality from their parents, according to SIECUS. Meanwhile, children are bombarded with messages about sexuality from the media, advertising, and peers. "There is no silence anywhere about sex," says Tatum, "except from the people who are supposed to care about kids"—parents and teachers. She and other experts believe schools have a responsibility to fill that silence, not merely with dry physiological facts but with comprehensive information about all important aspects of sexuality.

AIDS EDUCATION

SCOTT WILLIS

In a 7th grade classroom, a bag of ping-pong balls is passed from one student to another. Almost all of the balls are white—except one or two red ones. Each student pulls a ball from the bag. Those who pull white balls return them to the bag and pass it to the next student. Those who pull out a red ball, however, remove a white ball also and put two red balls into the bag. The bag continues on its round. Slowly at first, then faster and faster, the balls in the bag change from white to red. In a surprisingly short time, the bag is entirely filled with red balls.

The point of the lesson, explains Susan Levy, associate director of the Prevention Research Center at the University of Illinois–Chicago, is to make students understand how fast an infectious disease can spread. If a red ping-pong ball is equated with the HIV virus, then in short order the predominantly healthy class has become infected.

Such lessons are needed as part of a concerted effort to give students the facts about AIDS and how to prevent transmission of the HIV virus that causes it, as well as to raise their awareness that they can contract the disease if they engage in risky behaviors, experts say.

Anyone who doubts that some adolescents are at high risk for exposure to the HIV virus should consider these survey-based statistics recently reported by the U.S. Centers for Disease Control: Among high school students, approximately one in five has had at least four sexual partners, and about 3 percent have injected drugs.

Misconceptions about AIDS are also rife among teenagers, the survey of about 100,000 high school students in 30 states revealed. About half of the students responding believed that insects could carry the HIV virus, and about one-quarter believed that using public toilets or taking a blood test could put them at risk of contracting AIDS. (However, most students do understand the ways the virus is usually transmitted, the National Adolescent Student Health Survey found.)

Experts have cited such dismal statistics to make a strong case for comprehensive AIDS education in schools—an argument that is winning over many state legislatures and schools boards. Forty-six states and essentially all large school districts support AIDS education, and 30 states and the District of Columbia require it, according to the Guttmacher Institute.

AIDS education should not take the form of a one-shot crash course, experts agree. Instead, the subject should be made part of a comprehensive health education program, says Debra Haffner of SIECUS. "A special AIDS curriculum unit or school assembly is not enough to prevent the spread of AIDS among young people," states *AIDS and the Education of Our Children,* a guide for parents and teachers issued by the U.S. Department of Education in 1987.

Information presented about AIDS must be developmentally appropriate, experts stress. Elementary students need to feel free to ask questions about AIDS, says Marcia Quackenbush, coordinator of training with the AIDS Health Project, a program of the University of California–San Francisco. Junior high school students need information in a positive, prevention-oriented context, Quackenbush continues. At this level, the program should emphasize self-esteem, refusal skills, and the value of independence. At the high school level, students should look at broader issues, such as discrimination and the value of people's lives. At every level, she adds, educators should review the basic facts about the disease.

In the Alexandria, Va., public schools, for example, students in grades K–5 are given indirect information about AIDS as part of "helping them to understand about communicable diseases," says teacher-specialist Jean Hunter. In grade 6, students begin to receive specific information about AIDS, and in grades 7–9, they receive detailed information about the disease, focusing on prevention and on tolerance for those infected.

A Moral or Health Message?

While AIDS education has a broad base of support among the public, opinions clash regarding the treatment of such issues as abstinence and condom use.

The U.S. Department of Education's *AIDS and the Education of Our Children* recommends that educators should "help children develop clear standards of right and wrong," by teaching restraint as a virtue, presenting sex education within a moral context, "speaking up for" the institution of the family, and setting clear and specific rules regarding behavior.

Some AIDS experts have attacked the Department of Education's guidelines as overly moralistic, as "a moral message disguised as a health message." Haffner warns that such an approach runs the danger of causing students to tune out, because they will feel that adults are "using AIDS as a way to clobber them" into abstinence.

The goals Haffner recommends for an AIDS education curriculum are to reduce panic and misinformation; to help students delay sexual intercourse; to encourage condom use for sexually active students; to reduce experimentation with drugs; and to increase compassion for those infected.

While there is consensus among experts that abstinence should be taught as a strong option, views differ sharply about what to teach students who are and will remain sexually active. How to discuss condoms in

AIDS prevention lessons, in particular, has divided many educators. Discussion of condoms is a controversial issue, both because of the moral and religious beliefs some hold against them and because of the belief (discounted by experts) that telling students about birth control might increase their level of sexual activity.

The U.S. Department of Education's *AIDS and the Education of Our Children* states that discussion of condom use should take place with parental approval and occur in "an appropriate moral context." Such discussion "must not undermine the importance of restraint and responsibility in the minds of young people," the guide stresses. Further, "young people must know that the use of condoms can reduce, but by no means eliminate, the risk of contracting AIDS."

Quackenbush believes it is immoral *not* to teach about condoms. She also believes, however, that it is immoral not to emphasize that students can choose to be abstinent. Educators need to convey that "abstinence can be very hip," she says.

That message may be difficult to pitch to students in high-risk areas such as inner cities, however. In high-risk communities, says Levy, the norm of early sexual activity is so strong that it can't be changed by advocating abstinence. Such an approach might, at most, postpone sexual activity for a year, she predicts.

Levy is studying the effects of a 7th grade AIDS curriculum in high-risk communities, where, she says, students "are serially monogamous every three weeks"—that is, they tend to be sexually active and to change partners frequently. On the positive side, these children generally want to use contraceptives; typically, what holds them back is fear of what others will say. For example, Levy says, in the Hispanic community a girl who carries a condom might be branded "a slut." Part of the school's job, she believes, is to persuade students that taking precautions against disease is a way of showing care, not distrust.

Levy stresses that it is important to focus on the real risks that students are likely to be running. Intravenous drug use has never been common practice among students, she notes; students are much more likely to run risks from needles through ear piercing, tattooing, or injecting steroids. Therefore, she says, the curriculum should dwell on those risks.

Like the students with the bag full of red ping-pong balls, American society has recognized the danger posed by AIDS if the disease is allowed to spread unchecked. Whatever they believe about the proper emphasis of the curriculum, experts in the field of AIDS education agree that educators must inform all young people about the disease and how to prevent it.

◆

DRUG AND ALCOHOL EDUCATION

SCOTT WILLIS

Despite recent statistics showing that drug use among young people has declined slightly, the use of drugs and alcohol among U.S. students is still alarmingly widespread. Over 3.5 million students between the ages of 12 and 17 have tried marijuana, and one-third of them are regular users; while 39 percent of high school seniors surveyed report getting drunk within the past two weeks, says *Code Blue,* the report of the National Commission on the Role of the School and the Community in Improving Adolescent Health. And a person under the legal drinking age is almost twice as likely to die in an alcohol-related car crash as an adult over 21, according to the National Commission Against Drunk Driving.

Schools have a responsibility to help students stay clean and sober, experts say, not only because substance abuse poses a serious danger to their health and lives, but also because it precludes learning. "A child that's high on drugs can't learn," says Huntley Cross, coordinator for drug and alcohol programs in Anne Arundel County, Md. And if a student is preoccupied with getting high, "you couldn't teach him to spit if he had a mouthful of water," Cross adds bluntly.

A drug and alcohol prevention program can be effective whether it is infused throughout the curriculum or taught in a separate course, experts say. The mode of delivery doesn't matter as long as there is adequate reinforcement, says Mary Cobbs of the National Parent's Resource Institute for Drug Education (PRIDE). "Many schools target only one or two grade levels," she says, thereby failing to provide enough reinforcement to drive lessons home. Given this type of one-shot delivery, many students miss drug education entirely, she adds.

Programs that seek to prevent alcohol and drug use among students must go beyond the "just say no" approach, experts agree. "We make it sound so easy," says Clay Roberts, a Seattle-based health education consultant and former teacher. "But it's not enough to say 'just say no'," he insists. "You need to teach them *how*."

Children are usually exposed to drugs by a good friend or sibling, Roberts notes, and they fear that saying "no" will jeopardize the relationship. Therefore, students need to learn that "you can take a stand and still have friends." Most important, they need to have the social skills that will enable them to act on their decision to abstain.

One program that focuses on social skills is the curriculum used in Project ALERT, an $8.8 million study sponsored by the Conrad N. Hilton Foundation and conducted by the RAND Corporation in 30 junior high schools in California and Oregon. The curriculum includes eight weekly lessons in 7th grade and three booster sessions during 8th grade.

The Project ALERT curriculum is based on the premise that "kids begin using drugs because peers and influential adults are using drugs," says Abby Robyn, director of curriculum implementation for the project. Therefore, the curriculum focuses on developing resistance skills and on motivating students to resist peer pressure to use drugs. Some of the techniques the curriculum uses are "trigger" films to provoke discussion, role playing, scenarios that illustrate different resistance responses, and films modeling successful resistance.

A recent study of the effects of the Project ALERT curriculum showed that it was successful in curbing students' use of marijuana and cigarettes. Among the 4,000 students aged 12 to 14 who were subjects, initial use of marijuana was cut by a third, as compared to a control group; among students who had experimented with cigarettes, the number who became heavy smokers was cut in half. The curriculum works, Robyn contends, because students who feel they are *able* to resist pressure to use drugs or alcohol are much more likely to do so.

Educators should not forget that teaching refusal skills reaches only those students who are not already confirmed users of drugs, experts caution. Such strategies work only with students who *want* to say no, Roberts points out. Students who are already harmfully involved with drugs or alcohol need intervention, he stresses.

Educators often find it difficult making students realize that the negative consequences of drug and alcohol use are things that could actually happen to *them*. "Kids think they're immortal," says Ellen Ficklen, a writer and consultant who has served as a panelist for the U.S. Department of Education's Drug-Free Schools Recognition Program. "Kids live for the here and now," adds Roberts. "Fourth graders don't worry about lung cancer."

One way to personalize the consequences of drug and alcohol use, experts say, is to emphasize the short-term effects. The Project ALERT curriculum, for instance, emphasizes that students will get yellow teeth and bad breath from smoking cigarettes and may lose control over their actions if they drink or get high, says Robyn. Students *do* worry about avoiding these consequences, she adds.

SEND A NO-USE MESSAGE

Many experts recommend that schools send a strong no-use message to students, in contrast to the "responsible use" message sometimes conveyed during the 1970s, which implied that "drug use is okay if you don't abuse drugs, or hurt anyone."

PRIDE, like the U.S. Department of Education, advocates a total abstinence approach. "The overall intent is to prevent these behaviors ever happening," says Cobbs. She criticizes the "responsible use" approach as a mixed signal. "Drug use is an illegal activity and the curriculum should reflect that," she says.

Teachers should give students a strong, explicit no-use message because students don't have the experience or maturity to make good decisions, believes Lee Dogoloff, executive director of the American Council for Drug Education. But, he adds, "we need to make a good case as to why" students shouldn't use drugs. Dogoloff also believes that schools tend to place too much emphasis on what's taught in the classroom and not enough on school policy and climate.

Cobbs agrees that school policy and climate must be consistent with the messages sent in the classroom. Schools do "a vague two-step on alcohol and tobacco," she says, by telling students not to use them while tacitly accepting such behaviors by providing smoking areas and designated driver programs. The most consistent approach, she says, is to establish a no-use policy and enforce it.

Roberts agrees that educators should convey a clear no-use message, but cautions that speaking only in terms of abstinence misses experimenters who are still reachable. And the ultimate goal of the such "practical options" as safe ride programs, he says, should be to get students to change their behavior.

The Anne Arundel public schools are noted for their tough, consistent drug policy, under which students caught once with drugs or alcohol are suspended, while repeat offenders—or dealers—are expelled. Undercover investigations have shown that the policy has sharply decreased the incidence of drug possession and distribution in Anne Arundel schools.

Such a tough policy can be helpful in ridding a school of drugs, says Cross. But he emphasizes that the county's policy is "a compassionate mechanism" to provide help to student drug users.

Students can earn their way back into school by revealing the source of the drugs or alcohol, signing an agreement to remain drug-free, and attending eight hours of drug-education instruction and five hours of counseling. Most students disciplined under the policy do come back to school, and there has been a "fairly high rate of success" with those who have returned, says Cross.

Even the most effective drug policy, however, needs to be supported by a drug prevention curriculum. *Learning to Live Drug Free*, a curriculum issued in July by the U.S. Department of Education, suggests ideas for integrating lessons about substance abuse with regular curriculum content in grades K–12. A mathematics lesson for 4th–6th graders, for example, calculates the societal costs of drug use, while an art/music lesson for 7th and 8th graders examines the impact of messages conveyed by various media, including movies and advertising.

Learning to Live Drug Free is "user-friendly, simple, and straightforward," says Dogoloff. But he sees it as "the floor, not the ceiling," as something schools can build on. The curriculum is "a good starting place," agrees Ficklen.

"No one curriculum is going to be the answer to everyone's dilemma," Cobbs points out. Those selecting a curriculum for a particular district, she advises, should survey the grade levels they want to target to determine when usage begins and what drugs are used. Then, they should develop or purchase a curriculum that meets the specific needs of those students. The best curriculums, she notes, are "modified or developed by the school district itself."

INDEX